"BEGOTTEN, NOT MADE"

Figurae

READING MEDIEVAL CULTURE

"BEGOTTEN, NOT MADE"

CONCEIVING MANHOOD IN

LATE ANTIQUITY

Virginia Burrus

Stanford University Press, Stanford, California 2000

Stanford University Press
Stanford, California
© 2000 by the Board of Trustees of the
Leland Stanford Junior University

Printed in the United States of America
on acid-free, archival-quality paper

Library of Congress Catalog Card Number: 00-105468

Typeset by James P. Brommer in 11/14 Garamond

Original printing 2000

Last figure below indicates the year of this printing:
09   08   07   06   05   04   03   02   01   00

FOR MY FATHER, SIDNEY,
AND MY MOTHER, MARY

We believe in . . . one Lord Jesus Christ, the Son of God, begotten as only-begotten of the Father, that is of the substance of the Father, God of God, Light of Light, true God of true God, begotten not made, consubstantial with the Father.

—NICENE CREED (325 C.E.)

In fact, man is engendered, not created. Yet, it is as if, in wishing to be God, man has lost the culture of his own body. As if he has yet to attain human status. We would seem to be a species of living beings in search of our identity, as men and women.

—LUCE IRIGARAY,
I Love to You: Sketches of a Possible Felicity in History

Acknowledgments

I am sharply aware that neither these brief remarks nor the text that follows will adequately acknowledge my many debts. Nevertheless, both Drew University and the American Council of Learned Societies must be thanked for their material support in enabling a sabbatical leave for the academic year 1997–1998, during which I finally produced these pages. Bill Regier, who was at the time director of the Johns Hopkins University Press, offered enthusiastic encouragement at a crucial stage; Helen Tartar, of Stanford University Press—an editor of rare grace, insight, and caring—finally gave the manuscript a home and turned it into a book. I am more than ever conscious of all I owe to my teacher and friend Rebecca Lyman, who first instilled in me a passion for the Arian controversy and for the history of theological ideas more generally, while also encouraging me to approach patristic thought as an aspect of late-antique culture. Drew University's Graduate School, where I have taught since 1991, has housed an incomparable company of faculty members and students joined in productively undisciplined conversation at the interstices of history, theology, and feminist theory; if I have achieved any apparent freshness or inventiveness of phrasing or thought, I have likely borrowed it from such "Drew school" collaborators. ("On the sly, I stole myself"—to snatch yet another line, this one from Hélène Cixous.) Finally, a fluidly constituted field of scholars of Christian antiquity has proved remarkable, in my experience, for its intellectual openness and lively sociability, consistently providing a welcoming home for my work (as well as my play), whether at the meetings of the North American Patristic Society or the American Academy of Religion or in other, frequently less formal settings. Many have thus nourished this work with their conversation and encouragement. Among those who actually read and commented on portions (or in some cases the entirety) of the manuscript are Sharon Betcher, Daniel Boyarin, David Brakke, Elizabeth Castelli, Elizabeth Clark, Jim Goehring, Patrick Gray, Catherine Keller, Derek Krueger, Vasiliki Limberis, Rebecca Lyman, Harry Maier, Neil McLynn, Patricia Cox Miller, Stephen Moore, Peter Savastano, Karen Torjesen, and Mark Vessey. Three in particular have aided and abetted my crimes of scholarly passion (or at the very least tactfully looked the other way)—Daniel Boyarin, Catherine Keller, and Mark Vessey. Without them, this book would have been inconceivable. I confess that, owing either to stubbornness or to lack of skill, I have failed to respond effectively to many of the most insightful criticisms and suggestions I have received. The text remains strangely mine, even as it now takes on a life of its own.

V.B.

Contents

Abbreviations

The following abbreviations occur in citations in the text. Information on particular English and original-language editions used is given in the notes and bibliography.

Anim. et res.   Gregory of Nyssa, *De anima et resurrectione* (On the soul and the resurrection)

Apol. sec.   Athanasius, *Apologia secunda contra Arianos* (Second apology against the Arians)

Ar.   Athanasius, *Orationes contra Arianos* (Orations against the Arians)

Decr.   Athanasius, *De decretis* (On the Council of Nicaea)

De virg.   Gregory of Nyssa, *De virginitate* (On virginity)

Ep. Aeg. Lib.   Athanasius, *Epistula encyclica ad episcopos Aegypti et Libyae* (Encyclical letter to the bishops of Egypt and Libya)

Ep. Afr.   Athanasius, *Epistula ad Afros* (Letter to the African bishops)

Eun.   Gregory of Nyssa, *Contra Eunomium* (Against Eunomius)

Fid.   Ambrose, *De fide* (On the faith)

H.e.   Eusebius, *Historia ecclesiastica* (Ecclesiastical history)

Inc.   Athanasius, *De incarnatione Verbi* (On the incarnation of the Word)

Off.   Ambrose, *De officiis ministrorum* (On the ministerial duties)

Opif.   Lactantius, *De opificio Dei* (On the workmanship of God)

Spir.   Ambrose, *De spiritu sancto* (On the Holy Spirit)

Syn.	Athanasius, *De synodis* (On the councils of Ariminum and Seleucia)
V. Anton.	Athanasius, *Vita Antonii* (Life of Antony)
Vid.	Ambrose, *De viduis* (On widows)
Virg.	Ambrose, *De virginibus* (On virgins)
V. Macr.	Gregory of Nyssa, *Vita Macrinae* (Life of Macrina)
V. Mos.	Gregory of Nyssa, *Vita Moysis* (Life of Moses)

Prologue

Interdisciplinary Plots

G raduate studies undertaken in Berkeley in the 1980s equipped me for professional play in that corner of church history known, rather pointedly, as "patristics." Formed by a discipline that bore the very name of the Father(s), I resisted what seemed to me its most punishingly patriarchal practice: the study of authoritative theological doctrine. I found an ally—as well as an alibi—in the version of late Roman religious history frequently tagged "late antiquity" and particularly associated with the work of Peter Brown. Having already imbibed feminism at the subversive edges of my undergraduate classics curriculum, I also eagerly read the available writings of Elizabeth Clark and the few other women historians working on what we sometimes referred to (with both humor and a certain ferocity) as "matristics." The approaches of social and cultural history promised to open up room for women and other "others" (historical and contemporary) in the field of ancient church history. Thus might an academic enterprise that had begun as the study of doctrine's "Sitz im Leben" finally put the Fathers and their teachings in their place—possibly even cut them down to size. After all, they had been taking up almost all the space for a virtual eternity, and some of us were impatient for change.

This book on manhood and the Trinity, written as I approach my fortieth birthday, may appear to expose my failure to live up to the aspirations of my twenties. Much as I have tried to elude their authority, the Fathers have continued to loom large in my view, and I seem destined to be a perversely loving daughter (even when equipped with cutting edges). Why not, then, surrender to destiny? I have asked myself. Wrapping the patristic authors tightly in a "context" has not, after all, diminished the sprawling literary body (evidently not yet a corpse) that remains at the center of ancient Christian historical studies. Thus, I have pursued a different strategy in these pages, encouraging the Fathers to grow and swell. I have let them overwhelm and engulf me. And then, with nowhere left to go, I have crawled into the skins of their lively and capacious texts. If I have brought my old interdisciplinary allies—"late antiquity" and "feminism"—inside with me, I am finally also ready to confide in them about the mysteries of doctrine buried in the heart of the patristic corpus, to which I am bound (as it now seems to me) by ties of desire as well as discipline.

~

It is a coarse view of history which can see nothing
in it but the flash of swords.

—*Henry Melvill Gwatkin,*
Studies of Arianism

Like the Arian marginalia that first cite, then dispute, and finally largely ignore the Nicene texts inscribed in the centers of the pages of a fifth-century manuscript,[1] the present study emerges as a series of digressive glosses on Henry Gwatkin's 1882 historiographic judgment. Gwatkin argued that "ecclesiastical history"—including the history of Christian belief—could not remain insulated from "secular history." However, he also sharply resisted the reductive secularization of church history that would convert ancient theological debates into mere wranglings for power, lamenting the selectivity of vision that could descry only "the flash of swords." His own goal was, rather, to produce a single, inclusive, "organic and indissoluble" account of the Nicene-Arian struggles, an account that would take seriously the extent to which ecclesiastical history was the "counterpart of secular" history, both "pervading it and permeated by it with the subtlest and most various influences."[2]

To a scholar writing near the turn of the millennium, the totalism of Gwatkin's vision may seem not merely naive but even sinister in its ambition. Yet it is perhaps easier than ever to sympathize with his insistence on the complexity of the causalities at work within a history that remains open-ended, as well as with his particular resistance to the foreclosures effected by narrowly politicizing interpretations of theological disputes. In this work, I have deliberately taken what might at first glance appear to be a "coarse view of history" (in Gwatkin's terms), adding another layer to recent reassessments of the Arian controversy by writing a new chapter in the history of masculine gender.[3] Indeed, it is by attending closely to the rhetorical "flash of swords" in the doctrinal debates of the fourth century that I hope to show how, in the late Roman Empire, theological discourse came to constitute a central arena in which manhood was not only tested and proven but also, in the course of events, redefined: when the confession of the full and equal divinity of Father, Son, and Spirit became for the first time the *sine qua non* of doctrinal orthodoxy, masculinity (I argue) was conceived anew, in terms that heightened the claims of patriarchal authority while also cutting manhood loose from its traditional fleshly and familial moorings. My aim is not, however, to *reduce* theological texts to sources for a cultural history of masculine gender but rather, precisely by *also* reading them as such, to enable the flashing swords of ancient manhood to vivify theological material that has become so deadeningly familiar that we can no longer perceive some of its most fascinating and indeed downright queer aspects. By opening our eyes to (re)conceptions of manhood, we may gain deeper insight into the powerful paradox of God's singular multiplicity. The credal formula "begotten, not made," gives birth to a sublime patriliny, as masculinized, sexualized, and pluralized theological metaphors are balanced against the one God's transcendence of a humanity defined by sexual difference and the generative flux of the flesh.

Where I depart from Gwatkin's actual historical practice—while still, I think, adhering to his asserted methodology—is in refusing to protect doctrine, the authoritative teaching of the church, from the effects of time.[4] As Maurice Wiles has phrased it, "a question does need to be asked about the degree of continuity between the revisionist Trinitarianisms of the present moment and the orthodox Trinitarianism of the fourth century." Adopting and adapting Wiles's language, I further acknowledge that my own framing of that question "will no doubt be influenced" by deeply personal preoccupations and communal commitments.[5] When I argue that fourth-century trinitarian doctrine both pervades and is permeated by emergent late-antique claims for masculinity, I am implicitly placing Wiles's question about doctrinal continuity into the context of contemporary concerns about gender, sexuality, and the body. The answer to the question will not, however, be a simple affirmation of discontinuity—not least because the very act of addressing the difference of the past always implicates the present in the past (and vice versa). If I call for critical—and critically intertwined—reassessments of both theology and gender in antiquity, I am attempting to shift readings of history; but in so doing, I am also attempting to revise present conceptions of God and manhood. The more carefully I resist collapsing distinctions by meticulously reconstructing the particularity of the past, the more intimately I weave myself into the texture of my history. Continuity and discontinuity are not, perhaps, so much opposite ends on a spectrum of historiographic options as necessarily twinned aspects of the relation of the present with the past, of relationality itself. A trinitarian doctrine that allows itself to mingle with the body of secular history will (dis)continually reconceive its truths under "the subtlest and most various influences." To retell the history of doctrine is to rewrite theology.

Inevitably, then, what I have above named a redefinition of manhood becomes visible primarily through my own re-marking of the traces of gradual, ambiguous processes sometimes resistant to the inscription of boundaries and the recording of shifts in terrain that are so beloved by historians, cartographers of time. To map out a plot, to write history at all, is perhaps not only to force one's "material" but also, and more to the point, to coerce one's readers. Yet every writer of history is herself first of all a reader of history, coerced but also actively struggling, writing *back*, *re*marking upon an always already marked page. Here, then, I add my marginalia to an ongoing historiographic tradition.

"We must . . . take up the neglected data," writes Gwatkin.[6] Must we not therefore take up the neglected matter of man? As we shall see, a decisive shift in ancient Mediterranean ideals of masculinity had taken place by the end of the fourth century. (Around this "shift"—inscribed as a re-mark on Gwatkin's text—pivots the drama of my own historical narrative.) Furthermore, the production of a sophisticated and tightly interwoven body of Christian literary texts contributed powerfully to the consolidation of that broader cultural shift. The emergent corpus of "patristic" writings, authored predominately by ascetic bishops deeply involved in the trinitarian controversies of their day, now stands on the near side of a chronological watershed that it initially helped to create: receding is the venerable figure of the civic leader and familial patriarch; approaching is a man marked as a spiritual father, by virtue of his place in the patrilineal chain of apostolic succession, and also as the leader of a new citizenry, fighting heroically in a contest of truth in which (as Gregory of Nyssa puts it) the weapon of choice is the "sword of the Word."

I am not really asking "whether . . . a watershed was passed" (to borrow Peter Brown's phrasing) but instead "what it is like for a great traditional society to pass over a watershed."[7] Rather than straining to prove that a change had in fact taken place (for this account of change is, after all, simply another version of a fiction that historians have been telling and re-telling at least since Gibbon, indeed since late antiquity itself), I want to turn one aspect of this freshly remarked "fact" into a problem, so as to make it a matter of curiosity—and it is perhaps no small undertaking to render the "unchanging," unmarked, genderless gender an object of curiosity or questioning. I want to ask "what it is like" when certain of the more vociferous members of "a great traditional society" succeed in both raising the stakes and gaining the upper hand in the ancient contest of men by adopting a radically transcendent ideal of manhood that commands more of the cultural authority of virility than the traditional roles of father or husband, soldier or statesman, orator or philosopher.[8] Such is the wager of many of the surviving anti-Arian texts. That wager, I am arguing, in large part pays off: the most stridently (and innovatively) dualistic and transcendentalizing theological assertions of the fourth-century Nicene Christians usher in a new era in the history of masculine gender. The assertion of the Son's absolute divinity and the divinization of humanity anticipated in his incarnation register their historical effect in the rigid discipline of fourth-century bodies resisting their own carnality, and in the sclerosis of words fixed in transcendentalized corpora of Scripture and creed, dogmatic commentary and liturgical text. A particular narration of salvation history, shot through with cosmological implications, sinks itself into the lives of those who incarnate it in the telling: as the Son attains full divinity in theological discourse, men begin to groom themselves for godliness, even as they also attempt, more audaciously than ever, to bring heaven down to the earthly city.

One of the paradoxes to be explored in this book is the extent to which a hypertranscendent masculinity incorporated characteristics or stances traditionally marked as "feminine"—from virginal modesty, retirement from the public sphere, and reluctance to challenge or compete on the one hand, to maternal fecundity and nurturance on the other. Indeed, feminization itself was frequently—though not inevitably—a device by which the new ascetic order of maleness distinguished itself from the female-identified carnal order it claimed to supersede. This was not an entirely unprecedented development in the history of the ancient Mediterranean. Nicole Loraux has argued that Homeric epic and later heroic legend perpetuate "a tradition that . . . postulates that a man worthy of the name is all the more virile precisely because he harbors within himself something of the feminine."[9] She goes on to suggest that Plato, in resistance to an ideology of the classical polis that defined "the man/citizen according to a notion of virility that is impermeable to anything feminine,"[10] retrieved and partly transformed this heroic ideal of a manhood that encompasses the feminine, most notoriously in his use of the metaphors of pregnancy and birthing to articulate the intellectual potency of the philosophic man.[11] Carlin Barton has tracked broadly analogous patterns of resistance to the Roman Republican ideal of a hard (*durus*) or weighty (*gravis*) manhood, as these emerge in the period of the civil wars and early Roman Empire: "In the besieged city one could sport. Now the 'heavy' and 'light' were equally weightless. The Roman male, liberated from rigid masculine sex roles, delights in the freedom of playing a slave and a woman."[12] In such a context, the transgressive fantasies of persecuted Jews and Christians, who imagine themselves "mothers" giving birth in suffering to their own ultimate triumph over their oppressors, begin to seem less marginal as cultural products.[13] The later subversions of classical ideals of civic manhood by a Christian elite under imperial patronage likewise contain echoes of the feminized virility of the wounded hero, echoes partly mediated by the Greek Platonic tradition and the early imperial fascination with figures of noble slavishness, triumphant victimization, and salvific suffering.[14] Or, to turn the argument the other way around: the particular "heroism" of the Platonic philosopher and the Roman gladiator (as well as the Jewish and Christian martyrs) have been mediated for later readers—to a greater extent than is perhaps generally acknowledged—by a late-ancient Christian ascetic ideal of masculinity.[15]

Although the very notion of analyzing fourth-century trinitarian doctrine in terms of the history of masculine gender might seem impossibly "coarse" to some, my intention is not to elide theological issues by suggesting that the long-enduring Nicene doctrine of God—with its explicit and virtually unprecedented preoccupation with the concepts of Fatherhood, Sonship, and the transcendence of the Spirit—is simply a residue of late-ancient gender politics. (Nor do I wish to fall into a theological reductivism that errs in the opposite direction, positioning the roles of men and ideals of manliness not as the cause but as the effect of doctrine—for of course it is also not my view that late-ancient concepts of masculine gender are merely by-products of a masculinist trinitarian discourse framed in the terms of a highly dualistic cosmology). As a cultural historian interested in ideas about gender, I remark on what appears to me remarkable—namely, that Nicene Christianity's contested articulation of the roles of Father, Son, and Spirit emerges as one of the most potent sites for reimagining manhood in the late Roman Empire. As a historical theologian, I interrogate ancient worlds of Christian thought and language that continue to grip me with the stubborn force of long centuries of habit—my ambivalent engagement and even identification with this history being a matter of fact, as I perceive it, rather than a confession or an assertion, far less a complaint. "Coarseness" is merely a ploy for disrupting a scholarly tradition that cannot imagine commingling talk of a trinitarian God with the delicate topics of human desire, fecundity, and the gendered body. What I strive for, finally, is not the drama of an apocalyptic exposé of history but rather the nuance of an attentive, inquisitive, and intimate reading of theological literature, a reading that preserves the subtle weave of the ancient texts more or less whole—if by no means leaving our understanding of them unchanged.

The Christian church was the *impresario* of a wider change. Its organization and the careers of its heroes made brutally explicit the consequences of the focusing of "divine power" on human beings. The Christian church produced the Apostles, whose deeds were remembered, and gained in the telling, in the Christian communities, the martyrs of the second and third centuries, the already formidable bishops of the later third century, and finally, the success of great holy men of ascetic origin who ringed the settled communities of the Eastern Mediterranean, from Saint Anthony onwards.

—*Peter Brown,*
The Making of Late Antiquity

I have suggested that this study may be read as an extended marginal gloss on a passage from Gwatkin's 1882 *Studies of Arianism*. But it is equally important to acknowledge that this study is written between and indeed sometimes layered over the lines of Peter Brown's 1978 *The Making of Late Antiquity*. In that work, Brown argues that "the locus of the supernatural had come to shift significantly" between the second and the fifth centuries, and he charts the effects of this shift on "the claims of particular human beings to represent the supernatural on earth," proposing that "what gives Late Antiquity its special flavor is precisely the claims of human beings."[16] Frequently positioning Christianity not as the cause but as the symptom of social and religious currents arising within ancient Mediterranean culture, Brown also assigns to Christianity a paradigmatic or even directorial role as "*impresario* of a wider change."[17] This concise formulation bears tremendous weight in *The Making of Late Antiquity* and in Brown's oeuvre more generally; indeed, one might say (as Brown later says of ancient Christian discourse itself) that it encapsulates a "facilitating narrative that [holds] in suspense precisely what we should now call 'the problem of Christianization.'"[18] According to Brown's own script, "the Christian church" staged the show of late antiquity and thus may also function in his text as a metonym for "late antiquity" itself. "The church's" key agents or players were figures like Cyprian and Constantine, Antony and Pachomius—the bishops, emperors, and "holy men" who emerged as the leading human claimants to divine power in late antiquity, in the wake of the shift in the "locus of the supernatural." "Agents of the supernatural," these men "had brought down into the dubious and tension-ridden world beneath the moon a clarity and a stability associated with the unchanging heavens."[19] The paradoxically all-too-human institutional foundations and stellar careers of such "upstart heroes" possessed of "*mens caelestis, pectus sublime*"[20] came both to overshadow the traditional social structures of the city and to outshine the starry canopy that had shed its soft glow on the men and women of earlier centuries. Although initially also identified with bishops and emperors, the heroes who interest Brown most are, finally, the desert ascetics who quickly displace bishops and emperors in his text. "Constantine, the 'man of God' and his new [episcopal] colleagues were not the only bearers of that title," he notes. "They were the younger contemporaries of men who had begun to carry the role in society of the 'friend of God' yet one stage further. . . . In the making of Late Antiquity, the monks of Egypt played a role more enduring than that of Constantine."[21] If Christianity is a metonym for late antiquity, the ascetic holy man is a metonym for late-ancient Christianity, and Brown's making of late antiquity also makes the holy man. The desert is the new city, and the city remakes itself in the image of the desert, as the monk overtakes the bishop and an asceticized episcopacy displaces both philosophers and magistrates in their roles of civic leadership.[22]

My own narrative consciously replays Brown's at many points, an act of homage no less where it may seem least faithful. By proposing that readings of a restricted set of Christian theological texts might add up to a study of "the making of late-antique *man*," I am taking the considerable liberty of relabeling Brown's own accomplishment while also implicitly reproducing —indeed potentially intensifying—his positioning of Christianity as the "*impresario* of a wider change." In repeating his narrative move, I do not intend simply to affirm Brown's assertion that Christianity is both distinctive relative to contemporaneous paganism and prototypically "late antique"; nor do I choose to criticize directly a narrative history of "late antiquity" that consistently makes Christianization the central plot. It is in order to explore and expose its effects—rather than defend or dispute its accuracy— that I inhabit one contemporary, ambiguously secularized version of a story of Christian triumph, a story that, as Brown (among others) points out, was originally authored by the late-ancient Christians themselves.[23] My argument also implicitly cites Brown's plot insofar as I, too, am interested in the link between shifts in the roles of men and ideals of masculinity, on the one hand, and shifts in cosmology, on the other. For Brown, what "makes" late antiquity is in large part the collective imaginative construction of a new "world," or a novel way of imagining the universe, centered in the perceived closure of what had been a fluid and "open frontier" between the human and the divine realms.[24] According to his account, the new men of late antiquity, as "agents of the supernatural," emerge partly in order to negotiate the hard boundary between heaven and earth freshly inscribed on the map of the cosmos. These "upstart heroes"—combining an exaggerated "upper-worldly" orientation with an almost unprecedented level of "worldly" authority[25]—arise at the paradoxical joint of the newly estranged realms of heaven and earth.

While Brown's narrative will be foundational for my own in these ways and others, I will also overwrite some of the palimpsest's lines rather thickly, in the course of bringing out my own arguments. First, as I have already indicated, this work will deal extensively with the interpretation of theological texts and themes, focusing particularly on the sedimented language of late-fourth-century trinitarian discourse. To encroach very far into territory jealously guarded by historians of Christian doctrine is an act understandably avoided by many secular scholars of late Roman religion and culture, especially those interested in downplaying the often exaggerated uniqueness or centrality of Christianity in its late-antique setting. In addition, Christian anthropology and Christology have seemed far more useful to the more down-to-earth purposes of cultural historians than have the high reaches of the doctrine of God.[26] And yet, as I am suggesting, it is trinitarian thought—characteristically patrilineal in its preoccupations and transcendentalizing in its tactics—that reveals most fully and directly the impact of shifts in cosmology and social roles on the positioning of *men*.

Second, I must introduce an explicit and critical analysis of gender into the text, if Brown's making of late antiquity is to accommodate my own account of the making of late-antique man. Attentive to the realm of the performative in a culture in which the actors are almost always male and gender is the performance par excellence, Brown brightly illumines the shifting contours of manly roles played out in late antiquity, but for the most part he carefully avoids naming masculine gender as such.[27] In *The Making of Late Antiquity* he speaks generically of "the claims of human beings," and elsewhere in his writings he enlarges the category of "holy men" to include "holy women" as well—rhetorical strategies of inclusion that partly mask perduring gendered distinctions (historical as well as contemporary). Recently, however, Brown has remarked directly upon the "stolid male identity" of the "holy man" and begun to interrogate not only the exclusion of women from that "highly public, even confrontational role" but also the transformation of masculine gender: the "imaginative alchemy" by which a man "turned . . . completely from the procreation that defined male gender in the normal world" might become, like an angel, "an unfailing source of hyperprocreativity in the world around him."[28] Thickening such a line of interpretation in order to mark more clearly the turning and bending of ancient norms of masculinity, I will seek both to reinhabit the world of the ancient texts and to extricate myself from the enveloping fabric of a male-centered "late antiquity." At this point, the endeavor is perhaps similar to Simon Goldhill's attempt (framed in response to Brown's treatment of asceticism in *Body and Society*) to loosen the weave of a scholarly narrative that may, at points, leave too little room for dialogic play and ironic distancing. The "problem," however, from the perspective of this study, lies not with the inherent didactic sternness of the theological or (as Goldhill puts it) "homiletic" sources used by Brown but rather with a particular performative mode of interpretation that tends, in the service of directly reproducing a "world," to elide the creative work of texts and the critical agency of (other) readers and writers (as Goldhill also suggests).[29] Here, it is partly by explicitly enacting my own role as a (writing) reader that I attempt to open gaps in the world of late antiquity so as to gain critical purchase on the *textual* production of late-ancient man.

Finally, I will also continue to expand the view of late antiquity to encompass the "settled communities" of the late empire, as these appear through the idealizing lenses of the bishops who inhabit them: the desert—despite its widespread metaphoric currency—was not the only theater, and its "holy men" were not necessarily the most representative or revealing icons of "late antiquity" or even of "late antique Christianity."[30] The ascetic authors with whom I am primarily concerned were preoccupied with the imaginative reinterpretation and reoccupation of the city, rather than with its abandonment. For these bishops, an already ancient version of patriarchy remained firmly in place, as the male body was not simply dissolved through its transformation into angelic status but rather subtly remolded to fit the context of a new patrilineage and novel modes of rhetorical competition and civic governance. Making such continuities visible so as also to clarify the variety of mutations taking place will involve shifting some of the emphases of a historiographic tradition heavily influenced by models of "privatization" and the "fall of the city." Such models are partly driven by an otherworldly Christian teleology that may prove inadequate not only for the interpretation of "late antiquity" more broadly but also for the interpretation even of Christianity's most outspoken ascetics.

The Copernican revolution has yet to have its final effects in the male imaginary. And by centering man outside himself, it has occasioned above all man's ex-stasis within the transcendental (subject). Rising to a perspective that would dominate the totality, to the vantage point of greatest power, he thus cuts himself off from the bedrock, from his empirical relationship with the matrix that he claims to survey. To specularize and to speculate. Exiling himself ever further (toward) where the greatest power lies, he thus becomes the "sun" if it is around him that things turn, a pole of attraction stronger than the "earth." Meanwhile the excess in this universal fascination is that "she" also turns upon herself.

—*Luce Irigaray,*
"Any Theory of the 'Subject'"

In order to put a new spin on the late-ancient revolution of manhood, I will sometimes find it necessary to veer away from the historical page altogether: this work is, finally, explicitly transgressive of even those wide-flung disciplinary boundaries that encompass the well-glossed and multilayered texts of both "patristic" and "late Roman" history. Here, epigraphs and embedded citations are intended to gesture toward a hypertextual superfluity buried within and spilling beyond the interpretation of history, to map—and thereby make partly accessible—a terrain of interwoven textuality that might accommodate the looping path of analysis pursued by a scholar who not only revolves around a transcendent masculine subjectivity but also "turns upon herself." Revoicing words received from the Fathers, I seek to capture late-ancient manhood's rays and send them "curving to and fro in turn with [my] cycles." My aim is thus not simply to reflect (upon) masculinity flatly or "objectively," with the rote fidelity of one positioned as the mirroring object of the singular sex of man. Rather, reading mimetically while remaining in motion, I hope also to insinuate difference into the apparent sameness of the texts, frequently twisting the inexactitude of repetition into the service of parody. Such an interpretive technique functions as a disciplined refusal of the choice between the light and the serious, the faithless and the faithful, or the critical and the apologetic reading. A parodic reflection of and upon late-ancient theological writings will take the shape of a convex mimesis,[31] on the one hand, enhancing and exposing the swell of a "masculine" discourse, while also conforming to the complex contours of concavity, on the other, giving a new turn to a tradition of theological speculation that thereby begins to curve in on itself, seeking the shining inner spaces of its own "feminine" excesses.[32]

Fragmentary interpolations of the poetic philosophizing of Luce Irigaray and the philosophical poetics of Hélène Cixous will play a particularly strong—if intentionally unsystematic—role in the attempt to open this study out onto a broader, interdisciplinary conversation that is yet continuous with (perhaps even, as I am suggesting, imaginably contained within the subtle folds of) the patristic writings themselves. Both Irigaray and Cixous can be named "feminists of difference," whose response to the political problem of sex is not to attempt to rise above a linguistic economy of gender in which woman is always marked as man's "other" but rather, working from within that economy, to decenter man by actively multiplying the sexes. In their writings, sexual difference is produced through the elaboration of a discursive position for a woman who does not merely serve as man's reflective object but also—on the basis of her very exclusion from rationality, on the discourse's own terms—remains "elsewhere," as Irigaray puts it.[33] If ancient Christian writings have been understood to adopt a dominant strategy of transcendence in relation to sexual distinctions by allowing (some) women to join men in shedding their gender—an approach both criticized and effectively appropriated by their feminist interpreters[34]—I have now chosen also to read those works for the traces of sexual difference that are simultaneously created and negated, contained and excluded, within fourth-century trinitarian discourse. Reading and writing to mark and thereby make a difference turns out, however, to be an immensely difficult project, constrained by a theological tradition that appears to be fundamentally oriented toward the task of reproducing one and the same Man. Indeed, despite more than two decades of patristic scholarship devoted to the study of "women" and the "female," the very attempt to shift the interpretive focus away from the category of the generic "Man" toward that of the sexed "man" meets with resistance at almost every turn. The theoretical problem presented by masculine gender, not only for late-ancient Christian discourse but also for the subsequent philosophical and theological tradition, has been framed by Irigaray, ironically, as the failure of an intellectualizing transcendence. The masculine subject of historical record is founded on the refusal to recognize the particularity of manhood;

systematically mistaking the limit of his gender for a principle of universality, "he dreams that he alone is nature and that it is up to him to undertake the spiritual task of differentiating himself from (his) nature and from himself."[35] If "the Copernican revolution has yet to have its final effects in the male imaginary," as Irigaray phrases it whimsically, this is because, even now, the philosophic implications of the ("feminine") earth's movements for the ("masculine") sun's position have not been grasped.

The discipline required for the resexing of man involves the skills of both the critic and the lover. My own narrowly focused genealogical interrogation of late-ancient manhood will frequently intersect with Irigaray's wide-ranging analysis of the male subjectivity produced and transmitted in the texts of a European-centered philosophical tradition.[36] In particular, Irigaray's subversive reading of Jacques Lacan's interpretation of Freud will resonate at many points with my assessment of the ideational habits of masculine self-formation that, as I am arguing, crystallize clearly and sharply for the first time in fourth-century Christian texts. These include the translation of human generativity "upward," from the site of the body to language or word, that is, logos; the identification of the disembodied and idealized realm of logos with power, creativity, order, knowledge, insight, and virility itself; the dissociation of the phallicized logos from the sex of man; and the implicit (and productively disingenuous) claim that this veiling of male bodily particularity potentially cancels the significance of the hierarchy of gender and indeed of sexual difference itself.

Just as Irigaray's critique of the Western philosophical tradition resonates with my own reading of ancient trinitarian theology, so does her readerly technique of parodic mimesis, erotic both in its intimately attentive and evocatively disruptive style and in its explicit attempt to insert a female body and desire into the metaphors of and for language. Literary critic Hélène Cixous is perhaps even more deeply committed to the explicit feminization and eroticization of language—or rather, more specifically, of writing—pursued not least through her elaborate reworking of a literary culture's heritage of metaphor and myth, in interpretations that themselves effectively dissolve the distinction between the figurative and the literal, text and body. Reading, according to Cixous, is "writing the ten thousand pages of every page," making the text "grow and multiply," "making love to the text." Reading and making love are "the same spiritual exercise."[37]

Such a close identification of the sexual and the interpretive realms is also crucial to my understanding of my task. Reading the Fathers sensitively and responsively—but also assertively and without too much fear of the friction experienced in the encounter, so as finally to put the sex back into late-antique man—is for me necessarily an explicitly erotic, as well as a profoundly spiritual, practice. However, it is not, strictly speaking, a "heterosexual" erotic practice. If (adapting Irigaray's language) "the option left to me is *to have a fling with the Fathers*, which is easier said than done," the goal is not to reproduce two sexes—which turn out to be no more than one—but rather to give rise to a "sex which is not one"—that is, to a "sex" that is multiple and fluid.[38] My reading of the patristic texts frequently exposes what Irigaray dubs a "hom(m)o-sexual" economy of discourse ("consider the exemplary case of father-son relationships");[39] a pneumatic exchange, lip-to-lip with the garrulous Fathers, will, however, lead to still queerer encounters.[40] "There are possibilities that have never yet come to light," Cixous reminds us. "Others entirely unforeseen that have come over us only once. Flowers, animals, engines, grandmothers, trees, rivers, we are traversed, changed, surprised."[41]

~

This study begins with a narrative introduction to the precursors of late-antique masculinity. In order to plot a historical argument, I will consider briefly the trajectory of manhood's cultural evolution in the second and third centuries, presenting the fourth-century developments in a chronological context that highlights both their continuities and discontinuities with the immediate past. The main portion of the text, however, is neither narrative nor chronological in its primary presentation. I have chosen to explore fourth-century masculinity by reading certain major works of three prominent and roughly contemporaneous Fathers—Athanasius of Alexandria, Gregory of Nyssa, and Ambrose of Milan—each of whom played a crucial role in defending Nicene trinitarian doctrine as the touchstone of "orthodox" and "catholic" belief. If Athanasius retroactively created the reputation of Nicaea's council and creed (325), Gregory participated in the Cappadocian effort to consolidate Athanasius's success in the Greek-speaking East, which effort institutionalized that success through the decisions of the ecumenical Council of Constantinople (381). For his part, Ambrose notoriously carried the victory for the Latin West, as performed locally at the Council of Aquileia (381).

The choice to work with only three figures results first of all from the most basic methodological considerations, my aim being—putting it simply—to balance the specific and the general in exploring a historical phenomenon as broad and elusive as the conception of masculinity within late-ancient Christian discourse. I have also chosen to limit interactions with scholarly works: although the notes record some of my most direct and immediate debts and occasionally clarify points of agreement and disagreement with other interpreters, I do not attempt bibliographic comprehensiveness; on the contrary, I am deliberately and idiosyncratically selective in my engagement of passages from scholarly works. My hope is that sustained readings of influential writings attributed to a single historical figure, seasoned with spirited and often playful dialogue but relatively unencumbered by conventional scholarly polemics, can show how an individual textual corpus both constructs "man" as an authorial persona and weaves a coherent theory of gendered subjectivity across a broad loom of works traditionally categorized variously as doctrinal, moral or ascetic, and historical or biographical. By juxtaposing three such sets of readings, dealing with figures neither historically unrelated nor closely linked, I can explore points of overlap and collusion that point toward broader cultural patternings, without simply repeating the coercive inscription of consensuality by which an authoritative patristic body of literature is continually reconstituted as such—not least via lengthy catenae of citations meant to demonstrate widespread ancient unanimity on a given point.

Triadic patterns are, finally, also intended to hint at ways of reconceiving both masculine gender and trinitarian theology along paths neither sharply discontinuous nor straightforwardly in line with the patristic texts that have engaged me. In playing with various possibilities for casting Athanasius, Gregory of Nyssa, and Ambrose in the roles of Father, Son, and Spirit, respectively, I am attempting not only to reveal how narrative and figural representation shape and reshape a historiographic tradition—in this case, the story of the "triumph" of Nicene orthodoxy—but also, and more importantly, to open space for ongoing reconceptions of divinity and the cosmos, transcendence and particularity. Such reconceptions might accommodate the fecundity of gendered desire and embodiment *differently,* while yet remaining in intimate—indeed fertile and transporting—conversation with the Fathers themselves. Framing this agenda is an ironic reclaiming of the Nicene assertion that the Son is "begotten, not made," by the Father, with its concomitant, paradoxical disavowal of any literalized biologism: interpreted as a sign of resistance to the frequently posited dichotomy of "sex" and "gender," "natural essence" and "cultural construction," this compact credal formula may (I am suggesting) be fashioned anew as the linguistic matrix of a sublimely supple sexuality and a fluidly engendered transcendence.

Introduction

The Lineage of Late-Antique Man

Manliness was not a birthright. It was something that had to be won.
Perhaps physical strength once had been the definitive criterion of masculine
excellence on the semi-legendary playing fields of Ilion and Latium, but by
Hellenistic and Roman times the sedentary elite of the ancient city had
turned away from warfare and gymnastics as definitive agonistic activities,
firmly redrawing the defining lines of competitive space so as to exclude
those without wealth, education, or leisure. Political and legal rivalries filled
varying proportions of the leisured gentleman's time, depending on the size
and relative independence of his native city; competitive displays of wealth
(mostly liturgical extravagance in the Greek cities, mostly private
extravagance at Rome) consumed varying proportions of his capital—
but the form of competitive masculine activity that proved most
electrifying as a spectator sport was rhetoric.

—*Maud W. Gleason,*
Making Men: Sophists and Self-Presentation in Ancient Rome

I dentifying rhetorical performance as the primary locus of masculine
self-fashioning in the early empire, Maud Gleason undertakes to
read second-century manhood through the careers of two dazzlingly successful public speakers, both associated with the cultural movement commonly known as the "second sophistic." Favorinus of Arles, a congenital eunuch, and Polemo of Laodicea, author of a physiognomic treatise equipping
spectators to distinguish real men from counterfeits, were not only professional rivals but also visible embodiments of what Gleason names "opposing paradigms of masculinity."[1] Depicting "opposite poles of possibility in
masculine deportment"[2]—flamboyantly sensual effeminacy on the one
hand and rigidly controlled hypermasculinity on the other—these two rhetoricians engaged in a public competition that enacted the extremes of gendered self-stylings available to the elite men of a society for which "nature,

as a category, [was] a creation of culture."[3] Gleason explores the era's preoccupation with the arts by which manly nature was cultivated, a consciousness attributable not only to the relatively continuous conditions of life in the competitive, face-to-face communities of the ancient Mediterranean, "where one's adequacy as a man was always under suspicion and one's performance was constantly being judged," but also to the particular destabilization of the social roles of the civic elite that came with the advent of "an increasingly centralized imperial government."[4] Following a hint from Michel Foucault,[5] she identifies as typical of the imperial age both Polemo's overtly conservative impulse to articulate and enforce a "sign-system of status" hitherto wordlessly transmitted and Favorinus's contrasting emphasis on a highly individualized technique of self-definition seemingly cut loose from the constraints of convention.[6]

Both styles of masculine self-cultivation weighed heavily on the malleable body as the bearer of the essential truth about a man. In this, they may perhaps be interpreted not as opposing poles but rather as two sides of the same coin. Polemo's investment in the complex arts of physiognomic discernment, by which a man's inner character, whether "effeminate" or "virile," might be carefully deduced from the external signs of his movement, stance, gaze, or voice, finally posits not anatomy but deportment—the *trained* body—as the site of masculine self-definition. What is implicitly sought, in other words, is a successfully naturalized manhood, a flawlessly embodied performance of a culture's conception of virility—hard rather than soft, erect rather than slack or aslant, dry rather than moist or slippery, and rough or hirsute rather than smooth. Favorinus's mercurial displays of meticulously crafted, mobile personae—an improvisational narrative technique enhanced by the self-proclaimed paradoxes of his identity as an innately womanish man, a Greek-speaking Gaul, and a philosopher who had survived an emperor's disapproval—likewise drew attention to the power of artfully assumed roles to create and reshape a man's natural superiority. For both Polemo and Favorinus, masculinity was defined by the cutting edge of risk and uncertainty, the threat that a performance might fail or a mask slip. Favorinus brashly, indeed manfully, courted this danger by flaunting his sing-song, high-pitched voice and androgynous appearance, while the vigilant Polemo fortified his defenses against an ever-encroaching effeminacy. In so doing, both acknowledged the fundamental indeterminacy of a manliness that was, as Gleason puts it, "not a birthright" but "an achieved state."[7]

The second century initially seems a precarious moment in the history of ancient Mediterranean masculinity. When competing styles of virile self-definition had come to rely so heavily and self-consciously on naturalizing strategies of embodiment, the "unnatural" effort required to maintain such diverse enactments of native masculine authority might appear in constant danger of exposing its own contradictions. Yet Gleason skillfully argues for the stability of the competitive economy inhabited by Polemo and Favorinus, in which a struggle for power explicitly framed in terms of contested definitions of masculine gender was used both to define class distinctions and to negotiate status among elite men. Each rhetorician thrived on his rivalry with the other, and such rivalries contributed to the vitality of a municipal ruling class now largely constituted as such by the power of the performed word.[8] In fact, as Gleason suggests in closing, it was not until the late fourth century, when political power had finally moved away from the city and the civic elite had been largely absorbed into the late-imperial bureaucracy, that rhetorical performance lost its power to produce manhood and gendered invective could no longer be risked by a tradition-based aristocracy whose power was rapidly waning. As Gleason puts it, late antiquity begins when the cities grow silent and men no longer have to play to their audiences but "start to draw on extra-social sources of validation, bypassing the approval of their peers to a hitherto unparalleled extent"; it is this change that "fostered the eccentric behavior of larger-than-life personalities in the fourth century, the age of Antony, Athanasius, Constantine, and Julian."[9] Despite her emphasis on the sharpness of the social and cultural shift taking place in the late empire, Gleason is able to see foreshadowings of late-antique manhood in both Polemo and Favorinus. If Polemo presents himself as "a man of almost occult insight" and Favorinus places immense confidence in "the transcendental nature" of ongoing self-transformation, both of these representatives of second-century styles of manhood may be understood to anticipate the audacious claims of the fourth-century "holy man."[10] Indeed, Gleason hints that the "temporal security provided by the church" partly reduplicated "the immense security of the *Pax Romana*" that afforded local aristocrats the luxury of challenging each other's very manhood.[11]

My aim here is to follow Gleason's lead in extending the account of second-century fashionings of manhood into the third and early fourth centuries, finally homing in on those particular "larger-than-life personalities" of the late empire with whom this work will be primarily concerned. The popular appeal of Favorinus's assertively effeminate self-styling (which Gleason, despite her persuasive efforts at interpretation, claims to the end to find slightly puzzling)[12] may have had as much to do with adaptation to the waning of civic autonomy in the early empire as with the reassuring stability of the *Pax Romana*—as Carlin Barton's study of the seductive figure of the gladiator and its Christian counterpart, the martyr, suggests by analogy.[13] In other words, a showcased preoccupation with the fragility of masculine gender may be less an indication of the luxury of the secure than an instance of making a virtue out of necessity. Empire had reshaped the city into a stage for agonistic performances of a multifaceted manhood distinguished by its power to turn vulnerability—frequently figured as a capacity for feminization—to advantage. And yet, where vulnerability could be turned to advantage, fragility might begin to be as much a part of the habitual structure of masculine subjectivity as a reaction to external circumstances.[14] By the late fourth century, the stance of the suffering martyr, whose disciplined body bespoke an inner virtue, was being adopted by Christians who not only avoided a state execution but also allied themselves ambiguously with imperial power; similarly, the feminizing tactics of a Favorinus were successfully accommodated—but also carefully disciplined—within a more stridently monologic and radically transcendentalizing ascetic masculinity whose particular incarnation owed at least as much to Polemo as to Favorinus. In commenting on the penchant of late-antique men to "draw on extra-social sources of validation" while ignoring the opinions of their peers, Gleason cannot mean to be taken too literally. Her point is both that what counted for a social peer group had partially shifted away from the community of local notables and that the strategies of self-presentation that could be relied on to persuade even a local audience had likewise subtly changed. At any rate, she is surely right to imply that the highly centralized autocracy by which the late empire was governed contributed to the conditions wherein male subjects began to style themselves more transcendently. Yet continuities with the deeper past remained significant—as she puts it, invoking the language of Pierre Bourdieu, "the *habitus* dies hard!"[15]

Although the rules that implicitly governed public speech changed rather dramatically by the late fourth century, and the written text came to vie with the authority of the spoken word, the cities did not, after all, fall silent. Indeed, as Averil Cameron frames it, the growing influence of Christianity was largely a triumph of discourse, a mark of the success of men who "talked and wrote themselves into a position where they spoke and wrote the rhetoric of empire."[16] More often than not, local communities remained the sites in which the men of a new elite performed their "most electrifying" claims to an achieved transcendence—even when this involved elaborate appeals to offstage presences both human and divine.

When so much continuity is woven into the texture of the most remarkable cultural discontinuities, even historians taking on the dubious— but finally also unavoidable—challenge of producing overarching narratives often do best to attend to particulars. Accordingly, I will attempt to bridge the gap between the second and fourth centuries, between a predominately pagan and a more preponderantly Christian society, by focusing on three relatively contained but evocative intervening textual moments. The first is the record of the disciplining of Paul of Samosata, bishop of Antioch in the late third century, by an extralocal assembly of bishops and other leading Christians. The second is Eusebius of Caesarea's restyling of the portrait of Christian manhood via his idealizing life of Origen, written at the opening of the fourth century. The third is Lactantius's contemporaneous depiction of the ideal man from the perspective of divine providence. Both Eusebius and Lactantius are cultural apologists for Christianity, living through not only the Great Persecution but also the conversion of Constantine to Christianity. They are thus poised on the cusp of the turn in political and religious life strongly associated in scholarly tradition with the dawning of "late antiquity."

Spectacle of Shamelessness: The Condemnation of Paul of Samosata

Gleason closes her work by posing a question: does Polemo's self-styling, seemingly more conservative than Favorinus's, perhaps look "forward to that vast cultural shift now called late antiquity," while Favorinus's diasporic and restlessly self-transcending manhood, apparently so radical, remains the artful product of a highly traditional culture? When the scholarly gaze shifts forward a century, similar paradoxes and questions, likewise explicitly raised from the perspective of hindsight, haunt readings of the flamboyant performer Paul of Samosata, bishop of Antioch, and his uncompromisingly sober opponents. Peter Brown sees signs of "the Christian bishop of the future" in Paul's popular theatrics.[17] Richard Lim, however, detects the onset of late antiquity in the strategies of Paul's rivals, who, circa 268, finally shut down the Antiochene show by producing stenographic documents that flattened the give-and-take of oral debate into an unforgiving record of heretical belief.[18]

Whatever such stenographic *acta* may have contained (and they were still circulating decades later), the outrage of the bishops and other Christian notables who flocked to town to bring Paul to order seems to have been provoked less by the transcript of his speech than by the text of his body. Like Polemo, Paul's opponents read the corporal text closely, and with immense suspicion. They not only read; they also reinscribed what they saw in the case of Paul, addressing a letter to "all our fellow ministers throughout the world" (*H.e.* 7.30.2).[19] At issue is Paul's straying from the straight way of the "canon" or "rule," his false turn toward "bastard and spurious" teachings (7.30.6). Presumably such errors of doctrine were evidenced in the lost *acta*—which were perhaps attached to the letter—as well as reiterated in portions of the letter that have not been preserved. "Paul is not willing to acknowledge with us that the Son of God has come down from heaven," his opponents complain at one point in the extant text; but they have time to do no more than "anticipate" a more expansive description of the beliefs at issue, in their hurry to give the fullest possible account of the life exhibited (*H.e.* 7.30.11). Initially adopting a pose of indifference toward the behavior of one whose thoughts already place him "outside" the fold (7.30.6), the authors of the letter thereby demonstrate their own high-mindedness—only to proceed to itemize in some detail all of the charges they will *not* bring against the outrageous Paul, who "sets his mind on high things" (7.30.8). Their letter thus asserts, by means of a seeming negation, the conviction that the outer signs of a man's life encode his inner character.[20]

The Antiochene bishop's offenses include extreme upward mobility: born poor, he has not taken up any ancestral trade but gained wealth through his glibness, arguing cases and arbitrating disputes, always to his own material advantage. He adopts the props, clothing, and titles of high-ranking public officials. Strutting in the marketplace, he reads and dictates letters ostentatiously, surrounded by a crowd of clients. In church gatherings he plays to the crowd, posturing impressively. Adopting high rhetorical style, "he smites his hand on his thigh and stamps the tribunal with his feet," thereby evoking—indeed explicitly demanding—the most enthusiastic of responses from his unruly audience. Shamelessly, "he brags about himself as though he were not a bishop but a sophist and charlatan." Women are trained to sing hymns to him during worship; outside the church, they proclaim him an angel from heaven. Indeed, Paul is quite a ladies' man: like others among the local clergy, he cultivates asceticism by cohabiting with virgins in luxurious style, as if to flaunt a manly virtue that is proof against any temptation. From the perspective of the letter, it matters little what Paul might *not* be doing behind closed doors: the problem lies with outward appearances and "the suspicion that arises from such a practice" (*H.e.* 7.30.7–15).[21]

The authors of the letter—who had, as they recount, previously gathered for disciplinary purposes with less decisive results—now represent themselves as "compelled" to appoint in Paul's place another man who, as son of a former bishop of Antioch, "is adorned with the noble characteristics proper to a bishop" (*H.e.* 7.30.17). A more appropriate and legitimate patrilineage is thereby established with the removal of the upstart Paul, purveyor of "bastard" doctrines, from the seat of ecclesial governance. We might have been left to wonder about the success of this act of epistolary excommunication, had not a later reporter chosen to inform us of the conflict's eventual resolution. When "Paul refused on any account to give up possession of the church-building," his opponents approached the emperor Aurelian, who subsequently directed that the building be handed over to those Antiochene Christians in communion with Rome and the Italian episcopacy. "Thus, then," the report concludes, "was the aforesaid man driven with the utmost indignity from the church by the ruler of this world" (*H.e.* 7.30.19)—and also apparently with immense difficulty, the careful reader notes.

In the terms of a culture inclined to equate womanizing (or sensual indulgence more generally) with effeminacy, Paul of Samosata seems in many respects a worthy successor to the versatile and seductively androgynous Favorinus, whom Polemo denounced as a "sophist," crowd-pleaser, seducer, and "charlatan."[22] Moreover, Paul may be represented in his own moment as the winner, as much as the loser, in his competition with his opponents, which was finally turned against him only by documentary tactics, enforced through imperial intervention. However, it is also possible to follow Lim in finding hints that the new Polemos—equipped not only with stenographers and imperial patronage but also with "an almost occult insight" into the secrets of the soul—were indeed winning the day for a more rigidly controlled style of masculine deportment that would exclude a performance whose unabashed theatricality marked it as effeminate and "from below," insulting to the dignity of the divine Word and its more decorous episcopal representatives.[23] The very existence of such sustained rivalries undoubtedly played a role in creating the class of Christian clergy, but the ultimate outcome of this conflict appears also, however ambiguously, to have limited the options for the self-fashioning of men. At the same time, such conclusions must be held lightly. As Brown's remark also suggests, late-antique bishops would retain a measure of the mobility of the "eunuch" as self-made man, by forging an innovatively asceticized masculinity more heavily invested than ever in the hope of self-transformation through the power of word.

Unseen Acts: Eusebius's "Life of Origen"

Eusebius of Caesarea preserved the letter of the Antiochene synod, along with a framing narrative, in book 7 of his *Ecclesiastical History*. His brief account of Paul of Samosata is preceded (per the dictates of chronology) by a lengthy and artful narration of the life of Origen, which dominates book 6. The reader of Eusebius's history thus encounters the third-century polemic on the profligate and sophistic Samosatene after Eusebius's own instructively contrasting depiction of the virtuously philosophic Origen.[24] Such a reader might note that many of Paul's opponents numbered among Origen's former students and that their role in his condemnation echoes (perhaps even lightly parodies) Origen's own carefully scripted role as the masterly persuader of heretics. The account of Origen is not, however, simple eulogy. Among the several nodes of ambivalence that complicate Eusebius's biography are his hero's failure to achieve martyrdom and the folly of his purported youthful self-castration.

Eusebius offers two explanations for Origen's castration, each of which proves curiously problematic.[25] First, the man whom we already know to have been, since his earliest childhood, "not satisfied with reading the sacred words in a simple and literal manner" (*H.e.* 6.2.9) here errs precisely by taking the scriptural reference to "'those who make themselves eunuchs for the kingdom of heaven's sake' in too literal and extreme a sense," according to Eusebius. Second, Origen is said to be concerned to "prevent all suspicion of shameful slander on the part of unbelievers"; Eusebius adds by way of explanation, "for, young as he was, he used to discourse on divine things with women as well as with men." Eusebius immediately insists, however, that Origen fully intended his act to remain a secret and was careful "to escape the notice of the greater number of his pupils." Diverting his readers with the acknowledgment that, "wishful though he might be, it was not possible to hide a deed of this nature," Eusebius colludes in unveiling the lack that Origen was purportedly trying to hide, even as he dodges the further contradiction he has introduced into his own narrative. If Origen's castration was intended to protect his reputation for chastity, a successful cover-up would have rendered the act potentially irrelevant. Only if he were seen to be unmanned could he be known to be chaste despite the mixed company he kept. However, evidently Origen's condition *was* seen, by some if not by all his pupils, and his bishop, Demetrius, "got to know of it later." And of course Eusebius's readers all know of it now. At the time, bishop Demetrius, "while he marvelled exceedingly at the rash act, approved the zeal and the sincerity of his faith," reports Eusebius; later, however, when Origen was ordained a presbyter outside his own jurisdiction, the envious Demetrius "attempted to describe the deed as monstrous to the bishops throughout the world" and "spread grave scandal about the deed that he had committed long ago when a boy." Thus, the hidden act that, if known, should have prevented scandal, when made universally known became itself the source of scandal. Seemingly, Eusebius can do no more to unsnarl this tangle of his own making than attempt to underline Demetrius's initial, already ambivalent judgment: Origen's self-castration "gave abundant proof of an immature and youthful mind, yet withal of faith and self-control" (*H.e.* 6.8.1–5).

This anecdote recalls an earlier incident, in which Origen had missed what was perhaps his best chance at martyrdom. During the Severan persecution, the very young Origen was—for the first but by no means the last time in Eusebius's account—filled with desire to claim a martyr's death. His mother resisted him, acting on behalf of "divine and heavenly Providence," as Eusebius tells it (*H.e.* 6.2.4). When Origen finally learned that his father had been imprisoned, the boy could scarcely be detained. His mother then played her last card: "she hid all his clothes and so laid upon him the necessity of remaining at home" (6.2.5). Origen's nakedness is unveiled by his mother, and this is his undoing, from the perspective of his own deepest longings. Avoiding one scandal, he incurs another—for he remains merely a near-miss martyr. Throughout his lengthy account of Origen's life, Eusebius bypasses no opportunity to bring Origen into as close proximity as possible to martyrdom, surrounding him with crowds of dying witnesses, and leaving him finally abandoned in the midst of gruesome tortures (6.39.5)—but he cannot give him the death he desires.

A near-miss martyr and a near-miss man,[26] Eusebius's Origen is beset with contradictory needs to veil and to consummate his manhood, and there appears to be no full resolution to his predicament available, within the logic of Eusebian Providence. He comes very close indeed to succeeding, however. Eusebius's text not only invites readers to scrutinize Origen closely but also shows him constantly on exhibit in his own world, in circles that widen as his fame spreads. And, most of the time, viewers see precisely what they should. "For in his practical conduct were to be found to a truly marvellous degree the right actions of a most genuine philosophy (for—as the saying goes—'as was his speech, so was the manner of life' that he displayed, and 'as his manner of life, so his speech'), and it was especially for this reason that, with the co-operation of the divine power, he brought so very many to share his zeal" (*H.e.* 6.3.6–7). Origen "continued to live like a philosopher," practicing the most stringent asceticism of fasting, minimal sleep, poverty—and shoelessness (3.9–12). Those "who saw him" followed suit, a course that led them quite naturally not only to asceticism but onward to martyrdom (6.3.13). He was sought out by pagans, heretics, and heresy-hunters alike, and women as well as men were prominent among his patrons and disciples. At the height of his celebrity, Origen was summoned by Mamaea, the mother of the emperor himself, and also—as Eusebius adds—"a most religious woman." "She set great store on securing a sight of the man, and on testing that understanding of divine things which was the wonder of all." Apparently, she was disappointed neither by what she saw (or did not see!) nor by what she heard. "And when he had stayed with her for some time, and shown her very many things that were for the glory of the Lord and the excellence of the divine teaching, he hastened back to his accustomed duties" (6.21.4).

Despite the significant gaps that remain in Eusebius's text, his life of Origen at least partially succeeds in shifting the reading of the physical marks of both the eunuch and the martyr toward an interpretation that does not so much transcend the carnal sense as blur the distinction between carnal and spiritual meanings, making visible what is not actually seen. The embarrassments of Origen's purported success at self-castration and his failure at martyrdom are thereby made useful to the apologist, who can represent Origen *the ascetic* as both a *virtual* martyr and a *spiritual* "eunuch for the kingdom of heaven." Unmanned by his own desire, and panting for the fatal plunge of the executioner's sword, Origen's wondrously disciplined body bespeaks a virility that borrows from the feminine only what it needs in order to move beyond a merely carnal manhood.

Veiled Truth: Lactantius's 'On the Workmanship of God'

In his treatise *On the Workmanship of God*, roughly contemporaneous with Eusebius's *Ecclesiastical History*, Lactantius chooses not biography but a theologically framed discourse on human nature to display in more generic fashion the workings of Providence in the making of man. During a period of persecution, when the Greek-speaking bishop Eusebius attempts to refashion Origen into an ascetic "holy man" recognizable to a pagan as well as a Christian audience, the Latin rhetorician Lactantius likewise draws upon the philosophical tradition, most notably Cicero, in order to depict an ideal of manhood whose competitive claims on behalf of Christianity remain, strategically, merely implicit. On view once again is the body of the disciplined, philosophic man. Lactantius's physiological discussions already encode rules of decorum, in the manner of physiognomic discourse: to present the body as it was divinely created is to establish a standard by which a man's successful conformity to his nature can be judged.

Lactantius's musings on human physiology initially locate themselves
in the broader context of zoology. The contrast is between two classes of
animals, the "human," which stand tall, and the "other animals," which
are pressed to the earth. Yet Lactantius admits that there is also a "third
class," namely birds, and his striking preoccupation with birds in this text
seems to derive from the perception that this anomalous class of airborne
creatures may offer a challenge to his representation of humanity as the
"highest" of all animals. Like humans, birds take much care in raising their
young: "For they either build their nests of mud, or construct them with
twigs and leaves, and they sit upon the eggs without taking food; and since
it has not been given to them to nourish their young from their own bodies, they convey to them food, and spend whole days in going to and fro
in this manner; but by night they defend, cherish and protect them. What
more can humans do?" (*Opif.* 3). Indeed, as parents, humans surpass birds
only in the longer endurance of their bond to their children. It is thus not
surprising that Lactantius attributes to bird parents "something of human
intelligence" (3), since sociability is one of the distinctive marks of humanity: "If the human . . . did not stand in need of the assistance of any
other, what society would there be? . . . But since he is feeble, and not able
to live by himself apart from humanity, he desires society, that his life,
passed in intercourse with others, may become both more adorned and
more safe" (4). Birds are also like humans in their highly developed capacities for vocalization (10)—capacities the rhetorician is well positioned to
appreciate. In bird fetuses, the eyes are the first organ to develop, and although Lactantius cites the authority of Varro and Aristotle for the view
that the heart (being the source of life and wisdom) is the first part to take
form in the human being (*Opif.* 12), his interest in the human eye makes
the bird example here again alluring. Finally, birds, having wings, are not
earth-bound, and thus in some sense birds even more than humans would
seem to be the logical counterpart to the "other animals" who are "depressed to the earth." Lactantius's task, then, in relation to his "third class"
of animals, is to disrupt similarities so as to displace onto the human form
the transcendence so easily claimed by the bird body. To this end he establishes a competition between wings and hands, in which he may assert
the superiority of hands, "which are produced . . . for acting and controlling" (*Opif.* 5). "The free course of birds through the air [is not of such

consequence] that you should be without hands," he assures his reader (3). More important, though, than asserting the superiority of hands over wings is getting the human body into the sky.[27]

This act of levitation is in large part accomplished by Lactantius's emphasis on the unique stance of the human being. It is the divine decision to make the human being, alone of all animals, a "heavenly" creature that prompts God to "raise him erect and make him a biped" (*rigidum erexit bipedemque constituit*), for the explicit purpose that the human might "contemplate the heavens" and "look toward the place of his origin" (*Opif.* 8).[28] For Lactantius, what marks the firm, straight human body as transcendent is not only the upward thrust of that body but also the ascending trajectory of its gaze, which defies the drag of the earth and finally even of the body itself, tracing the path toward its only true parent, "God the Father" (*Opif.* 8). It is through the eyes that the mind—identified as the "true human being" (1) who is "hidden within this body" (19)—"being situated in the highest part, the head, as in a lofty citadel, looks out upon and observes all things," thereby exercising its "rule not only over the animals which are on the earth, but even over its own body" (8). The "citadel" or "palace" of the mind is "like an orb and a globe, because all roundness belongs to a perfect plan and figure" (8). Exquisitely set into the orb of the head are the globular eyes, "the acuteness of which is especially inexplicable and wonderful; for he covered their orbs, presenting the similitude of gems in that part with which they had to see, with transparent membranes, that the images of objects placed opposite them, being refracted as in a mirror, might penetrate to the innermost perception" (8).

Despite his use here of language of penetration, Lactantius immediately contradicts the common interpretation of the mind as passive in relation to the images or to the sense organs themselves, "lest you should happen to think that we see . . . by the striking [*incursione*] of the images" (*Opif.* 8). Instead, he underlines the mind's agency and power: "it is the mind which, through the eyes, sees those things which are placed opposite to it" (8). Here the eye is compared not to a mirror but to a window, "covered with pellucid crystal or transparent stone"—through which the mind not only sees but is also at least partly exposed (8; cf. 9).[29] Finally, Lactantius is concerned with the orientation of the gaze, as well as its agency: suggesting that the human body is anatomically endowed with a celestial view (never mind that eyes are not actually in the top of the head!), he translates rules of comportment into physiological signifiers of transcendence.

While he subsequently claims to leave the shameful "genital members" themselves "veiled with a cloak of modesty" (*Opif.* 13), Lactantius does make so bold as to probe the workings of the "inner parts" of the reproductive organs "concealed in a secret place" (12). His initial representation of those "inner parts" and their functions is elaborately symmetrical with respect to the sexes, emphasizing that both male and female organs produce seed necessary for conception, and noting that either the paternal or the maternal influence, or a mixture of both, may predominate in the progeny, regardless of the child's sex. Having already observed that both male and female organs are separated into a right, or "male," and a left, or "female," part, Lactantius then explains, "When a seed of the masculine stock perchance falls in the left part of the uterus, the conjecture is that a male is begotten, but because it is conceived in the feminine part, it has more of the feminine in it than male honor suffers. . . . Similarly if a seed of feminine kind flows into the right part, a female is begotten, but because it has been conceived in the masculine part, it has in it some virility beyond what the order of the sex permits. . . . If the masculine comes to the right, the feminine to the left, both fetuses develop appropriately" (*Opif.* 12). The original symmetry of Lactantius's presentation is here disrupted, as the right/left division of the male testicles and seminal ducts is displaced onto seed "of the male stock" or "the female kind," and the maternal seed drops out of the text altogether, so that only the gendered space of the uterus remains. The paternal seed determines sex; however, the female receptacle is not altogether passive but may blur or confuse, as well as strengthen, the sex of the child.

Lactantius's gender categories are most elaborately articulated in his descriptions of problematic blurrings of sex. The feminine male, he reports, is marked by excessive simplicity, smooth body, delicate manners, short stature, soft voice, and feeble soul. The virile female, on the other hand, is characterized by strong limbs, tallness, dark color, hairy face, unbecoming visage, robust voice, and bold soul. The unambiguous male whose gender safeguards the "honor of nature" is described as "preserving virile hardness as much in the mind as in the body." Having invoked the image of "virile hardness," Lactantius is moved to laud the providential "enticement of *voluptas*" through which the survival of the species is ensured.[30] He then observes that etymology attributes to the male (*vir*) both greater power (*vis*) and virtue (*virtus*) than to a woman (*mulier*), who is etymologically characterized by a contrasting "softness" (*mollities*). Female "softness" is represented both in woman's submission to the "marital yoke" and in her nurturing capacity as breast-feeder. On the subject of the maternal breast, Lactantius gushes: "swollen breasts distend with sweet juice and the full bosom abounds with milky fonts for the nourishment of the one to be born" (*Opif.* 13). In only one other passage outside Lactantius's discussion of the reproductive organs does a specifically female body intrude into his text; significantly, it is his description of the human breast, characterized as uniquely broad, "open and erect," adorned with nipples, "given to females for the nourishment of their young, to males for grace only, that the rest might not appear misshapen and, as it were, mutilated" (*Opif.* 10). The male body is not "mutilated" but whole, he insists; yet at the same time its own softnesses, swellings, and effluence remain "veiled with a cloak of modesty" in this text.

This brief discussion of gender betrays the implicit masculine ideal that underlies Lactantius's generic representation of the human body as erect, firm, tall, and domineering. Indeed woman, associated with submission and nurturance, seems to find her place more easily within the category of those "other animals" "depressed to the earth," "subservient to their appetite and food," "ruled over" and "looked out upon" by a virile mind housed in a bodily citadel—the human head—that possesses a countenance "closely resembling God his Father" (*Opif.* 8). Yet, as the lesson in reproduction (which gives rise not to two but to four sexes) has already taught, maleness and femaleness are not simple categories. Even as Lactantius's text participates in the physiological naturalizing of sexes fixed in the moment of conception, the assertion of complexity that is part of the attempt to stabilize even ambiguous genders through an appeal to biological determinism also indirectly introduces questions about the permanence of sexed identities. Real men are begotten and not made, according to Lactantius; yet the signs that betray the difference between the virile and the effeminate male encompass gesture, voice, hairiness, and the demonstration of "boldness of soul," potentially manipulable aspects of self-presentation.

"The human being can neither be touched, nor looked upon, nor grasped, because he lies hidden within this body, which is seen," notes Lactantius in closing. What is essential about man is veiled. Tension remains in a textual representation of an idealized humanity that claims radical noetic transcendence while manifesting itself visibly as an ascetic effect of corporality. "And if he shall be more luxurious and delicate in this life than its nature demands, if he shall despise virtue, and give himself to the pursuit of fleshly lusts, he will fall and be pressed down to the earth; but if (as his duty is) he shall readily and constantly maintain his rightful position, and if he shall not be enslaved to the earth, which he ought to trample upon and overcome, he will gain eternal life" (*Opif.* 19). For Lactantius, the invisible and intangible human subject can be apprehended only via bodily practices and postures that are themselves, paradoxically, the veilings or displacements by which materiality is disavowed. Interweaving a stoicizing anthropology with a more dualistic ontology, he strongly asserts the transcendence of mind while yet linking it inextricably to a naturalized bodily performance.[31]

Realizing a providential masculinity is finally as elusive yet as accessible as learning to walk upright with eyes raised to the heavens. Indeed, the achievement of manhood lies in creating the illusion of a subject who floats birdlike *above* the earth, "ever and again return[ing] to plant his foot" upon the ground of his corporality "in order to spring farther, leap higher."[32]

Anticipations

From the perspective of later history, Eusebius and Lactantius, each articulating a version of philosophic Christian manhood, present themselves as "old" men already leaning heavily into a "new" future. These two writers are the primary transmitters of the accounts of the emperor Constantine's conversion to Christianity in 312 and leave us with some of our most striking impressions of the dramatic change experienced by Christians living through the shift from the Great Persecution to the troubled peace of the church. While it is debatable to what extent Christianity owed its fourth-century successes to the patronage of Constantine and subsequent emperors, the strong impact of imperial patronage on Christian life and practice is undeniable. Especially evident are the effects of such patronage on those techniques by which Christianity traditionally constituted itself, both discursively and institutionally, as an "orthodox" or "catholic" church. The material resources and imaginative conceits of empire opened up new possibilities for concretizing the church's symbolic unity. In the process, however, not only was existing diversity made painfully visible, but new mechanisms of council and creed, excommunication and exile, by imposing their brisk clarities on the more gradual, ambiguous, and localized patterns of diversification, polarized and multiplied differences at an often bewilderingly rapid pace. Eusebius himself would be awkwardly drawn into the early stages of the trinitarian debates, whose processes and products equally reflected the new conditions of the Constantinian age. That his reputation for orthodoxy was only barely preserved indicates (among other things) the extent to which his conception of manly excellence remained liminally positioned, caught in the turning of an era. Lactantius likewise appears unsteady in his accounts of both transcendent manhood and trinitarian doctrine, when viewed from the perspective of later developments.[33] The fourth-century theological debates that quickly overtook these two men directly engaged and decisively transformed both the cosmological framing of human subjectivity and the positioning of masculine gender. With the assertion of the absolute difference of deity and the accompanying suppression of the subordinationist Logos Christologies that had prevailed in the pre-Nicene era, divine Sonship became the site for the articulation of culture's triumphant subsuming of nature. Henceforth, men were "begotten, not made," and the observable arts of male self-fashioning—practiced more assiduously than ever—came to be read as signs encoding the mysteries of a purely transcendent procreation.

It is not my task to retell the history of the Arian controversy from the outside, as it were[34]—nor, for that matter, to address the Christianization of the empire, the rise of asceticism, or the evolution of the episcopacy. Rather, my analysis will remain local, as I undertake to inhabit the texts and discursive worlds authored by three Nicene Christian bishops and to explore the masculine subjectivities produced within their writings. My wager is that this kind of reading will finally add something significant to what we "know" about trinitarian theology, gender, sexuality, asceticism, episcopacy, and Christianization in late antiquity, and about the relevance of these historical phenomena to our own lives and cultures. Although there will be an

element of chronological as well as geographical arrangement in what follows, as a "story" moves lightly both forward and out, the primary interpretive mode is synchronic and multilocal, the technique juxtapositional
rather than progressive or even explicitly comparative. By reading Athanasius of Alexandria, Gregory of Nyssa, and Ambrose of Milan both sepa-
rately and together, I will try to show fourth-century textual performances
of manhood at their "most electrifying," in such a way as to preserve the
differences among them while pointing toward the forging of a patristic
corpus as bearer of a single, transcendent sex of man.

CHAPTER I

Fathering the Word
Athanasius of Alexandria

So for the sons of the Book: research, the desert, inexhaustible space,
encouraging, discouraging, the march straight ahead. For the daughters of
the housewife: the straying into the forest. Deceived, disappointed, but
brimming with curiosity. Instead of the great enigmatic duel with the
Sphinx, the dangerous questioning addressed to the body of the Wolf:
What is the body for? Myths end up having our hides. Logos opens
its great maw, and swallows us whole.

—*Hélène Cixous,*
"Coming to Writing"

P eter Brown's *The Making of Late Antiquity* evocatively casts "the
Christian church" as the "*impresario* of a wider change."[1] In its
epoch-making role, the church produced "holy men" Antony and Pachomius as the "upstart heroes" of a classical Mediterranean world thus
broadly transformed.[2] Athanasius, bishop of Alexandria during the life-
times of Antony and Pachomius, never makes an entry in Brown's text.
This is not because he has missed his cue: his absence may be read as an
indirect allusion to the behind-the-scenes activities of a figure who powerfully embodied the ecclesiastical role of impresario in the original "making
of late antiquity," which Brown's work re-presents. Serving as scriptwriter,
stage manager, and publicist for the early desert ascetics, Athanasius was
among the first to take the Egyptian show on the road with his *Life of
Antony*—a text that got the distinctly late-ancient genre of Christian biography swiftly off the ground. It is true that Brown downplays the well-
crafted *Life of Antony* in favor of the loosely collected "sayings" of the
desert fathers in his own sinuous remaking of late antiquity and its holy
heroes.[3] Pushing aside the muffling veils of textuality, he ushers his readers into a quasi-oral realm in which the gritty "experiences" of the ascetics
might, he suggests, be "entered into" and "reconstructed" *sans* authorial
mediation.[4] As Brown suppresses the figure of Athanasius as the holy

man's maker, he simultaneously distracts attention from his own refashioned authorial role. However, the evocative power of Brown's written works indirectly reintroduces questions about the place of narrative, "representation," and textual production in the formation of "late antiquity" —then as now.[5] The literary exertions of Athanasius and other "sons of the Book" who followed his lead contributed hugely to the first cultural making of the desert fathers, marking them as both heroes and harbingers of a new age.

Athanasius is adept at setting a scene—or, better yet, weaving a world —in text. In his early treatise *On the Incarnation of the Word*, the Alexandrian bishop had already used the field of christological doctrine to work out one version of the sharply bifurcated cosmology that, according to Brown, would foster the emergence of those ascetic "agents of the supernatural" who set the trends for fourth-century fashions in holy manhood.[6] Whereas in the third century "the frontier between the divine and the human had lain tantalizingly open," writes Brown, in the fourth "the upward ceiling of human contact with the divine has come to be drawn more firmly";[7] moreover, with the heavens and earth no longer perceived as porously interpenetrating realms, the human community was apparently willing to grant more power to those few exceptional "friends of God" who might be thought to keep the narrowed channels of access open. Athanasius seems to confirm Brown's characterization of the world of late antiquity: his theological writings exhibit overall a striking preoccupation with the boundary between the created and divine realms, as well as the frontier zones of human possibility. It is thus not irrelevant that by the time Athanasius assembled the *curriculum vitae* of the holy man Antony, he had not only published his christologically refracted cosmological views but was also well-launched in his self-appointed task as archivist and propagandist for the Council of Nicaea. As he defended it forcefully in text after text, the Nicene Creed came to function as the touchstone of a newly crystallizing orthodoxy that would eventually both fix the masculine terms of theological language and pull down the cosmic veil separating the transcendental triad of Father, Son, and Spirit from material creation.

Marching straight ahead, Athanasius almost single-handedly made the reputation of Nicaea and thereby affirmed the essential and incomparable bond uniting the divine Father to his "co-essential" Son, through his promotion of the creed's controversial term *homoousios.* He did so not least as part of a strategy to make his own reputation as legitimate son and unique successor to *pappas* Alexander of Alexandria, whose paternal authority Athanasius linked tightly with that of the council itself. Rather than suppress the precariousness of his much-contested position as Alexander's heir, Athanasius published the facts of his own repeated oustings, exiles, and departures. He thereby not only reaped the benefits traditionally awarded to the persecuted witness for Christian truth but also (and in so doing) drew a sharp line between the all-too-worldly political events of his beleaguered career as bishop of Alexandria and his sublime governance of a new *politeia,* discursively constructed at the intersection of a fictive civic council and an imaginary desert city—a Christianized metropolis that was and was not Alexandria. Virtually motherless but well fathered, wifeless but ordained to generate many sons, an exile sometimes seen lurking within city limits with the unworldly scent of the desert on his ragged sheepskin cloak, Athanasius may have come very close indeed to repressing the bodily "real" in his innovative, transcendentalizing strategies of self-representation. However, he never abandoned the claimed status of either father or civic leader—roles lacking motherhood's apparent fleshly self-evidence and thus conveniently tinged with the fictive from the start. Fighting to retain certain social positions, the value of which had only been increased by their spiritualizing transmutation in the heady symbolic realm generated by his own discourse, Bishop Athanasius notoriously remained up to his neck in the muck of high-risk and morally dubious power plays.

Scholarly accounts often awkwardly reproduce the contrast between the sublime worlds spun in Athanasius's less agonizingly agonistic texts and his low-down political career as bishop, the details of which surface in his shrill and repetitious polemics and in papyrus letters that seem to preserve the complaints of his enemies.[8] A troublemaker in his own day, Athanasius continues to create problems for his most loyal interpreters, who must acknowledge him as "an unscrupulous politician" capable of the worst kind of "gangsterism," while upholding him as "a genuine theologian" whose "achievement in his doctrinal works was a great one"[9] and lauding "the clarity and consistency of his theological thinking" and "sincerity of his belief" despite "the stormy events of his life and the various charges brought against him."[10] But it may be possible to take a slightly different tack. Rather than simply reduplicating a split initially opened up by Athanasius himself, or (worse yet) papering over the crack with a thin allusion to the compromises entailed in the bishop's pastoral role, one might identify the disjunction between Athanasius the dirty politician and Athanasius the orthodox theologian (between the realms of corruption and divinity more generally) as the effect of a consistent schema reproduced throughout his literary works. This sustained dichotomy helps structure a subjectivity that paradoxically both inscribes a sharp cosmological opposition between the human and the divine and reassigns "divine" status to men—disowning the messes made on the earthly plane, which are swallowed up by the "great maw" of the salvific Word. The strained and straining structure of this emergent late-antique self, whose constitutive disavowals and sublimations become tangibly fixed in their textualization, is crucial to the fourth-century reconfigurations of the roles of men in the family and the city, social shifts embedded in discursive reweavings of a radically idealized masculinity. Put otherwise, Athanasius's more theoretical and theological works are of a piece with his polemics and politics, and both reflect broader social and cultural shifts under way in the fourth century that were to leave a lasting imprint on conceptions of masculinity.

Keeping one eye focused on the ever-materializing costs of Word's repressive hegemony, costs borne, differently, by both men and women, I am not perhaps easily numbered among Athanasius's "most loyal interpreters." However, I am not altogether disloyal either, insofar as I remain interested, to put it simply. Not a son of the Book but a daughter, desiring to write nonetheless, I approach the Word of Athanasius both eagerly and warily. Gazing intently at features that have become all too familiar, I am still, like Hélène Cixous's fairy-tale heroine, capable of surprise. The bodily particularity of the "gramma-r wolf"[11] gradually captures my attention, disclosing the embarrassed maleness of the incorporeal Word, which I am not supposed to see beneath the Word's cross-dressed disguise—which has furthermore surely encrypted, but never yet utterly destroyed, so many of the grandmothers. In brimming curiosity lies hope for the one who strays from the path. A stream of sincere but slyly posed questions may not merely postpone the inevitable moment of her own devouring but yet pull off the trick of a revelation of Logos that defies that inevitability.

A Theory of the Subject: 'On the Incarnation of the Word'

Men have their masculine identity to gain by being estranged from
their bodies and dominating the bodies of others.

—*Jane Gallop,*
Thinking Through the Body

We can properly describe this doctrine as a "Space-suit Christology."
Just as the astronaut, in order to operate in a part of the universe where
there is no air and where he has to experience weightlessness, puts on
an elaborate space-suit which enables him to live and act in this new,
unfamiliar environment, so the *Logos* put on a body which enabled him
to behave as a human being among human beings. But his relation to
this body is no closer than that of an astronaut to his space-suit.
The *Logos*, says Athanasius, "though he was God had his own body and
by using this as an instrument (*organon*) became man for our sakes."

—*R. P. C. Hanson,*
The Search for the Christian Doctrine of God

R. P. C. Hanson's assertion to the contrary only serves to plant the suspicion that there is something *im*proper—as well as naggingly insightful—
about his designation of Athanasius's doctrine of the incarnation as "Spacesuit Christology." Indeed, Hanson may have committed more than the
single slight impropriety of a deliberate anachronism. The playful textual
antics of this seasoned scholar productively confound and complicate our
reading of Athanasius's *On the Incarnation*—and not merely by hinting
that this early work penned by the bishop of Alexandria might be most
helpfully regarded as the boyish performance of an unripe theologian.[12]
The point is: at first glance, the astronaut metaphor is *not* so very apt a description of Athanasius's Christology. Hanson's space traveler is equipped
with "an elaborate space-suit" that simulates the comforting tug of earth's
gravity and its damp, oxygen-rich atmosphere; thus outfitted, he may venture—like a born-again babe—into a "new, unfamiliar environment" lacking the conditions hitherto vital to his survival. The Logos of Athanasius's
On the Incarnation is, however, traveling in the opposite direction, so to
speak, and he has no need of umbilical supply lines or portable support systems. He is, rather, an extraterrestrial alien, proper inhabitant of a realm of

inexhaustible space, located both everywhere and nowhere: "He has filled all things everywhere, remaining present with His own Father" (*Inc.* 8.1); "He . . . was actually in everything, and while external to the universe, abode in His Father only" (17.4).[13] "Incorporeal by nature" (1.3) and thus essentially unlimited, the cosmic Word, who is also the supracosmic Son of a purely acosmic Father, dons the superficially transformative costume of corporeality in order to visit a perishing race on Mother Earth. "For . . . the Logos disguised himself by appearing in a body, that he might, as a Man, transfer men to Himself and center their senses on Himself" (16.1). This sky-born Savior thus responds to the gravity of a situation by taking on substance as ballast, so as not to float above the realm of human perception. But he surely does not contaminate his heavenly being by inhaling the cloying air that clings to earth's surface, any more than he actually ingests terrestrial food and water (18.1); "not defiled by being known in the body" (17.7), he remains insulated from such strangely unstable stuff, from the instability of stuff itself. If the Logos's insulating earth-suit—a genuine body, after all—does eat as well as breathe (and even cry crocodile tears!), its wearer contrives this not for the sake of his own survival but rather for the sake of appearances, crucial for his propagandizing mission. More mysteriously and significantly, the flesh's material interpenetrability enables the Logos to enact his own sublime metabolic process on the whole of human creation—transforming it from corruptibility to incorruptibility and thereby also from ignorance to knowledge—through his infectious proximity to the single body he has made his own. "Whereas men had turned toward corruption, He might turn them again toward incorruption, and quicken them from death by the appropriation of His body and by the grace of the resurrection" (*Inc.* 8.4).

Hanson insists that we note the presumably troubling fact that the chillingly soulless Logos's "relation to this body is no closer than that of an astronaut to his space-suit"—or more "properly," as I have suggested, of a space-alien to his earth-suit. Hanson also remarks, with the same flash of humor, that Athanasius seems to imagine that the salvation of humanity effected by the incarnation "is a kind of sacred blood-transfusion . . . almost independent of our act of faith."[14] Hanson's second metaphor, layered over the first, suggests that Athanasius depicts the human creature as a passive (even anaesthetized) recipient of an alien grace administered by a supremely impersonal, all-powerful medical authority, who asks only whether a patient (reduced to humanity's lowest common denominator of "flesh") is insured. However, such telling comparisons can perhaps also convey a slightly different tale. Late-modern technology has partly blurred the boundary between what is organic and what is artificial, what is proper or natural to the body and what is not. Though alien blood can be rejected, it can also be assimilated, appropriated, and made the body's own. Moreover, under the right conditions, an astronaut might develop a far closer, more complex, and more profoundly cooperative "relationship" to his (or her) prosthetic "suit" than Hanson appears able to imagine. If, for the Athanasian Christ, "embodiment . . . is prosthesis,"[15] divine simplicity here resists the threat of prosthetic—or incarnational—hybridity through an assimilative process that actively reconstitutes "wholeness."

By re-angling Hanson's metaphors to slightly shift our reading of Athanasius's text, we can savor the scholar's pungent insights while also taking seriously the claim that the *organon* of the body "wielded" by the Athanasian Logos (*Inc.* 17.4, 42.6), a body admittedly "owned" not as "nature" but as "property," nevertheless stands in some kind of meaningfully close relationship to that Logos by which it is "quickened." Still more, if Athanasian soteriology suggests a process not unlike a sacred blood transfusion, this can be taken to describe not simple human passivity but rather a complex responsiveness: a suffering self receives, assesses, adapts, and finally appropriates—at the most intimate, particular, and undeniably material level—an animating substance that enhances his or her liveliness, that may mean the difference between life and death. Some interpreters have attempted to intellectualize Athanasius's soteriology radically, locating the glue of salvific relationality in human rationality and its communion with Reason itself.[16] However, the specific incarnational emphasis of Athanasius's Christology and theory of human salvation seems to require that we imagine the Logos and flesh of Christ, life-sustaining Word and otherwise-moribund body, as intimately interwoven, almost as two aspects of the same entity—"a life wound closely to a body" and "a body wound closely to the life" (*Inc.* 44.5–6)—*even as the sharply dualistic cosmology in which that Christology is framed makes the imaginative leap nearly impossible.* If *On the Incarnation* demands to be read on its own, complex terms and not reductively simplified or marginalized as "immature" in relation to a slightly later "orthodoxy" (as Hanson might have it), this is not because its successes outweigh its failures but because it is a straining, ambitious text, often most successful when inadvertently calling attention to its own failures, reworking its own contradictions into gestures toward the not-yet-articulable, imagining divinized matter or materialized divinity within the dualistic framework of a profound cosmological estrangement. If, on the other hand, the text needs to be subjected to a critique even sterner than Hanson's, this is because its contradictions lapse back too easily into corrupt half-truths that produce the logistical coup of creation's shame and the cover-up of the body of man.

But I am getting ahead of myself. I have not yet even posed a crucial question: To what extent is the Athanasian Christ, who stands upon a cosmological fissure so freshly incised in the fourth-century imagination, a model of or for man and therefore legitimately read as a vehicle for the articulation of a human subjectivity? To what extent *can* he be? A figure intended to bridge the gap between heaven and earth, this celestial Savior may, nevertheless, be attached so tenuously to materiality that he risks disqualification from any solidarity with created beings.[17] The Logos does not even seem to have his heart in the pedagogical task of demonstrating the "how to's" of human perfection and knowledge; sooner or later, he will just do it for us—in fact, it seems he *has* to. And yet Athanasius also insists on both the ontological continuity between material creation and its incarnate redeemer, on the one hand, and the crucial teacherly or revelatory role of the embodied Logos, on the other.[18] Once again, the question must be posed: Are these the contradictions that mask a lie when in fact Athanasius is *really* a "Docetist," as implied in Hanson's bald statement, "whatever else the *Logos* incarnate is in Athanasius' account of him, he is not a human being"?[19] Or are such fundamental inconsistencies rather the chaotic upshot of a fertile text that sometimes exceeds its own principles of ordering? Both, I think, and simultaneously. Athanasius's Christology *is* covertly—and insightfully—"docetic." The partly repressed representation of a Christ who only "seems" (deceptively) to have anything of humanity in his nature may stand in for a man who only "seems" to be compromised by materiality. On this reading, the lying Christ uncovered in Athanasius's veiled text exposes a truth about a human subjectivity erected upon a deception—the denial of the body—that nevertheless begets its own realities, and Docetism (as an indirect strategy for telling the truth about a powerful lie) proves far from incompatible with the assertion of Christ's exemplary role. On another, equally ambiguous reading, Athanasius's Christ is anything but docetic: as Rebecca Lyman puts it, in the terms of Athanasius's thought, "unless human nature were real, the enfleshment of the divine Son would not effect the necessary internal cleansing of the human body of the passions of birth and ignorance."[20] It is thus the *seemingly* irreconcilable opposition between divinity and corruptible materiality that is unveiled as a lie by his text's revelation of the incarnation of the Logos. However, such a revelation remains paradoxical, taking the form of a negation that, with every assertion of the almost-unimaginable miracle of a mediating embodiment of Logos, heavily reinscribes the irreducible difference of divinity.

It may be true, from a certain perspective, that Athanasius "develops no theory of humanity in his writings."[21] But it is also true, I am suggesting, that he develops no christological theory that is not always also deeply preoccupied with the status of humanity, and furthermore, that his very choice to frame anthropology in the terms of Christology, however typical of Greek patristic thought, deeply affects the positioning of the human subject. In *On the Incarnation*, Athanasius begins not with Christ but with the creation of humanity, an account that in turn anticipates a narrative of redemption-as-re-creation: "for in speaking of the appearance of the Savior among us we must also speak of the origin of humanity" (*Inc.* 4.2). Citing the support of Genesis, Hermas, and Hebrews, Athanasius asserts, "Out of nothing, and without its having any previous existence, God made the universe to exist through His word" (3.1). Although initially meant to affirm both God's omnipotence and the goodness of a cosmos of purely divine origins, the forced concept of a creation eked out of nothing quickly begins to show symptoms of stress, bearing as it does unprecedented explanatory weight in Athanasius's text.[22] Athanasius's all-powerful God—boasting, in essence, that only weaklings use preexistent matter—can barely keep his handiwork from unraveling, and the good cosmos seems destined for a bad end. As Lyman puts it, somewhat more mildly: for Athanasius "divine nature and will are good and eternal, yet the effect of divine will in creation is surprisingly weak."[23] "By virtue of the condition of its origin"—that is, having been wrenched out of nonexistence—

the human race is unstable from the start. Attempting to stave off the disaster ensuing from a mutability that (according to Athanasius's theory of matter) leads inevitably to an absolute dissolution in death, the divine creator provides extra protection for the privileged (or perhaps the most fragile) among his creation, namely, a share in "the power of His own Logos." With the aid of rationality, the otherwise inconstant earthlings might hope after all to "abide ever in blessedness" (*Inc.* 3.3). To the gift of rationality, God quickly adds the gift of the law (νόμος) to steady further the still-wavering human will (3.4).

If the reader begins to sense that Athanasius's Creator is fighting a losing battle in these repeated attempts to stabilize a fundamentally and indeed fatally shifty creation, that is not only because she has also read Genesis 3.[24] Athanasius's suspicion of matter and its mutability, a suspicion vastly exceeding the terms of the biblical account or even its earlier Christian readings, permeates a narrative in which fall and redemption are already inscribed in humanity's origin, through the dual assertion of corruption as the natural condition of created matter and incorruptibility as the gift of the uncreated Logos. It may be the case that the first humans are not strictly predestined to disobey the divine law and so to fail to live up to the promise of their rationality; but when they do disobey, their backsliding appears natural enough to Athanasius. "Transgression of the commandment was turning them back to their natural state, so that just as they have had their being out of nothing, so also, as might be expected, they might look for corruption into nothing in the course of time" (*Inc.* 4.4). Athanasius repeats that "it followed naturally" that "they should be disintegrated and abide in death and corruption" (4.5), being "by nature corruptible" (5.1). Unable to feign surprise at a dissolving "fall" into nothingness encoded as destiny in an origin *ex nihilo*,[25] Athanasius is also convinced of the profound seemliness of an "escape" from this "natural state" owing to the stabilizing grace of the Logos, which was also bestowed at the moment of humanity's creation (5.1), a gift repeated and finalized in the incarnation of the Logos as Christ, in which the creation of humanity "in the image of the Logos" is renewed and perfected (13.7–9).

At this point we might consider whether Athanasius proposes a "Spacesuit *anthropology*" with his description of salvation as a kind of "unnatural" perversion of a humanity now bent in the direction of divinity: "He was

that we might be made God" (*Inc.* 54.3). Tugged heavenward by
of the Logos, the cosmically cross-dressed Athanasian man in-
on something like an "elaborate space-suit"—the protective en-
velope of his divine aspirations—which not only equips him for celestial
life but also covers up something else, the shifty materiality that is the
mark of created nature. It is humanity's superimposed destiny to escape the
flux of material existence, framed by Athanasius as a prior, original incli-
nation to slide back into the abyss of nonbeing, and this "escape" via "divinization" *both is and is not* represented as a process of transubstantiation
that constitutes a suppression or supersession of the materiality created *ex
nihilo*, making way for the acquisition of something essentially "other."

This crucial ambiguity in Athanasius's soteriology—producing, I think,
a fruitfully unresolvable contradiction—is concisely built into the assertion
that "God did not simply create man, as He did all the irrational creatures
on the earth, but made them after His own image, sharing [μεταδὺς] with
them even of the power of His own Logos" (*Inc.* 3.3). On the one hand, the
gift of being made in the image or participating in the power of the Logos
completes the process of creation with which it is continuous, adding
merely the final ingredient of stability. On the other hand, this gift exceeds
"simple creation," making humanity *more than* creaturely, even *other than*
creaturely, thus not only leaving open the question of the status of nonhu-
man creation but also introducing a conflict into the structure of the human
subject. The Logos's gift of stability is posited as alien to a materiality defined by its self-dissolving tendencies, according to an Athanasian principle
that all change is for the worse and disorder is not the matrix of (re-)creation
but the extinction of final death; yet that corruptible materiality remains the
fundament of human "nature."[26] Athanasius's difficult description of the *incarnation of the Logos* is thus entirely consistent with the tensions and ambiguities already present in his account of the creation of humanity as the *sublimation of the body*. His incarnational Christology directly implies a theory
of human subjectivity, while his teleological theory of the subject is necessarily represented via its partial displacement onto the ultimately inaccessible figure of a saving Christ.

Holding the line between humanity and divinity, on the one hand,
and insisting on the divinization of humanity as the goal of salvation and
the end of creation, on the other, Athanasius's treatise mobilizes an incar-

national Christology—itself the product of a fractured and polarized cosmology—in such a way as to take the transcendentalization of the human subject to the limit. Setting his sights upon the model of a re-creation performed by Christ, Athanasius expects the human subject to supersede his own natural mutability through the granted stability of divine incorruptibility. Yet insofar as Athanasius will not—and indeed cannot coherently—permit the ontological opposition between God and creation to be even partially dissolved, the incarnate Logos is an idealized "exemplar" but *not* a representative "example" of humanity. *This distinction is crucial to the structure of subjectivity theorized by Athanasius*: as Christ, the Logos *em*bodies and thereby signifies what humanity desires and emulates but *as body* will never really "have," namely, absolute transcendence of materiality, the status of undefiled Word or Image, and (as we shall see) the stable security of ontological Sonship. The divinization of humanity thus comes in the (dis)guise of a put-on, a cover-up, a veil, shrouding the ebb and flow of bodily existence. The veil of immutable divinity is itself configured as a site for the erection of a "logical" subject or talking head. Man becomes Word, a "signifier" who has purposefully misrecognized his material matrix as a referent in turn conveniently misplaced. The loss of the generative body is itself endlessly fertile: repeatedly rediscovered somewhere else, the body reproduces itself eternally in the sublime sowings of interpretive re-creations of that Word "spoken and written by God" (*Inc.* 56.2).

Essential Masculinities: 'Orations Against the Arians'

When the crucial intergenerational link is between father and son, for which birth by itself cannot provide sure evidence, sacrificing may be considered essential for the continuity of the social order. What is needed to provide clear evidence of social and religious paternity is an act as definite and available to the senses as is birth. When membership in patrilineal descent groups is identified by rights of participation in blood sacrifice, evidence of "paternity" is created which is as certain as evidence of maternity, but far more flexible.

—*Nancy Jay,*
Throughout Your Generations Forever

> In his desire to refute Arian misconceptions, Athanasius pursues the topics
> of Father, Son, and salvation in *Contra Arianos* with a relentless
> thoroughness which borders on the obsessive. . . . It is possible certainly
> that the association of God as Father with the ideas of primacy and source
> reflects the influence of third- and fourth-century assumptions about
> fatherhood, generation, and authority. But if the association does
> reflect such an influence, it is in no way obvious.
>
> —*Peter Widdicombe,*
> The Fatherhood of God from Origen to Athanasius

Peter Widdicombe's provocative proposal that the systematic analysis and elaboration of fatherhood as a central theological category emerged relatively late—indeed, "not until the fourth century with Athanasius"—raises the daunting question "of how this dominant theme began and why it was so influential."[27] The question itself ultimately creates, for Widdicombe, the necessity of setting bounds on answers, a task to which he turns in an epilogue, at the limit of his own text. Leery of certain reductivisms, he reminds his readers of what is *not* considered relevant: "In Athanasius's theology, the term Father implied anything but sexuality and gender in the divine nature"; indeed, he explains, a "correct context of reference" for the interpretation of theological language "does not include facile references to, and explorations of, human experience."[28] Although he elsewhere remarks that God functions in Athanasius's text as the "causal exemplar" who sets the standard for correct speech "about the human experience of the father-son relation,"[29] here (at the end) he cherishes doubts about whether Athanasius or other patristic authors "even unwittingly drew on contemporary discussions of fatherhood in the larger Greek culture to help them in their thinking about the fatherhood of God." At any rate, if there was such "influence," he concludes, "it is in no way obvious."[30]

The Athanasian paradoxes reproduced in Widdicombe's text are once again tensely balanced; at points, only the emphatic assertion of an "anything but" seems to keep the conceptual structure from collapsing into blatant contradiction. On the one hand, "influence," articulated in the form of linguistic comparison, may flow in only one direction, from theology to anthropology, with the result that tremendous weight is placed on divine self-revelation via the Scriptures. On the other hand, according to Athanasius's interpretation, the biblical text itself emphasizes the fundamental fatherhood of God, language that does, after all, seem to introduce an explicit comparison to human relations structured by "sexuality and gender." Frances Young notes that, in order to stress that "God's begetting cannot be of that kind," Athanasius must introduce "an external hermeneutical principle" so as to produce a reading "which is not strictly literal."[31] The designation of Athanasius's interpretation as "not strictly literal" may, however, release too much of the tension sustained within texts that place unprecedented weight on the letter of Scripture and the bodies of men.[32] Like incarnation, the metaphor of fatherhood—if indeed it can properly be described as a metaphor—is theologically indispensable as well as authoritatively revelatory, from an Athanasian perspective. For the Alexandrian Father, as Widdicombe argues persuasively, there is no substitute for "paternity" as an expression of God's essential generativity, in which divine will and being are perfectly united. Considering possible alternatives by way of testing his thesis, Widdicombe ventures that Athanasius "might have had difficulties" with the language of "parenthood," which "he might have found slightly too abstract," as well as "too functional." As for "maternity," the concept is perhaps not quite abstract enough: although Widdicombe acknowledges that it does, like "paternity," appropriately imply both "shared being" and "a relation of love," he concludes (with Athanasius) that a maternal God is ruled out for reasons of both history and revelation, since "in the event" Jesus "is seen in the Bible to address God not as mother or parent but as Father."[33]

By demarcating "sexuality and gender" as the no-man's-land at the borders of his own historical-theological enterprise, Widdicombe also maps the frontier zones now open for a woman's off-trail "explorations" of the historic contributions made by Nicene theology to the structuring of "human experience." Although seemingly uncertain about *why* the concept of divine motherhood might have caused "difficulties" for Athanasius, Widdicombe feels sure that it would have: he is here (as elsewhere) an insightful reader of this Father. In the discursive world woven by Athanasius, paternity and maternity are scarcely interchangeable, for reasons that perhaps after all have something to do not only with bodies but also with cultural "assumptions about fatherhood, generation, and authority." If a Father God is deemed essential, this theological claim encodes the assertion that mere human paternity does not suffice—even by way of analogy—to secure "shared being" and "a relation of love" for the son. Indeed perhaps mere human paternity, "for which birth by itself cannot provide sure evidence," is never enough: fatherhood remains a supernatural achievement, so long as only maternity can be reduced to a carnality as "definite" as it is "available to the senses." The strictest logic of patriliny would seem to demand that maternal birth be disavowed, and Athanasius's texts conspire to construct a radical patriliny (which is also to say a radically sublimated paternity) that cannot even tolerate the *explicit* exclusion of the mother, lest discourse be tainted by materiality through her very negation.

In Athanasius's patrilineal trinitarian theology, as in his incarnational Christology, the "influence" of the flesh must be made "in no way obvious"; fatherhood is about "anything but" sexuality and gender; the divine "person" produced is a disembodied neuter, *like* a man but *not* comparable to a woman. In Athanasius's anti-Arian works, the Logos will be decisively named the true Son of a paternalized God, in keeping with Athanasius's earlier wish to secure the Word's claim to the legacy of a saving divinity. His soteriology dictates that human creatures straining toward divinity will get as close as they can to what they can never really have, namely, a share in that essential, bodiless Sonship. If "divinization" (θεοποίησις) as the goal of human salvation is also framed as "filiation" (υἱοποίησις), some may find that adoption as a virtual son comes more naturally than it does to others. A very few, like Athanasius, will almost succeed in escaping the mortality of the mother-born by inserting themselves into a chain of male succession in which material birth is replaced by a transcendentalizing rite —which is also a right—of sublimated blood sacrifice. Nancy Jay remarks, "When Christianity became the established religion of the Roman Empire in the fourth century, sacrificing and sacrificially maintained hierarchical social organization simultaneously took great leaps forward. . . . Apostolic succession and priesthood are identified by sacrificial power over the Eucharistic body."[34] Athanasius was not uninterested in upholding his sacramental role as bishop; indeed, according to one tradition, he commissioned a member of his clergy to destroy the chalice that had been used "to administer the blood of Christ" in eucharistic rites performed by a presbyter whose ordination Athanasius considered invalid (*Apol. sec.* 11). However, Athanasius's most lasting influence on the broad development alluded to by Jay lay more in the conception of an imaginative world dominated by a Father and his only begotten Son than in the enactment of the ritual practices that materially reproduced the lineage of divine patriarchy on the earthly plane.

Athanasius's *Orations Against the Arians* here claim our attention. Written circa 340 (which is to say perhaps no more than a few years after his *On the Incarnation*), these three volumes are among Athanasius's earliest explicitly anti-Arian writings.[35] They also constitute his most substantive and enduring contribution to the formulation of a masculinized Nicene trinitarian theology. As in the earlier christological treatise, he begins his written account at the beginning of "the writings" themselves, that is, with the Genesis tale of creation and fall. His interest is now slanted less toward genetics than toward genealogy, though he will return to ground his sociology of familial succession in a quasi-biologized ontology. Insinuating accusations of illegitimate birth, he opens by positioning his opponents as contrivers of heresy who have "walked out" on their kin, and in so doing demonstrated that their minds were never really "with" the family of Christ at all. It follows that they were always already fallen, the dupes of the devil; and if the dupes, then also the descendants; and if descendants of the devil, then not sons but "daughters." In line with this train of logic, the so-called Arian heresy is assigned the trickster role of the littlest sister in a partly feminized antifamily characterized by its conniving and contriving: "The Arian, as it is called, considering that the other heresies, her elder sisters, have been openly proscribed, in her craft and cunning, affects to array herself in Scripture language, like her father the devil, and is forcing her way back into the Church's paradise."[36] This youngest daughter shoves her way back into the lap of creation's garden, and does so not only violently but duplicitously, by playing the man: although (as Athanasius explains) there is nothing of the well-reasoned (εὔλογον) in her (she doesn't have the Logos!), "made up" (πλάσασα) as a "Christian," she nevertheless deceives some with the persuasiveness of her irrationalities (παραλογισμῶν). Indeed, she tickles more than the ears of her victims with her honeyed lips, for "taking, with Eve, they taste" and mistake the bitter for the sweet. Thus it is that Athanasius finds it necessary to "rip apart the folds of the breastplate of this loathsome heresy" and expose the stink of her frothy senselessness (*Ar.* 1.1).

As I mentioned above, Athanasius proceeds by insinuating accusations of illegitimate birth so as to reconfigure the family of Christ and thereby rhetorically excise certain members—Christians who do not, however, actually align themselves with the discredited and deceased presbyter Arius but rather "boast of patronage of [more powerful] friends and authority of [the emperor] Constantius" (*Ar.* 1.10). Illegitimacy—the denial of the link to the divine Father—is here defined not in terms of a mother's transgression but in terms of a child's brutally exposed sex. *There is no mother* in these opening lines written against the Arians. There are only rival fathers and children, some of whom are marked as "daughters" and thereby assigned a perverse or diabolic paternity. The "daughters," partly identified with the seduced Eve, stand on shifty ground, or rather, they stand in for the shiftiness of any created foundations. The matter of pretense having been raised, the "made-up-ness" of matter becomes once more unavoidable: the gaping nothingness at the beginning and the end that is the womb's sole offer of certainty is all the space a seemingly envious fatherhood is willing to grant maternity.

The association of illegitimate sonship, deception, and a "daughterly" effeminacy continues as Athanasius interweaves his discourse on those who forsake the "name" of Christ (and thereby betray their lack of true sonship) with his portrait of Arius, which casts the heretic as rivaling the daughter of Herodias in his blasphemous twirlings and dancings, and as imitating the poet Sotades in the castrated and effeminate tone (τὸ κεκλασμένον καὶ θηλυκὸν ἦθος) of his writing (*Ar.* 1.2). The only ones who retain the name of Christ, according to Athanasius, are "those who remained with Alexander"; those who "walked out" with Arius "left the Savior's name to us who were with Alexander," he repeats. Athanasius's rhetoric gains momentum as the argument hits still closer to home: "Behold then, after Alexander's death too, those who communicate with his successor Athanasius, and those with whom the said Athanasius communicates, are instances of the same rule; none of them bear his name, nor is he named from them, but all in like manner, and as is usual, are called Christians. For though we have a succession of teachers and become their disciples, yet, because we are taught by them the things of Christ, we both are, and are called, Christians all the same. But those who follow the heretics . . . " (*Ar.* 1.3). Well, by now we can guess: mislabeled, girlish, they do not bear the Name of the Father's true Son but instead are called "Arians." Or at least that is what Athanasius calls them, now that Arius is as dead as Alexander. And paternity is, after all, largely a matter of name-calling.

I am tempted to say that all the significant pieces of Athanasius's argument are already in place three brief paragraphs into this multivolume work. Patrilineal succession has been announced as the theme that will thread its way through the layered discussions of theology, salvation history, and episcopal politics. The basic strategies for constructing (and unraveling) filiation have been established. Seven more paragraphs remain, however, to round out the introductory section of the *Orations Against the Arians* and to establish the specifically *bookish* terms of Athanasius's debate. At the center of this introduction, and following the passages just discussed, citations and paraphrases of Arius's *Thalia* are embedded (*Ar.* 1.5, 6). Here Athanasius artfully re-creates a text that can serve simultaneously as foil and as pretext for his own polemical writing, offering an "Arian" cover for the diverse range of positions with which he will contend in the later portions of the work. As he pours the *Thalia* into the mold of his own treatise, Athanasius is able to extract from it the cherished doctrines perniciously negated by his opponents: the necessary eternity of divine Fatherhood and the concomitant eternity, omniscience, and ontological stability of the Father's immutable Logos, whose Sonship is *not* "constructed"—that is, merely bodily, created out of nothing—but "essential."

The textual centerfold of Athanasius's introduction—with its shocking figuration of a pseudo-Son whose createdness, subordinate status, and alterability mark him as an unreliable Savior at best—effectively symbolizes heresy as an antidiscourse, a mode of writing marked by impotence and frivolity, lacking the Logos's driving force. "These are portions of Arius's fables as they occur in that jocose composition," Athanasius remarks dismissively at the end of his recitation (*Ar.* 1.6). Later he depicts the *Thalia* as vomit and as a "container of all impiety," comparing the trashy text to the beckoning body of Dame Folly in Proverbs 8, into whose female depths the ignorant may plunge, only to find themselves in the abyss of Hades in which the "giants" (γηγενεῖς; literally, "earth born") perish (*Ar.* 1.10). This feminizing abjection of the form, content, and author of the *Thalia* is underlined by the framing of its citation: immediately surrounding the central presentation of the heretical text are passages that pick up and elaborate the previously introduced images of the author Arius as a vulgar poet, a dancing girl, and the serpent seducing Eve. Composed by one who "dances against the Savior," Arius's "loose and dissolute meters" betray "the unmanliness of his soul [τὸ τῆς ψυχῆς μὴ ἀνδρῶδες] and the corruption of the writer's thought," according to the principle that "a man [ἀνὴρ] is known by the issue of his word [ἀπο ἐξόδου λόγου]." A snaky character, he "twists to and fro" (*Ar.* 1.4). Singing and prancing about as if onstage, when he writes of God he is "like the serpent counseling the woman" (1.7). A writhing effeminacy of word is the shifty mark of the illegitimacy by which he, Arius—motherless like all the sons in this work—is unmasked as the offspring not of God the Father but of Satan the antifather, disseminator of the "mania" of heresy. Later, Athanasius will describe the Arian heresy as "foreign and not from our fathers," positing a Son who is "made" and not a "proper offspring"; and again he will return to the pseudo-proof of invented patronymics: "being Arians, they are not Christians" (*Ar.* 1.8–10).

"Turning away from the Word of God and making up for themselves one that does not exist, they have fallen into nothingness," continues Athanasius. "For this reason also the ecumenical synod cast Arius out of the church when he said these things and anathematized him, not tolerating such impiety" (*Ar.* 1.7). He has already brought his episcopal predecessor Alexander into his text in order to secure his own right to bear the name of the Father and to counter the rival claims of the "Arians." Now he briefly cites Nicaea as the disciplining arm of the law. But it is Athanasius himself, as author of the *Orations*, who will effectively take up the mantle of both Alexander and the council in order to deflate the pretensions of the *Thalia*, a frivolous word puffed up *ex nihilo*. He will do so by building his own textual fortress on the immovable foundations of Scripture, veritable Word of God, not concocted out of nothing but divinely generated. For Athanasius, to write is not to invent but, reading the Word already sown, to harvest meaning like sons. Men, destined for divinity, are not made but begotten. Materiality is the realm of what is contrived or fictive, and a corruptible and changeable creation is the natural ally of the Deceiver and his daughters. Maternity's stubborn particularities are what finally come to "nothing," disappearing almost entirely from Athanasius's text, while a paternity wholly sublimated—pure culture, one might say—lays claim to what is essential, giving the name to an identity more natural than nature itself.

"If God be not as a man [ἄνθρωπος], as He is not, we must not impute to Him the attributes of man." With this passage, which draws us into the main body of Athanasius's text, we return to the question raised at the outset: what can a blanket denial of human attributes possibly mean, in a discussion in which Athanasius insists on the necessity of thinking of God as a Father and his Word as his begotten Son? It is characteristic of both rational and irrational creatures, Athanasius continues, to be "begotten according to a line of succession [κατὰ διαδοχῆς ἀλλήλων γεννῶνται]," with the result that identities multiply and shift, as one who was once a son to a father becomes in turn also a father to a son. "Hence in such instances, there is not, properly speaking [κυρίως: authoritatively], either father or son, nor do the father and the son stay in their respective characters [ἔστηκεν ἐπ' αὐτῶν: stand erect and on their own]." Although he has here drastically reduced the complexity of family structures to the clean linearity of a continuous chain of fathers and singular sons whose ongoing regenerative processes achieve a *virtual* "eternity," Athanasius remains troubled by the lingering specter of change and multiplicity that is the mark of creatureliness. "But it is not so in the Godhead," he reassures his readers. "It belongs to the Godhead alone, that the Father is properly father and the Son properly son, and in them and them only does it hold that the Father is ever Father and the Son ever Son" (*Ar.* 1.21). The formula is by now familiar: perfection is an exclusively divine property, yet humanity strains to conform itself to the unachievable standards of a divinity in which fatherhood and sonship are immutably sunk into being itself. Leapfrogging over the deadly alterability of the mother-born, Athanasius will not even settle for an unbroken and undefiled succession of human fathers and sons but aspires instead to the perfected security of relational identities put permanently on ice. Frozen, fixed, essentially Father, essentially Son, his theological personae eternally beget their own divine certainties.

Small wonder that Athanasius is annoyed to find himself interrupted from contemplation of this static, crystalline dyad by the clamor of Arian pollsters in the marketplace quizzing children exuberantly about the freedom and movement of the Son and questioning "little women" (γυναικάρια; cf. 2 Timothy 2.6–7) in flowery terms concerning their memories of childbirth (*Ar.* 1.22). Such strategies have the processes of knowledge and salvation exactly backwards: the point is not to reduce God to the level of humanity but rather to stretch humanity in the direction of divinity.

Athanasius is particularly disturbed by the approach to women for theological insight, an issue to which he returns. Indeed, it is on account of the easily deceived "little women" that he undertakes to refute the heretics, as he claims (1.23). In response to the Arians' "very simple and foolish inquiry, which they put to silly women" about birth, he retorts that "it is not suitable to measure divine generation by the nature of humanity" (1.26).

If, however, the Arians want to drag human biology into the discussion, Athanasius will agree to meet them on their own terms. Biological generation underlines the essential and proper relation between parent and child, he affirms, while it can be proved from Scripture that even human fathers are in some sense eternally parents of sons: just as "Levi too was already in the loins of his great-grandfather, before his own actual generation, or that of his grandfather," so any man, upon reaching maturity, actualizes his ever-present potential fatherhood as "immediately, with nature unrestrained, he becomes father of the son from himself" (*Ar.* 1.26). But however useful, even necessary, such comparisons may be, they are also dangerous in their appeal to the flesh, and Athanasius must constantly repeat, even at the risk of seeming partly to contradict himself, that "divine generation must not be compared to the nature of men, nor the Son considered to be part of God, nor the generation to imply any passion whatever." He retreats to the title of Word, when the metaphor of "generation" brought in with "Son" gets too messy—which is to say, too close to the "passionate" body, which he prefers to identify as female. "So much may be impressed even on these men of folly; for as they asked women concerning God's Son, so let them inquire of men concerning the Word" (*Ar.* 1.28). We recall Jay's dictum that "birth by itself can never provide sure evidence" of paternity, and that it is precisely "evidence of paternity" that is required "when the crucial intergenerational link is between father and son." Thus, Athanasius directs our attention away from sons emerging in time from wombs, to sons eternally quiescent in fathers' loins; away from children born, to words uttered; away from female birthing, to a purely male generativity.

"Does the father replace the womb with the matrix of his language?" queries Luce Irigaray.[37] Ask men about the Word, instructs Athanasius. And what kind of a Word is it? Athanasius's filial Logos is, as we have seen, defined by its immutability, its fixed or static essence. In Athanasius's texts—in his sensitivity to "textuality" itself—we sense something of what

Ath. vs. Joseph Smith

Richard Lim describes as a late-antique trend toward a "growing reliance on textual authority," which went hand in hand with an "increasingly negative reception of public debate as a form of social competition and dispute settlement."[38] What will later become for Athanasius also an authoritative invocation of a creed is at this point primarily a resort to Scripture,[39] but in all cases the appeal is to a written word, fixed by the letter, fixed to the letter—sometimes truth is the matter of one iota! Sensitive to the fact that his opponents "blame the Nicene bishops for their use of phrases not in Scripture" (*Ar.* 1.30), Athanasius defends the concept of divine Fatherhood by leaning heavily on the authority of the biblical text: "For [Unoriginate] is unscriptural and suspicious, because it has various senses; . . . but the word Father is simple and scriptural, and more accurate, and only implies the Son" (1.34). His initial organization of his discussion based on certain theological "questions" (1.11–36) eventually shifts to a sequential treatment of key biblical passages (1.37–3.58). From start to finish, the Athanasian theory of divine Fatherhood and Sonship as developed in the *Orations Against the Arians* presents itself as a lettered phenomenon. The frozen words of Scripture deliver the certainties of an immutable patriliny, and the body of man is insulated from the material mess and ambiguity of the feminized realm of becoming and dying. To be begotten a son is to transcend maternal birth, and to transcend the flesh—to be made word—is to become a man.

"We can assume," writes Irigaray, "that any theory of the subject has always been appropriated by the 'masculine.'"[40] While stopping well short of attributing a unique generative power to the works of Athanasius, I *am* suggesting here that his writings exemplify and concretize a broader historical shift in Western theories of subjectivity and practices of theory, in which a radical suppression of materiality is accompanied by an explicit masculinization of the constructed "self," articulated in the theological terms of a motherless patriliny. In other words, Athanasius played a potent role in generating the "assumed" universality of the masculine appropriation of both theory and subjectivity, as the "logocentrism" of his treatise *On the Incarnation* gave rise, historically and (chrono)logically, to the "patricentric" and "filiocentric" masculinism of his anti-Arian trinitarian theology, which is (as Widdicombe argues) innovatively and almost obsessively preoccupied with the metaphors of fatherhood and sonship. If the particular masculinizing "theory of the subject" that was erected in late antiquity has come to seem numbingly familiar, we must push back behind boredom and learn again to feel surprised that the ongoing construction of a "neutral" subject should have been underwritten by the doubled and linked repressions of materiality and of the female.

Staging the Father's Council: The Apologetic Works

> To produce a single precise word, [our two lips] would have to stay apart.
> Definitely parted. Kept at a distance, separated by *one word*. But where
> would that word come from? Perfectly correct, closed up tight, wrapped
> around its meaning. Without any opening, any fault. . . . The unity,
> the truth, the propriety of words comes from their lack of lips, their
> forgetting of lips. Words are mute, when they are uttered once and for all.
> Neatly wrapped up so that their meaning—their blood—won't escape.
> Like the children of men?
>
> —*Luce Irigaray,*
> "When Our Lips Speak Together"

> In a traditional society, *logos* mediated the relations of social life and
> introduced a dimension of competitive fluidity that was not always
> welcomed. . . . The rise of traditional authority and hierarchical tendencies
> in philosophical and ecclesiastical bodies rendered clever words harmless
> by attributing more weight to written documents, and by favoring
> acclamatory (synchronic) and traditional (diachronic) consensus, thus
> returning the settlement of Christian disputes to the province of
> old-style power politics, away from the unpredictable sway of *tyche* in
> which fortune might favor talent and daring.
>
> —*Richard Lim,*
> Public Disputation, Power, and Social Order in Late Antiquity

Richard Lim traces the gradual solidification of the flow of words in the fourth century. A society that had begun to define itself through stiff public performances of unanimity, consensus, and fidelity to "tradition" intensified its policing of the supple lips and agile minds of men trained in the arts of dialectic and oral debate. Lim connects the rigidification and homogenization of a mute and lipless discourse in late antiquity with the increased importance of writing. The latter social development was itself linked to an emergent ecclesiastical conciliar process that entailed the meticulous recording and publication of minutes, decisions, and approved statements of belief. The *documentation* of councils—as sites of public debate—not only displaced the actual events after the fact but also contributed to the cramped style of the deliberations themselves: "The dynamics of public debate were altered dramatically when one could be held responsible for everything one said in the heat of discussion."[41] Interestingly, the Council of Nicaea, which inaugurated the history of the authoritative "ecumenical" councils, lacks written *acta*. The high level of dissension that gave rise to a council later reputed for its unity, Lim points out, may have "rendered a set of *acta* unnecessary and undesirable."[42] He goes on to discuss the late-fourth- and early-fifth-century literary representations of the Nicene council, which in the final event made such *acta* doubly superfluous. "The death of Athanasius, who attended the council as a young priest at the side of his bishop Alexander, marked the advent of the post-Nicene age. With all eye-witnesses dead, legends about Nicaea began to emerge."[43] Did the end of Athanasius's eye-witnessing, however, really mark the *beginning* of "legends about Nicaea"? It seems equally important to point out that Athanasius's death marked the *end* of a crucial phase in the literary invention of Nicaea, and that, furthermore, the layered inscription of his "historical" or "apologetic" texts—resulting in his retroactive construction of a virtual archive for the council—contributed heavily to the creation of a documentary habit that was, as Lim and others have demonstrated, crucial to the success of the late-antique council in producing "consensual" orthodoxy.[44]

Athanasius's apologetic corpus is a fruitful place to ask again "where would that word come from?"—a word "single," "precise," "perfectly correct," and "neatly wrapped," "like the child of men." A reading of his literary defenses helps explain how utterances detached from flesh and blood were reembodied in fixed texts, suitably rigid stand-ins for the unchangeable body that was the goal of the divinized man. Sorting through the complexly intercalated writings authored, ghost-authored, or edited and published by the bishop of Alexandria, we observe him constructing Nicaea, its frozen Logos, and indeed his own armored body through a series of very deliberate textual acts of self-defense. As Timothy Barnes comments, "Athanasius never forgot the controversy surrounding his election in 328."[45] What Athanasius never allows his *readers* to forget, therefore, is the authority of the Council of Nicaea, its participants, its decrees, and its all-sufficient definition of faith. In Athanasius's writings, Nicaea is re-worked into the matrix of an otherwise motherless paternity and sonship, giving rise to the 318 conciliar "Fathers," and also to their only-begotten credal Word, put forth as the touchstone of true and legitimate sonship within the ranks of episcopal leadership. Charles Kannengiesser empha-sizes that the "Arian crisis" was in large part a local, Alexandrian produc-tion,[46] and one might say the same of the "ecumenical" Council of Nicaea. Athanasius carefully positions Nicaea as Bishop Alexander's council, con-vened for the defeat of the "Arians," and he presents Alexander in turn as Nicaea's bishop: it is the council itself that—in the texts of Athanasius—both vests Alexander with fatherhood and marks Athanasius (then deacon) as his only son and heir. "Nicaea" was thus Athanasius's oft-repeated an-swer to "the controversy surrounding his election in 328," a controversy that Alexandrian church politics made it difficult ever to forget. His depo-sition at the Council of Tyre in 335 and the installations of the Cappado-cian Gregory as bishop of Alexandria in 338 and of George of Cappadocia circa 356 are only a few of the tense moments in the long career of this quintessentially controversial bishop—a bishop rarely able to inhabit the city whose churches' rule he claimed as a legacy.[47]

The consistency with which Athanasius links Nicaea to his tactics of self-defense is striking. But equally striking is the late date at which Athanasius began his apologetic construction of the ecumenical synod.[48] As we have seen, *On the Incarnation* seems to be Athanasius's earliest written treatise, along with its companion text, *Against the Gentiles*, and it includes no mention of Nicaea or the Arians, nor any autobiographical material. Only after the crisis of Gregory's entry into Alexandria in late 338 did Athanasius rediscover "Arius" (who had been dead since 335 or 336) and the usefulness of the label "Arianism"—although he was warming to the topic in the festal letter for 338, which contains his first recorded mention of "Ar-ians."[49] The *Encyclical Letter to All Bishops*, which he seems to have written in 339 on the point of his departure for Rome, following the appointment of Gregory as bishop of Alexandria, frames Gregory as an "Arian" but still does not explicitly mention Nicaea.

"Nicaea" enters Athanasius's texts on the heels of "Arianism," but initially with faltering steps. The earliest reference to the council in the Athanasian corpus occurs in the *Encyclical Letter of the Council of Egypt*, also written around 339. Preserved in a documentary collection probably first assembled by Athanasius in the 350s, this letter names Athanasius in the third person; however, it may well have been authored by Athanasius himself and was perhaps also circulated by him at the time of his departure for Rome, since it is addressed to "all bishops, and to Julius, bishop of Rome" (*Apol. sec.* 20). Prior to its inclusion in the *Second Apology Against the Arians* (357/358), the encyclical had already been constructed as a gathering place for other documents, several of which were originally attached to the letter but later redeployed within the *Apology*;[50] the letter thus stands at the beginning of the history of the Athanasian documentary project. The letter represents Athanasius as a persecuted witness for truth. It recounts how, in the period before Nicaea, Athanasius, "who was then a deacon," had already been harassed by the Arians because of the "familiarity" and "honor" with which Bishop Alexander, archenemy of Arius, regarded him. When Athanasius thereafter attended the Council of Nicaea with his bishop, he "spoke boldly against the impiety of the Arian madmen" (*Apol. sec.* 6). Nicaea, the site of Athanasius's witness, is the "true" council by virtue of both its large numbers, or "ecumenicity" (7), and its freedom from imperial coercion (8). Its judgments "against the Arians" deposed those very "Arian madmen" who later convened at Tyre to depose Athanasius. The letter thus pits the legitimacy and veracity of Nicaea directly against the illegitimacy and falsehood of Tyre, which merely parodied Nicaea when it claimed absurdly to depose Athanasius (7).[51]

The first *Oration Against the Arians*, which is difficult to date but may have been started as early as 339, makes brief mention of the council and also refers to Alexander and to Athanasius's place as his successor, as we have seen. But Athanasius does not really begin to elaborate his understanding of the council for more than a decade after that—that is, two and a half decades after the council itself—in a period when he once again was in danger of being cast as a bastard bishop by the appointment of another "Arian" rival to the see of Alexandria. Written up in stages long after the event, "Nicaea" has the air of neither accident nor inevitability in its emergence within Athanasius's texts—and thus also within Christian history more generally.[52] Edward Gibbon writes of the Alexandrian bishop: "The knowledge of human nature was his first and most important science. He preserved a distinct and unbroken view of a scene which was incessantly shifting; and never failed to improve those decisive moments which are irrecoverably past before they are perceived by the common eye."[53] These are intriguing lines. Indeed, what we have first encountered in Athanasius's writings is his self-proclaimed "knowledge of human nature," as presented in his earliest and most serenely nonpolemical work, *On the Incarnation*, and further elaborated through his account of divine fatherhood and sonship in the *Orations Against the Arians*. Having fixed his own nearly transcendent vantage point in those works, and at the same time framed the scene of an "incessantly shifting" creation, he is finally—much later— ready to let the cameras roll. It is his gaze that will pull together something "distinct and unbroken"—the clarity and permanence of Nicaea's singular word and his own dogged faithfulness as Alexander's only-begotten son— out of the chaotic history of the Arians' restless and contentious proliferation of synods and confessions of faith, from which he strives to distance himself, paradoxically, given the rehearsed vicissitudes of his own career. The view of human history requires improvements, and Athanasius does not fail to make them for the benefit of "the common eye." By 350 Nicaea was surely "irrecoverably past" without having yet been clearly "perceived": but Athanasius, from his elevated perspective, would do all he could to assure that his readers would henceforth encounter it as one of "those decisive moments."

On the Council of Nicaea is among the first of the extended apologetic texts probably composed after 350. Athanasius opens with a strong polemical alignment of the "Arians" with the "Jews." Like the Jews, the Arians deny the Lord; having denied the Logos, they are without reason and do not even deserve a rational response; he will, however, reply to those in his own camp who are disturbed by the issues raised by the Arians (*Decr.* 1, 2). Athanasius reminds his readers that the Arians were condemned at Nicaea and insists that the precise terms of the condemnation cannot be changed or even questioned; an Arian self-defense would have to consist in proving a change of heart, rather than in challenging the immovable Nicene language itself (*Decr.* 2). Hermann Josef Sieben points out that Athanasius here moves beyond the position of the *Encyclical Letter of the Council of*

Egypt: Nicaea "is no longer merely the pronounced sentence (κρίσις) that expels from the church . . . ; it is also the written, formulated judgment (ὁρισθέντα). . . . "[54] As he goes on to retell the story of the council in this text, Athanasius mocks those condemned at Nicaea for their internal divergences. At the same time, he stresses that those in the party of Eusebius of Nicomedia—whose followers are among Athanasius's contemporary "Arian" opponents—signed their agreement to the very terms (τοῖς ῥήμασιν) that they are now placing under dispute, namely the Son's status as begotten "out of the essence" and "homoousios" with the Father. From this, it follows either that the Eusebians changed their minds after the council, in which case their present disciples are the successors of shifty and wavering men, or that they remained true to their signed commitments, in which case the latter-day "Arians" fail even at loyalty to those whom they claim to honor as masters. At any rate, any who disagree with what "the Fathers handed on as doctrine" at Nicaea thereby diverge from the truth (*Decr.* 3, 4, 5). Sieben emphasizes that the move to identify the particular text of the Nicene credal formulation with the true doctrine "handed on"—namely, with apostolic tradition itself—is another bold innovation in this work and is directly linked with the unprecedented designation of the bishops who attended Nicaea as "Fathers." The introduction of such paternal terminology is a key factor in the evolution of Athanasius's concept of Nicaea: "Since those who attended Nicaea are in a conspicuous sense the transmitters and agents of the divine 'tradition' or 'παράδοσις,' that is, of the 'teaching' or 'διδασκλία' that is handed down from 'Fathers to Fathers,' they themselves are designated with this title, which is surely the highest that Athanasius has to bestow. And the more conscious Athanasius is of the fact that the Nicene faith in its positive formulation is the divine 'παράδοσις,' the more exclusively are the council's attendees designated by this title."[55]

The main body of the treatise *On the Council of Nicaea* consists of an extended defense of the two phrases attacked by the "Arians," "out of the essence" and "homoousios" (*Decr.* 18–24). In support of these phrases, Athanasius adds a short chain of citations demonstrating that the Nicene language had been transmitted "from Fathers to Fathers" (ἐκ Πατέρων εἰς Πατέρας) (*Decr.* 25–27), as well as a refutation of the proposal that God be defined as "unoriginate" (28–32). Paternal generativity as a theological *sine qua non* and patrilineal succession as the only reliable mode of transmitting theological truth are here more sharply defined and closely linked than ever, and both are mediated through the fixed text and lettered precision of the Nicene Creed. Athanasius insists on the need to distinguish between God's begetting of the Word out of the divine essence itself and his creation of Adam "out of the earth" (ἐκ γῆς) (*Decr.* 9). This is not, however, to imply either that God creates out of preexistent material or that he begets as human beings do. "For human offspring are a portion of their begetters, since the very nature of bodies is not simple but fluid and compounded of parts. And when humans beget they flow forth; and again nourishment flows into them when they eat." God, on the other hand, is Father of the Son without either division or passion, "for there is neither effluence of the incorporeal nor is there any influx into him, as with humans." And while humans may have multiple sons, the divine Father, in his simplicity, has only one (*Decr.* 11). If a fathering God is not subject to the ebbs and flows, the vacillating excitement and ejaculative mess, of male sexuality, Athanasius would like to assert the same of the "blessed Fathers" of Nicaea, who neatly beget texts as sons and sons like texts (27): "for even a human word is not begotten with passion or division," as he notes (11). Athanasius surely intends his reader to wonder, however, whether as much can be said of the seed-sowing devil and his untidily large and diverse family of girlish Arian sons (2, 27, 29).

As Timothy Barnes notes, manuscripts of *On the Council of Nicaea* attach to it "a sheaf of other documents" testifying to the condemnation of Arius and his allies. He speculates that this text and its "dossier" were composed in response to a letter from Liberius of Rome attempting to arbitrate the dispute between Athanasius and the Council of Sirmium, which had deposed Athanasius (yet again) in 352. Barnes concludes: "It has often been observed that the Nicene creed and its key term *homoousios* became prominent in theological debate only in the 350s. On the known facts, it can plausibly be claimed that it was Athanasius who brought it into prominence by sending his *On the Council of Nicaea* to the bishop of Rome in 352. He had devised a potent rallying-cry."[56] *On the Council of Nicaea* provided something else possibly as significant as the rallying-cry of "*homoousios!*"—namely, a literary format for paternity testing. The "dossier's" documentation of specific ecclesiastical alliances and enmities via letters of reference and the like is complemented by the introduction of what might now be named "patristic" prooftexts, demonstrating lineage by doctrinal affinity.[57] Athanasius repeats his innovative appeal to a literary body of "patristic" doctrine at greater length in the closely related Athanasian text *On the Opinion of Dionysus* and develops dossier-building into a fine art in the slightly later *Apology Against the Arians*. Such strategies attest to the evolution of techniques for providing evidence of a highly sublimated paternity "which is as certain as evidence of maternity, but far more flexible." In fact, Athanasian fatherhood becomes far *more* certain than maternity, once he has ontologically re-marked motherhood's fleshly self-evidence as shifty and translated its perceived certainties into a higher realm of being in which gender and sexuality are made invisible— which is to say, in which all generativity is "appropriated by the masculine" and paternity is the only parentage. Highly flexible indeed, such sublime fatherhood must be supported by a textual edifice strong enough to hold it firmly in place for eternity.

Subsequent works continue to repeat and develop the themes and techniques already mentioned, as Athanasius meets new rounds of opposition with similar responses. Written circa 356, once again from "exile," the *Encyclical Letter to the Bishops of Egypt and Libya* echoes many of the rhetorical strategies of the first *Oration*, making even more of the diabolical paternity of the duplicitous, hyperinventive, and ever-shifting Arians by refracting it through the story of the serpent's seduction of Eve. However, the Arians' frivolous *Thalia* is here explicitly contrasted with the written confession of the true faith at Nicaea, a move that Athanasius had not yet made in the earlier text. The Nicene Creed can now be represented as a concrete talisman; indeed, it is almost fetishized.[58] "Wherefore I exhort you," writes Athanasius, "keeping in your hands the faith which was written by the Fathers at Nicaea, and defending it with great zeal and confidence in the Lord, be examples to those everywhere" (*Ep. Aeg. Lib.* 21). Athanasius develops the figure of the "blessed Alexander" further in this letter as the one who ejected Arius from the church and "who contended even unto death against this heresy," coming very close to representing him as a martyr for the faith of Nicaea (*Ep. Aeg. Lib.* 8, 12, 18, 21, 23). *On the Councils of Ariminum and Seleucia*, another partly documentary work written a few years later still (circa 360), makes even more explicit the designation of the Nicene Creed as a literal inscription of the apostolic tradition: here "Nicaea," as Sieben phrases the point, "is essentially the apostolic faith, the literarily fixed Kerygma."[59] What the Fathers of Nicaea wrote down was, in Athanasius's words, "no discovery of theirs but is the same as was taught by the Apostles" (*Syn.* 5). It is therefore completely sufficient and makes any further councils superfluous (*Syn.* 6). Athanasius again picks up the point that Eusebius and others originally signed off on the Nicene Creed, now framing it in explicitly paternal terms: "What confidence can be placed in their acts," he asks concerning the Arian followers of Eusebius, "if the acts of their fathers be undone? or how call they them fathers and themselves successors, if they set about impeaching their judgment?" With a devious twist he wonders rhetorically, "how can they any longer be bishops, if they were ordained by persons whom they accuse of heresy?" (*Syn.* 13).

The synodal *Letter to the African Bishops* was probably written circa 370, that is, during the last years of Athanasius's life;[60] it thus locates us finally at that end point from which we of the post-Athanasian age inevitably begin to see Nicaea and its Word. "Ἱκανὰ μὲν τὰ γραφέντα," the letter begins: "sufficient are the writings." "Sufficiency" is one of the letter's leitmotifs, and it is by first lauding the "sufficiency" of certain Western synodal texts that the letter backs into the primary source and standard of "sufficiency," namely the faith "which Christ granted, the apostles preached, and the Fathers who gathered at Nicaea from all parts of our world have handed down." Going on to identify Nicaea's purpose as the refutation of the Arian heresy, the letter again underlines the council's completeness, in relation to which all other words, rulings, councils, and parental sources are seen to be excessive and thereby transgressive: "Sufficient then are those things agreed to at Nicaea, and enough in themselves [αὐτάρκη], as set forth, for the overturn of all impious heresy and for the security and succor of ecclesiastical teaching." Those who reject the council declare themselves Arians by that act and rightly share the heretics' punishment. The offense is cast more starkly than ever as a failure of filial piety: the opponents of Nicaea refuse to reverence the Fathers, who anathematized all who opposed their confession. The letter cites ominously from Scripture: "Do not remove the eternal boundaries which your fathers set in place" (Prov. 22:28). "Let the one who speaks evil of father or mother die the death" (Ex. 21:17) (*Ep. Afr.* 1).

"Who would not hate those who disregarded the acts of the Fathers?" the letter's authors query, expanding on the theme of filial loyalty (*Ep. Afr.* 3). The opponents of Nicaea are not sons of a father at all but come "from a dunghill" and "truly 'speak from the earth'" (John 3:31), in contrast to those bishops "who did not discover their phrases [λέξεις] for themselves but, having the witness from the Fathers, wrote it down accordingly" (*Ep. Afr.* 6). "The Fathers wrote down that the Son was *homoousius* with the Father . . . , not making up the phrases for themselves but learning them from those who had also been Fathers before them" (9). Establishing one's place as son in the patrilineal succession designated "apostolic" is at least as much a matter of repeating the right words as of performing the correct rites of episcopal generation: a man's concocted speech may always unmask a paternity that is merely excrement, marking him a creature of the earth, corrupt and changeable. "Why do they reject the synod at Nicaea, at which their Fathers too signed and agreed that the Son was from the essence and *homoousios* with the Father?" Refusing to own Nicaea's word on essential Sonship, their opponents put their own sonship in question: "Whose heirs [κληρονόμοι] and successors [διάδοχοι] are they then? How can they call Fathers those whose confession, well and apostolically written, they do not accept?" (*Ep. Afr.* 7). The Nicene Fathers signed; their signatures stand as witness; they wrote things down once and for all (*Ep. Afr.* 9). Their true sons—the letter's authors—do no more than retrace the letters already inscribed, writing with one pen—all 90 of them. Of one mind, they even sign for each other—in fact they "always" do!—should anyone happen not to be present (*Ep. Afr.* 10). True sons? Well, at least superior imitations of the immutable Son, close copies of the unerasable Word, brothers almost indistinguishable one from the other, like the children of men (cf. *Ep. Afr.* 7).

We note again, in closing, the strikingly close identification of the divinely begotten Word with the written texts that now incarnate "Nicaea"; the linking of legitimate episcopacy with an orthodox sonship defined by loyalty to the Nicene "Fathers"; the equation of such filial piety with willingness to sign on (quite literally) to the words inscribed by those Fathers at Nicaea; and, finally, the narrowing of those texts to the "confession" and its key word *homoousios*, so that the meaning wrapped up in the all-sufficient Nicene word—the begetting of the divine Son from the very essence of the Father—both mirrors and further sublimates the patrilineal structures in which its authority is embedded. As Sieben argues in his treatment of the development of Athanasius's "Konzilsidee," this complex web of argument—which forms a matrix for the linked emergence of fixed and universalizing credal texts, a "patristic" literary corpus, and an episcopacy sharply defined in terms of patrilineage—is not only innovative in relation to prior Christian tradition but also the culmination of 30 years of Athanasius's revisions of his account of Nicaea as an "ecumenical synod."[61] The process was clearly and explicitly rooted in his ongoing defense of the legitimacy of his own sonship as heir to the episcopacy of Alexandria, a legacy that remained insecurely defended—from Athanasius's perspective—so long as the status of Nicaea's text as the single, fixed authoritative "word" was uncertain.

For Athanasius, Nicaea materializes—as transmitted text—both the underlying theory and the concrete practice of constructing patrilineage. Putting pen to page, the Alexandrian Father conceives Nicaea as the "ecumenical" council of the Fathers who begat the immortal body of the written word. Drafted for the most part during periods of exile or withdrawal from Alexandria, when his episcopal identity was under the most intense threat of dissolution, Athanasius's apologetic works convey something of the high stakes of a such a radically sublimated conception of patriliny. Always vulnerable to the charge of fictionality (a fatherhood puffed up out of nothing!), this version of masculine succession nevertheless powerfully unites the authority of a transcendental—and therefore invisible—transmission of essential identity with the tangible certainty of irrefutable documentation. If the deposit of "apostolic faith" passed down from man to man turns out to be little more—and certainly no less—than the technique of patriliny itself, is this not enough?

The City a Desert: 'The Life of Antony'

> Gender is the repeated stylization of the body, a set of repeated acts within a highly rigid regulatory frame that congeal over time to produce the appearance of substance, of a natural sort of being.
>
> —*Judith Butler,*
> Gender Trouble

> Athanasius appears to have lacked a concept of an essential self or given
> personality; rather conformity to some model defined a human being's
> character, for good or ill. . . . [In the *Life of Antony*], Athanasius is clearly
> attempting to present not one model among many, but *the* model of
> the Christian life. His goal is to freeze the flow of imitation and to
> create a single icon, one powerful enough to mirror a diverse set of
> virtues into a single civic life. Antony is designed to join Athanasius's
> Bible as a "canon," the canon of the heavenly πολιτεία.
>
> —*David Brakke,*
> Athanasius and the Politics of Asceticism

David Brakke's observation that Athanasius "lacked a concept of an essential self" occurs in his discussion of Athanasius's appeal to "perverse" forms of divinization to explain the malleability of gender in the case of pathic males. As Brakke summarizes Athanasius's argument, "male worshippers of a female deity imitated their goddess by becoming more 'female' in their nature."[62] On this point at least, Athanasius and Judith Butler would seem to agree: a diversity of sexed identities emerge from sustained ascetic disciplines or iterative mimetic practices that "congeal over time" into *apparent* "natures" or "essences." However, Athanasius (unlike Butler) places the work of human cultivation in the context of the tension between a higher, divine "reality" and a lower "nature." Precultivated "nature" is characterized (as we have seen repeatedly) by the instability, fragmentation, and flux that has nonbeing as its matrix; materiality's chaotic default femaleness must be stabilized, simplified, and sublimated in the ascetic production of the divinized self as a virtual—though never quite "real"—man.

If, as Brakke suggests, Athanasius's *Life of Antony* narrates the mimetic process by which Antony congealed his identity as a holy man and thereby also draws the reader into a mimetic relation to Antony as the singular icon or "sufficient representation" (*V. Anton.* 1) of humanity's divinization, does this process not have something to do with producing the right kind of *masculine gender* in one who imitates not a goddess but a god addressed as Father and Son? In other words, should we not attend to the manhood as well as the holiness of the "holy man" or, to be more precise, to the holy aspirations of this particular, meticulously cultivated version of manhood? Brakke points us to Athanasius's interest in a version of political philosophy, manifested especially in the *Life of Antony*.[63] This highlighting of the significance of the political in Athanasius's text strengthens the suggestion that Athanasius's concerns here have particular implications for the positioning of *men*. Brakke more generally contrasts Athanasius's letters to female ascetics, which are designed to keep urban women off the streets through "the maintenance of proper gender roles," with his writings to and about the desert monks, which attempt to reattach male ascetics to civic life[64]—some version of which had, of course, long been crucial to the making of men. Robert Gregg and Dennis Groh have elaborated the case for the "anti-Arian" preoccupations of the *Life of Antony* that link the bishop's efforts to win the support of desert monastics quite directly with the factionalized theological controversy raging in the cities.[65] Susanna Elm stresses the Alexandrian center of Athanasius's ascetic preoccupations, going so far as to argue that even his "interpretation of 'rural' Egyptian asceticism" functioned to "control and organize inner-urban asceticism," while also acknowledging Athanasius's interest in disciplining the "rural" movement itself.[66] Clearly, then, Athanasius's vigorous attempt to win the support of the monks during his so-called "third exile"—following the installation of a second non-Nicene bishop, George, to Alexandria's episcopacy circa 356—served his own urgent and immediate political needs as an urban bishop on the run in the midst of a booming ascetic movement. The broader and more lasting result of his efforts is the reweaving of a partly unraveled continuity of masculine political identity: *anachoresis*, or "withdrawal," as Athanasius represents it, constitutes not a simple rejection of the city in favor of an alternative but rather a strategy for refashioning the city, to which there is never, in Athanasius's mind, any alternative.[67]

   In the *Life of Antony* and his other ascetic writings, Athanasius once again locates the body of the divinized man at the fulcrum of a paradox: corruptible materiality that has miraculously transcended its nature via the fixative gift of the Word, the body yet remains creaturely in every respect. Thanks to God's grace in the incarnation, all may now practice the ascetic disciplines that allow them to draw as close as possible to a perfect imitation of Christ. Through such discipline, sublimated bodies mime the incarnate Word, and adopted sons ape their only-begotten Brother in controlled performances that "congeal over time to produce the appearance of real substance."

However, in the dance of imitation, the balance between identity and difference is carefully calibrated, and Athanasius is alert to the possibility of misstep. Too much rigor might prove as dangerous as too much bodily laxity, and the severity of the lifestyles pursued by some monks seemed to ignore the fine line separating men's granted divinization from Christ's essential divinity. Resistance to such hubris is at stake when Athanasius suggests that the persisting flux of the male body reveals the limits of grace in humans—an argument that takes shape in a letter to the desert father Amoun addressing the question of whether nocturnal emissions rendered a monk impure and unfit to partake of the Eucharist.[68] Athanasius makes clear that even an ascesis centered on withdrawal could not stop seminal effusions, though it *was* (in his view) designed to reduce ejaculation to a matter of mere personal hygiene. As "natural" as nose blowing, spitting, urinating, or defecating, periodic nocturnal emissions were deemed by Athanasius "a physical necessity of animal life." Part of the body's involuntary response to material needs, ejaculation could not be eradicated, but it might be confined to the substratum of purely animal elimination that lay safely below the reach of human desire. "But when any bodily excretion takes place independently of will, then we experience this, like other things, by a necessity of nature," he instructs. Though elsewhere he is troubled by material instability and excess, in this letter Athanasius regards seminal effluence dispassionately as a stabilizing mechanism that prevents the build-up of excess by routinizing flux. "But possibly medical men . . . will support us on this point, telling us that there are certain necessary passages accorded to the animal body, to provide for the dismissal of the superfluity of what is secreted in our secret parts; for example, for the superfluity of the head, the hair and the watery discharges from the head, and the purgings of the belly, and that superfluity again of the seminative channels." He hastens to clarify that for the waking man, whose rational faculties are engaged, the only "use" of the particular "passages" in this God-created generative organ is "that lawful use which God permitted when He said, 'Increase and multiply.'" In Athanasius's text, desire is overtaken by will and, thus "rationalized," is sheered free of its moorings in sentient flesh; flesh is in turn reduced to a somnolent substratum of mute necessity, defined by the unchallengeable laws of "nature." Although the "needs" of the body persist, men schooled in the arts of nonresponsiveness may hope to achieve a transcendent numbness. Paradoxically, the sign of grace for those who choose the angelic way of celibacy seems to be the utter mindlessness of ejaculations that are always premature anyway. Too much cultivated bodily self-control, according to Athanasius in his letter to Amoun, raises suspicions of "filthy thoughts."

Although Antony's wet dreams and nose blowings go unspecified in the Athanasian *Life*, the hagiographic text does highlight the struggles in the borderlands of voluntary control, recording the shame with which Antony "used to eat and sleep and go about all other bodily necessities." "So often, when about to eat with any other hermits, recollecting the spiritual food, he begged to be excused and departed far off from them, deeming it a matter for shame if he should be seen eating by others" (*V. Anton.* 45). We recall that elsewhere Athanasius distinguishes humanity from divinity by the criteria of permeability and fluidity: "when humans beget they flow forth; and again nourishment flows into them when they eat" (*Decr.* 11). Pressing the limits of humanity, the nearly divine Antony draws a veil of shame over the realm of "bodily necessity," while drastically slowing the porous flow of corporality by restricting his meals—morsels of solid, dry loaves that remain "fresh" for up to six months are all he eats! (*V. Anton.* 12)—and curtailing sleep, with its vulnerable disengagement of will. Like Amoun, he is ashamed to expose his earthly flesh (*V. Anton.* 47, 60), preferring to fix his gaze on the incorruptible body that will be his heavenly inheritance (*V. Anton.* 16; cf. 91).

As has often been remarked, Athanasius's *Life of Antony* charts the holy man's transformation across space as well as time. "The desert alone, and Anthony's journeys within it, provided the map against which the *Life* plotted the profound changes in Anthony's person."[69] On the cusp of adulthood Antony leaves his Egyptian village, divesting himself of his landholdings, movable property, and family responsibilities (*V. Anton.* 2–3). Living at first on the margins of the village, "he confirmed his purpose not to return to the abode of his fathers" (3), dwelling instead among hermits who "welcomed him as a son" or a "brother" (4). During this period of explicit familial reconfiguration, Antony struggled particularly with the demons of sexual desire, which might come in the form of a woman or a dark-skinned boy (5–6). Having strengthened his soul's resistance to sensual pleasure and traditional family life, Antony moved further from the village to the site of some tombs (7–8). There his battles against demons wracked him with such extremes of bodily pain that his friends took him for dead. But when he finally learned to remain mentally detached from pain as well as pleasure, he was rewarded with an illumination of divine grace (8–10). Now physically deadened, he moved from the tomb to a still more remote site, where, having "built up the entrance completely" (12), he remained walled up in an abandoned fortress for twenty years. At the end of this period of fortifying self-encryption, he emerged as unchanged as if he had been embalmed: "he had the same habit [τὴν αὐτὴν ἕξιν] of body as before, and was neither fat, like a man without exercise, nor lean from fasting and striving with the demons, but he was just the same as they had known him before his retirement." Indeed, Antony had recovered the paradisal condition of a humanity whose nature had been stabilized through the grace of participation in the Logos: he was "guided by reason and abiding in a natural state" (14).

Athanasius concludes his account of Antony's emergence from the fortress with a now-famous flourish of rhetoric: "And thus it happened in the end that cells arose even in the mountains, and the desert was made a city by monks [καὶ ἡ ἔρημος ἐπολίσθη ὑπὸ μοναχῶν], who came forth from their own people, and enrolled themselves for citizenship in the heavens [ἐν τοῖς οὐρανοῖς πολιτείαν]" (V. Anton. 14). And again: "So their cells were in the mountains, like tabernacles, filled with holy bands of men who sang psalms, loved reading, fasted, prayed, rejoiced in the hope of things to come, labored in almsgiving, and preserved love and harmony one with another. And truly it was possible, as it were, to behold a land set by itself [χώραν τινὰ καθ᾿ ἑαυτὴν], filled with piety and justice" (44). Shortly after this second description of the transformation of the desert into a monastic city, Athanasius relates Antony's visit to Alexandria (46) and his subsequent return, whereupon he found himself besieged by visitors in his desert dwelling place and "not allowed to withdraw [ἀναχωρεῖν] according to his own intention, as he wished." In a final gesture of removal from society, Antony traveled three days and three nights, until he came to a high mountain in the "inner desert," at the foot of which flowed a cold and clear spring (49). "He loved the place," writes Athanasius, "recognizing it as his own home [ἴδιον οἶκον]." Wild palm trees offered Antony their fruits, and the soil, tilled and sowed by the hermit, yielded grain and a few vegetables

(50). This site of sufficiency remained Antony's permanent dwelling place. He lived 105 years—an inadequate hint of the vast stretch of eternity (16). At the end of his life "his eyes were undimmed and quite sound and he saw clearly; of his teeth he had not lost one, but they had become worn to the gums through the great age of the old man; he remained strong in both hands and feet" (93). Preserved through his ascetic practice and poised for rebirth into eternity, he took pains to ensure that his achieved fixity of bodily *hexis* should not be parodied according to Egyptian customs of conservation: he instructed that at his death he be buried in a secret place to await his resurrection into incorruptibility (91).

This narration of Antony's life lays ascent on its side, recasting the divinization of man horizontally by tracing the saint's movement away from the busy villages and damp fertility of the banks of the Nile and into the solitude and arid sterility of the desert's "inner mountain." Pushing at the outer edges of habitable land, Antony finds himself suddenly on the inside of a place he recognizes as "home." The desert—taking on Edenic overtones—gives forth water and a garden, so that the holy man no longer requires even occasional deliveries of bread. At the heart of the inhospitable wilderness, he has discovered the site of perfect plenitude, where there is neither lack nor excess: nearly desireless, he has come very close indeed to conforming himself perfectly to the template of Christ. And yet, however self-sufficient, Antony is still not alone; "he seems more accessible than ever."[70] Athanasius's mapping of the progress of holy manhood does not after all draw a clean line from village life to mountain solitude. The inner mountain proves far from impenetrable: Antony's vegetable garden is tended for the benefit of his visitors, and the monks, "like children mindful of their father," visit him every month (*V. Anton.* 50–51). More significantly still, Athanasius has structured his narrative so that Antony's journey ends roughly halfway through the tale, which subsequently doubles back on itself, topographically. The second half of the *Life* recounts Antony's numerous visits to the monastic colonies of the outer mountain as well as at least one trip outside the desert: "Then being summoned by the bishops and all the brethren, he descended from the mountain, and having entered Alexandria, he denounced the Arians, saying that their heresy was the last of all and a forerunner of Antichrist" (*V. Anton.* 69). Antony appears oddly at home during this carefully scripted visit to the big city. Responding to some of his supporters who had tried to shelter him from the crowds, "he said, undisturbedly, that there were not more of them than of the demons with whom he wrestled in the mountain" (*V. Anton.* 70). When he is shown declaiming and performing miracles in Alexandria and its outskirts, the scenes painted are almost indistinguishable from Athanasius's accounts of his healings and exorcisms, fatherly sermons, and philosophical debates in the outer mountain. There too, the hermit seems in his element. As Brown notes, the primary sign of Antony's transcendent state after reaching the inner mountain is, strangely enough, his "quintessentially fourth-century gift of sociability."[71] In Athanasius's *Life*, Antony's solitude is the inner lining of his vibrant participation in the society of the outer mountain, which Antony never really moves beyond; moreover, the outer mountain proves capacious enough to accommodate not only the inner mountain but also Alexandria itself.

Few readers have missed the point that Antony's withdrawal from village life leads paradoxically to the rise of a city in the desert, but most have emphasized Athanasius's establishment of a contrast between societies—as if foreshadowing the fading of the cities of the classical world, on the one hand, and the unearthly commonwealth of Christendom that proposes to displace them, on the other. What Athanasius's "outer mountain" is understood to provide is, in other words, the vision of an *alternative* citizenry. True enough; yet this account overlooks the complicating factor of the placement of Alexandria in the text. The two poles of the *Life* are the "village" (κώμη) and the monastic "city" (πολιτεία), and Alexandria is aligned not with the village but with the desert commonwealth. Indeed, this subtle association of the city at the mouth of the Nile with the city of the desert is crucial to Athanasius's textual strategy for winning asceticism for his own Nicene cause. Leaving the village, Athanasius's hero founds a new society; he never really leaves it; and the desert *politeia* bends around to Alexandria, whence Athanasius himself will indeed eventually return, with the support of much of Egypt's monastic community. In the meantime, "flight" from the city can always be retooled as that ascetic "withdrawal" through which the city is produced anew (*Apologia de fuga*);[72] "exile" helps create a flexibly transcendentalized sense of place that does not, however, completely renounce topical specificity. Athanasius, like Antony, is a man who knows "home" when he sees it. That home is not the occupied city represented by the effete urbanity of the Arian heretics whom he parodies in his apologetic works. But it *is* in some important sense still Alexandria, an Alexandria in exile, a city that traces a horizontal path of transcendence into the desert, where it is reconceived as a harmonious community of fathers, sons, and brothers, overseen by the orthodox bishop Athanasius, to whom Father Antony himself had bequeathed one sheepskin and the garment that Athanasius had given him long before (*V. Anton.* 91).

The *Life of Antony* makes two brief and conspicuously constricted references to Antony's ascetic sister. We are told that Antony commits his sister to the charge of some virgins known to him, "giving her to be raised in the convent [εἰς Παρθενῶνα]," as he sets out on his own monastic venture. Immediately thereafter Athanasius remarks that Antony initially pursued an ascetic life on the edge of his village because "there were not yet so many monasteries [μοναστήρια] in Egypt and no monk at all knew of the distant desert" (*V. Anton.* 3). Were there many "convents"? The question is not raised, and the silence instructs: "convents" are not relevant to the tale, which marches onward toward "monasteries" and the "distant desert."[73] Much later, we encounter the sister again. Antony has come down triumphantly from the inner mountain to be greeted as "Father" by those in the "outer monasteries" (μοναστήρια). No longer requiring supplies from them, he instead feeds his children with his own words; his very presence spreads joy. Athanasius continues, without further comment: "And Antony also rejoiced when he beheld the earnestness of the monks, and his sister grown old in virginity, and that she herself also was the leader of other virgins" (*V. Anton.* 54). Are we to imagine female "virgins" among the citizens of the desert *politeia*, or have these women traveled from their village to meet with Antony? Did they look upon Antony's sister as a "Mother"? Again, these are not questions the text invites us to ask; indeed, they seem to die on our tongues. The village, and with it the *parthenon*, has been left behind. The desert city is a place of *monasteria*. Antony's sister and her "virgins" function as a device of exclusion. Securing the masculine gender of the "monk" by evacuating the "monasteries" that constitute the "city," the virgins are marked instead as the inhabitants of a "convent" in a village. By their awkward and ambiguous placement, they effectively erase the space for female asceticism in this world of text.

In the *Life of Antony*, the desert becomes a place to rethink the city, to rethink man, to rethink a manly city. *Topos*—place itself—mediates between the cultivated body and civic culture of man. The technique of topographic thematization is applied in other ascetic works of Athanasius as well. The women pilgrims from Alexandria, whom he addresses in his *Second Letter to Virgins*, wept as they departed from the cave of Christ's birthplace, "which is the image of Paradise or, rather, which surpasses it." They shed streams of bitter tears; breasts grew damp with the mingled tears of the women and the virginal sisters to whom they bade farewell, as he imagines it (*Epistula ad virgines* 2.1).[74] Seemingly sympathetic, Athanasius nevertheless sternly exhorts his addressees not to seek to return to Palestine but rather, remaining in their earthly fathers' houses, to remake their own bodies and souls into the "holy land" of Christ's dwelling place (2.3–4). After all, they are his brides (2.7).[75] As early as his festal letter for 330, Athanasius had begun to unlink "the pattern of the heavenly Jerusalem" from the physical city of Jerusalem led astray by "the ignorant and fleshly Jews." This carnal Jerusalem was displaced and transformed by a "withdrawal" through the desert—with Moses—that was explicitly reconfigured as an "ascent to the city in heaven"(*Epistula festivalis* 24[2]).[76] The fecund caves and dripping peaks of one sacred land are thus first safely contained (in the fathers' houses) and then superseded by the arid purity and wombless sufficiency of another holy place. The desert fathers the holy man and also a city of men.

"The fusion of Desert and City is one of the most momentous of the changes in the spiritual landscape of Late Antiquity," declares Robert Markus.[77] He has in mind the particular "blurring of frontiers" produced as an innovation within fifth-century Gallic monastic culture. However, it is possible that the desert and city were never other than topographically overlapped in the late-ancient Christian imagination: the *Life of Antony*, a text that arguably did more than any other to map Christianity onto place by putting the desert on the Christian map, already makes the case that the desert *is* the city, in its most transcendent dimension. In the face of the "drastic alternative" represented by Christian asceticism's bid "to bring marriage and child-bearing to an end," some seemingly did hope and others doubtless feared that "the huge fabric of organized society would crumble like a sandcastle."[78] Meanwhile, men like Athanasius were far less interested in abandoning than in renovating the old structures of fatherhood and civic life, while drafting their schemes for improvement like so many castles in the sand.

Revaluing the Father

The pieces are all gathered and arranged, the achievement appears magisterial, and the effects have surely been long-lasting. An account of the creation of humanity as the sublimation of the corruptible body, overlaid with a highly dualistic incarnational christology, places the subject at the site of a doubled tension between "matter" and "divinity." Caught in the strain, the body itself fractures, defined by its audacious self-alienation. On the one hand, corporality is placed under a cloak of shame and thereby disavowed; on the other hand, spiffily decked out in its ethereal veil, corporeality is triumphantly turned against nature into something divine, impermeable, and unchanging. The innovative articulation of trinitarian theology in the primary terms of Fatherhood and Sonship (with the Spirit still hovering ambiguously in the wings) makes coherently explicit the gendering of Athanasius's theory of human subjectivity: in the absolutely transcendent divinity toward which the human subject stretches (but from which it is also finally barred), "essence" is conflated with the continuity of masculine identity, while the female is implicitly aligned with a corruptible materiality wrenched out of the womb of nonbeing. Athanasius's theological deployment of patrilineal terms also calls attention to the more concretely political aspects of the process of reconceiving masculinity. At stake was nothing less than the standards by which a father's potency, a son's legitimacy, and a leader's fitness would be judged, definitions sunk deep into the life of the body as well as the body politic. Antony as "holy man" was not merely a creature of the desert, standing in for an "alternative" to the life of the family and city. He was also the product of the literary campaign of a bishop caught up in a cultural movement that was decisively shifting the terms of masculine identity while remaining planted in the city and steeped in the language of family lineage and indeed biological connection.

"So for the sons of the Book: research, the desert, inexhaustible space, encouraging, discouraging, the march straight ahead." Reading Athanasius, I rewrite an account of the genesis of a fatherhood that begets by the book, of a style of manhood aesthetically best suited to the monotonous vastness of the desert, of a new heroics that arises not so much from the surge of the heart—*le coeur, courage*—as from the steady march of the mind. And if this masculine subjectivity results from the march of the mind, it has seemed necessary to ask: "What is the body for?" Is there more to the man than these eyes, these ears, this voluble, voracious mouth? Perhaps under the disguise there remains only a tomb that might swallow a girl whole, impregnating itself stiffly with a still-intact body, hiding the flesh while stealing its generative power so as to refashion itself into an invisible womb for the stingy utterance of a single Word. *Only a single Word.*

Recounting this legacy, I am forced also to count it partly my own: a theory of human subjectivity that arises at the impossible meeting point of radical transcendence and irreducible specificity; a situating of human sex and sexuality, gender and the fecundity of desire, precisely at that point of impossible conjunction; a close alignment of the materialization of desire's fertility with the practice of writing; and an ambivalent conviction that body and community are in large part our own fabrications. To say, with Athanasius, that this inherited treasure is "enough" is also to demarcate the space of excess, so that sufficiency gives birth to surfeit at every turn. Reading Athanasius, rewriting Athanasius, is *more* than enough. Are we not still reading Athanasius, excessively, women as well as men?

"Writing: a way of leaving no space for death, of pushing back forgetfulness, of never letting oneself be surprised by the abyss. . . . How often I've been there, my tombs, my corporeal dungeons, the earth abounds with places for my confinement. . . . But I feel, after all, 'at home.' What you can't have, what you can't touch, smell, caress, you should at least try to see. I want to see: everything. No Promised Land I won't reach someday. Seeing what you will (n)ever have."[79]

"Reading, I discovered that writing is endless. Everlasting. Eternal. Writing or God. God the writing. The writing God."[80]

Is this the voice of the Son of the Book or the daughter of the housewife?

CHAPTER 2

A Son's Legacy

Gregory of Nyssa

Is Tancredi a woman ending, or a man beginning to be a woman in order to
be a man? But my God, I am only me, I am only a woman, how can I
express what is more than me? I divine what is more than a woman, what is
more than a man, but above me everything sparkles and dazzles me and
merges into a single person with athletic aspirations, rather tall for a
woman, yes, she seems to me to be a woman but set naturally in the bearing
of a man, like my pearl in turquoise.

—*Hélène Cixous,*
"Tancredi Continues"

Gregory of Nyssa does not take his place easily in remakings of
Christian late antiquity. The "Cappadocians" get plenty of
press—that heroic trio who clinched the deal on trinitarian orthodoxy, as
Nicaea's creed was triumphantly reproduced at Constantinople in 381 by a
new generation of conciliar Fathers. However, scholarly accounts tend to
dwell most enthusiastically on the vigorous exploits of Nyssa's older brother
Basil and his well-matched (if somewhat high-strung) companion Gregory
of Nazianzus. These two move boldly in the society of men, striding
through courses of study in Cappadocian Caesarea, Antioch, and Athens
itself and returning to the province to whose municipal aristocracies they
belong, for alternating bouts of austere withdrawal and frenetic political
engagement as bishops. Nyssa, in contrast, scarcely seems to move at all:
his life is "singularly uneventful."[1] Left at home wrapped in the skirts of his
mother and sister, he is hesitant about his calling, ambivalent about married life, dreamy, impractical, and occasionally duplicitous. His role in the
threesome—not unlike that of the Holy Spirit—appears supplementary at
best: another brother, another Gregory, a scribe who will complete Basil's
tragically unfinished sentences, a rhetorician who will continue to perform
for the cause of orthodoxy when his namesake—momentarily presider at

Constantinople—has retreated from the conciliar stage. But even as a supplement is he enough? We are reminded of Basil's impatience with his kid brother, who could never seem to get it right. Or is he not rather too much? Indeed, there is something excessive about Gregory of Nyssa: his astonishing literary productivity, his highly cultivated style, his philosophic bent, and his panting desire for God all seem to overflow the bounds of sufficiency.

Perhaps the fascinating Nyssa is difficult to place because he is so at home in a terrain not of desert and city but of hills and streams and towns. Viewed from this perspective, he is not so much wimpy as wily, understanding how to fit into a landscape that presents no sharp alternatives: he neither retreats altogether from what he calls the "common life" nor joins in it wholeheartedly. In the damp world that Gregory inhabits, the definitively "uncommon" holy man must be distilled from the desert scenes of inspired texts, as in his *Life of Moses*, or represented as a Platonic prophetess with athletic aspirations, as in his portrait of Macrina. For Gregory, virginity is not necessarily a matter of avoiding marriage or sexual intercourse, and familial lineage need not be discarded but may be gently warped into new patterns. Bishops, who frequently turn out to be the very men who had been groomed for civic leadership all along, take their seats relatively easily and therefore also with relative unease: the formative trauma of Gregory's career was not exile (though this too he experienced) but a fraternally coerced episcopacy. If the ambiguities of such ambivalent positionings are second nature for a man like Gregory, his tentativeness may be read as a strategy rather than a sign of weakness. In his writings, the strained and paradoxical stretch toward an unachievable transcendence melts into the supple embrace of the infinitude of desire, as lack becomes for the mystic the source of plenitude and erotic passion less the problem than the solution to the puzzle of man's destiny.

The urbanity of the Cappadocians is well acknowledged. As Brown puts it, "Basil guaranteed that he and his followers would not vanish from the city. . . . The towns of Cappadocia were small, and men of the stature of Basil and Gregory of Nyssa could feel that they might, indeed, be able to make of them more truly Christian cities."[2] Basil has more often seemed to evoke the investment of the Cappadocian threesome in the life of the city, through his vigorous style of episcopal leadership and an appealing version of monasticism with a recognizable social conscience. However, his brother Gregory, notoriously late in abandoning his secular career and resistant to absolutizing renunciations as much as to worldliness, also models a fashion of manhood that remains inextricably woven into civic life while also always gesturing—indeed, already distinctly drifting—toward a more transcendent home.

Gregory's strong sense of familial heritage and loyalty, juxtaposed with his freedom in reconfiguring relationships, is even more striking to the reader than his seemingly persistent connection to town life. Indeed, one of the great accomplishments of Gregory's literary self-invention is his presentation of himself as a son and heir. This is partly the achievement of a trickster younger brother who has stolen the older sibling's birthright. Remaking the deceased Basil in the image of hero and father, Gregory positions himself humbly enough as his son, only to seize the mantle of Basil's authority as champion of the Nicene cause. With Gregory thus self-anointed as Basil's heir, it is their dyad that claims attention in the younger brother's writings—in which context the *other* Gregory begins to seem superfluous. A father's blessing is not, however, enough for this son: Gregory of Nyssa will also insinuate himself as the heir of his sister Macrina, yet another "other" Cappadocian. (Whether she is the third person in the trinity or some missing "fourth," as Jaroslav Pelikan designates her,[3] is no more or less clear than in the case of Mary, that other virginal mother to whom Gregory is drawn.) It is above all through his representation of the deaths of his older brother and sister that Gregory scripts them into the roles of father and mother, simultaneously depicting himself as a virtuously grieving son. He thereby not only puts a subtle spin on sibling rivalry but also thickens his genealogical narrative, layering on an extra set of progenitors in order to create a more nuanced tale of generational progress. While making himself heir of more, he defines that heritage with greater precision: The public dignity and genteel Christianity of his father—another Basil—is mediated by the stridency with which his fraternal "father," Basil, translated civic heroics into an embattled "orthodox" episcopacy. The deferred ascetic aspirations of his mother, Emmelia, are actualized in the life of his virginally maternal sister, Macrina. The scales are finally tipped in favor of a masculinized matrilineage: Macrina, credited by Gregory with having converted Basil himself to a dedicated ascetic life, correctively controls Basil's role in Gregory's texts by claiming to model manhood for Basil, and thus also for Gregory. Like the generative channels of water that Gregory loves to describe, these perfectly routed and modulated genetic streams converge gracefully at the point of the author's present. Lineage marks out the trajectory of destiny, and with his siblings' posthumous help Gregory will become the man that neither Basil nor Macrina could be. As Philip Rousseau notes, "the Christian family takes on a rather different appearance" for a younger generation of perfectionists inclined to dismiss their ancestral Christian piety as lukewarm.[4] Yet it is precisely the delineated legacy of a "Christian family" that remains crucial for Gregory, whose "dynastic leanings" may incline in new directions without by any means snapping the links of kinship.[5] Gregory of Nyssa, as Anthony Meredith remarks, "is full of his family."[6]

Gregory's masculinity is clearly a complicated affair. A "character all the more man in that he is more woman,"[7] Gregory assumes a role that might, in a staging of his life, be most convincingly played by an actress—like the knight Tancredi of Rossini's opera. Gregory punctuates his polemical writings in defense of Nicene trinitarian orthodoxy with rhetorical thrusts of the sword—a metaphor that he himself repeatedly invokes. Yet he prefers to think of himself as the boy David, merely borrowing Goliath's weapon in a moment of need, or even (according to the inverted principle that it is better to receive than to give) as one of Plato's responsive boys, accepting the seminal utterances of his teacher, bishop, and father and thereby conceiving right doctrine in the virginal womb of his mind. If Plato's much earlier (but already in some sense "postclassical") subversion of the masculine ideals of democratic Athens shifted female procreativity "to the side of the philosopher's mental creativity,"[8] Gregory's texts repeat and intensify that appropriation. Gregory (the Cappadocian who never made it to Athens) does, I think, intend his Christian works to be read "like Plato" as well as "like Moses," and he weaves his feminized masculinity Platonically, in resistance to dominant civic models of manhood. He is concerned not so much to include women in public life as to incorporate the female into the domain of a transcendentalized subjectivity that will itself subtly transform male social roles and reshape the society of men. However much in awe of his sister Gregory may wish to seem to be, it is not women who are privileged as receptive lovers of Christ within the highly charged, sublimated homoeroticism of his soteriology, which catapults "man" into the infinite pursuit of the transcendent Man, of transcendence, of Manhood itself. Gregory's Macrinan works—one dialogue and a biography—productively destabilize but do not by any means simply erase the androcentrism of his thought. If it is because she is a woman that Macrina makes such a good man, it is also because she has been made male that she can become such a good lover of Christ. The blurring of genders works consistently to the advantage of Gregory's manhood: he is quite certain that humanity was originally created sexless, a state of integrity to which it—or rather "he"—would return in the end.

Is Gregory "a woman ending, or a man beginning to be a woman in order to be a man?" It is difficult to place this writer, and difficult also to place myself, as "woman," in relation to . . . "him"? Squinting hard against the dazzle of the performance, I look at a man and see someone alluringly like me, only taller. Coming closer, I perceive that the woman is "set naturally in the bearing of a man." Absorbed by this capacious masculinity, I sense my own "ending," lurching abruptly into a "beginning," the beginning for a man, for the man I am becoming—having been absorbed. If (as Nicole Loraux notes) in such dizzying transactions "the man gains in complexity, while the woman loses substance," she is (I am) little more than a ghostly remainder, a spirit or an angel. Yet she also leaves her traces in his texts (not least as "spirit" or "angel"), footprints into which I may yet insinuate my soles. "If the mortal body, in *eros* and reproduction, is felt in a feminine modality, and the soul is lived in the mode of the body, the reason is that something of the body is always and forever lodged in the soul. And therefore, without his knowing it, the philosopher's soul contains something of the woman who, before finding a respite from the pains of childbirth . . . , wanders like Io, pregnant by Zeus's doing and hounded by the gadfly that pursues her."[9]

This Sex Which Is (N)one: 'On Virginity'

Do you prefer to spill over or to taste your depths? When you soar your highest, where do you go? What do you want, old man? To remove me from my fortune? Because both flowing over my banks and savoring my great depths are equal rapture for me. I do not wish to be measured out drop by drop.

—*Luce Irigaray*,
Marine Lover

Gregory explains the value of celibate life with a metaphor, comparing it to a canal that prevents water—our erotic inclinations—from spreading out all over in disorderly streams and thus being unable to reach the appropriate goal—"the truly good" (*De virg.* 6.2.1–31). A few chapters later, however, he modifies this image, explaining that a skillful farmer is able to make a small outlet in the channel in order to water an intermediate field—marriage and worldly business—without sapping the force of the main current to reach the end goal. The "inexperienced" farmer, however, is likely to bungle the task and, in opening a small outlet, inadvertently create a torrent (*De virg.* 8.7–21). . . . . These remarks . . . reveal that he has greater reservations concerning celibate life and ascetic renunciation than those which many other writers of this period stress. . . . . He is asking deeper questions concerning whether the renunciation of marriage and worldly business can lead to the most perfect or complete form of virtue.

—*Mark Hart,*
"Gregory of Nyssa's Ironic Praise of the Celibate Life"

There remain questions about the depth of Gregory's reservations concerning celibacy, as we shall see. However, his linguistic reservoirs appear practically inexhaustible: rhetorically speaking, his *On Virginity* is an extraordinarily well irrigated treatise. In this work, he likens the praise owed virginity to a boundless ocean, to which the orator contributes a modest drop of sweat (*De virg.* 1).[10] A swollen and tumultuous river stands in for the vicissitudes of worldly life (4). Flowing water is repeatedly offered as an illustration (ὑπόδειγμα) of desire, bubbling up from a spring, in danger of being diverted and dribbled out along sensual byways if not channeled through celibacy's conduit into a gravity-defying heavenward spurt (7, 8, 9, 21). Virginity's passionless passion may, alternatively, be reflected in a pool whose unruffled surface is guarded from the rippling disruption of a single carelessly hurled stone (14). Turning to biblical and biographical examples, Gregory reports that Moses walked lightly over the restless sea of life (18), whereas Miriam upstaged him by leading the women in a dance to the resonant beat of a timbrel, its taut skin "devoid of all moisture and reduced to the highest degree of dryness"—like virginity itself, as Gregory explains (19). By this point, the aqueous figures of speech have begun to run in crosscurrents, if not at cross-purposes. In what state of dampness or desic-

cation does Gregory intend to leave his readers? Not so much clarifying as
further complicating the flow of his logic, he cites the physician's elemental theory that health is the golden mean of moisture produced within the
human body by the "union" of the wet and the dry, which can be mediated
by a second contradictory pair when "the hot penetrate[s] the cold" (22).

At issue is not only how seriously to take Gregory's rhetorical excesses
but also how much to humor him, as Mark Hart points out. If most scholars have condescended (uneasily) to forgive Gregory for his stylistic "pre-
ciosity"[11] in a purportedly vacuous and overwrought treatise penned early
in his Christian writing career,[12] Hart prefers to credit him with the gravity of a substantial irony. The general public may have been intended to
read Gregory as giddily endorsing the celibate agenda touted by his brother
Basil, but more knowing readers of this sophisticated work would be expected to appreciate the text's winks, hints, and strategic contradictions.
The literal celibacy of monastic life is in fact being subtly demoted to the
status of second-best by this married ascetic author, argues Hart, as "virginity" and "marriage" are elaborately reworked into fluid metaphors for
psychic nonattachment and attachment. Hart's interpretation is, as we
shall see, strained at points. Nonetheless, I think he is right to perceive
deep waters precisely where the text has most often been gauged shallow.
For those with ears to hear, Hart suggests, Gregory's carefully chosen figures of speech, far from merely digressive, are profoundly telling; the hyperbolic overflowings of his denunciations of married life and praise of
physical celibacy are not lapses into a senseless virtuosity but calculated
parodies with a coherent—and finally very *serious*—message.[13] Judgments
of style thus turn out to be crucial to the interpretation of Gregory's argument, insofar as the artistry cannot be separated from the philosophy in
the work of a writer whose soaring love of abstract thought is carried by his
remarkable gift for vivid metaphoric expression.

Gregory's virginal doctrine of desire raises the question, "What does
the man want?" The answer—as Freud might have put it—"is certainly in-
complete and fragmentary."[14] It is true that the Cappadocian Father begins
his treatise straightforwardly enough: "The aim of this logos is to create in
its readers the desire [ἐπιθυμία] for the life of excellence." He immediately
identifies "the lifestyle of virginity" as desire's proper gateway, leading from
the entanglements of the "more common lifestyle" to the "holier course"

characterized by philosophical contemplation of the divine. What Gregory claims to want, and to want his reader to want, is "true virginity," which will direct the reader in turn to "the true object of desire, for which (and which only) we have received from our Maker our power of desiring." But how will the reader know the real thing—whether it be desire's means or its end—when he sees it, especially since Gregory warns that his discourse will often proceed by indirection: "while it seems to look elsewhere, [it] will be really tending to the praises of virginity"? He further declares that he will shun descriptions of the particulars of the virginal lifestyle so as to "avoid prolixity": "nothing important will be overlooked, while prolixity is avoided," he repeats. By this point, one already floundering in the murky waters of the Cappadocian's vague allusions and ambiguous assertions may have reason enough to doubt both statements. A promise of clarity appears once again when Gregory avows that he will be "compelled" to produce a parade of saintly exemplars (ὑποδείγματα) of celibacy, since (as he admits) a new course of life is most easily embraced when modeled by well-known figures. But the moment proves fleeting, for Gregory immediately dismisses such merely narrated models as inadequate in comparison with the power of living voices and active examples to stimulate excellence in others. Necessity further tightens its constraints on the author, who next represents himself as "compelled" to mention (albeit not before the end of his treatise) his own "most devout bishop and father, who alone has the power to teach such things." The delayed unveiling of the living "father" who supersedes all merely textual exemplars will, however, bring no full exposure, as it happens: reluctance wins out as Gregory warns in advance that he has no intention of identifying the father by name, even in conclusion; instead, "by certain tokens the treatise will speak riddlingly of the one indicated." He mumbles by way of explanation that later youthful readers of his treatise might otherwise either misunderstand or disregard his advice, as if he were directing them to attend to the lifestyle of one already deceased rather than urging them (as in fact he is) to seek their own living guides among those who have been raised up to the leadership of the "virtuous commonwealth" (τῆς κατ᾽ ἀρετὴν πολιτείας) (*De virg.*, pref.).

By the end of his preface, Gregory has his reader exactly where he seems to want him—yearning for he-knows-not-quite-what, as the "father" who is the living guide to the virginal life retreats just beyond his grasp. Who *is* Gregory's "father," leader of that most excellent citizenry? Is it or is it not his more famous brother, Basil? What *are* the mysteries of virginal desire that the "father" alone can impart, which are however paradoxically being transmitted by the father's son in this very text? With his name inscribed, any dad would become a dead letter, suggests Gregory. Veiled in signs that shimmer with the excitement of the enigmatic, the father may, however, continue to seduce readers unto eternity, thereby molding them as virginal citizens of his undying city. But it is through the son that they will know him.

As the elusive paternal guide withdraws behind his instructive discourse—or rather re-embodies himself *as* this logos on desire—"virginity" remains the center of attention, luring the reader on, so that longing doubles back on itself and becomes its own inexhaustible object. Beckoning with all its transcendent powers of attraction "while it remains in Heaven with the Father of spirits, and moves in the dance of the celestial powers," virginity "stretches out hands for man's salvation." Not only the object but also the copulative vehicle of desire itself, virginity is "the channel which draws down the Deity to share man's estate." At the same time, it "keeps wings for man's desires to rise to heavenly things, and is a bond of union between the Divine and human" (*De virg.* 2). Desire's desire having been thus vividly configured in terms both spillingly liquid and reachingly ethereal, the treatise advances with a skittishly manly ardor. Skillfully elaborating a rhetorical commonplace, Gregory protests his humility by representing himself as lacking what he nonetheless dares to praise. He returns to the two courses of life initially contrasted and expresses regret that his own knowledge of virginity's beauty is like water placed out of reach of a thirsty man—"vain and useless." "Happy they who have still the power of choosing the better way, and have not debarred themselves from it by engagements of the secular [τῷ κοινῷ...βίῳ] as we have, whom a gulf now divides from glorious virginity" (*De virg.* 3). In a state of lack, Gregory is also in a state of yearning for what he lacks (for what no one really *has*?)—no less a good than the incorruptible divinity of the spiritual realm, as he has defined the virginal condition (1–2). Gregory does not possess virginity, but he hints that he is in pursuit of it insofar as he is capable of recognizing the poverty of the "common life" and thus of longing for something better (3).

At this point Gregory seems suddenly to digress, as he warned he would. And, yet, veering off to discuss the pitfalls of the "common life" in the guise of marriage, he is indeed still praising virginity; shifting to consider not lofty ideals but "the actual facts" (τὰ πράγματα), he plunges deep in order to achieve exalted rhetorical heights. His troublingly uncompromising denunciation of married life, famous for its rhetorical virtuosity, proceeds by cataloguing at length the daily course of intimacy between spouses, parents, and children, which repeatedly wounds men and women by the grief that necessarily accompanies any finite love. As Michel Barnes has shown, Gregory's description of married life draws heavily upon Stoic tradition, while placing new emphasis on the paradoxical conjunction of joy and sadness that is part of the fabric of mortal existence.[15] "They are human all the time, things weak and perishing; they have to look upon the tombs of their progenitors; and so pain is inseparably bound up with their existence, if they have the least power of reflection." Page after page, he sustains the spectacle of familiar suffering in an excessive yet seemingly insufficient attempt to answer his own challenge: "How shall we really bring to view the evils common to life?" Setting out to write of life as a tragedy, as he puts it, he raises his voice in the hyperbolic language of lament, which both performs and interprets the tumultuous flood of mortal life itself. As author, he has the role attributed to the servants who, "like conquering foes, dismantle the bridal chamber" of the young wife who has died in childbirth: "they deck it for the funeral, but it is death's room now; they make the useless wailings and beatings of the hands." In exuberant, exaggerated speech, Gregory pours out the uncontainable grief of mortality until it overflows, spilling into the hope of eternal life. Subsequently he will offer the illustration of "a winter torrent, which, impetuous in itself, becomes swollen and carries down beneath its stream trees and boulders and anything that comes in its way, . . . death and danger to those alone who live along its course" (De virg. 4). Here he creates a torrential flow of words in order also to exhort and enact their transcendence.

Calmer now, Gregory assures readers that a man who "lifts himself above the struggling world . . . , in a way exiling himself altogether from human life by his abstinence from marriage" is exempt from worldly trials. "His thoughts are above, walking as it were with God"; he "gazes as from some high watch-tower on the prospect of humanity." The "lofty mind" "is fixed on heaven," in contrast to the "grosser mind" that "lives for gorging and still lower pleasures," "as sure as the sheep stoop to their pasture." Gregory cites the Scripture as witness that those who live loftily for the spirit "neither marry nor are given in marriage" (*De virg.* 4). The life to be avoided by the Christian contemplative who would achieve "divinity" thus *seems* clearly and most concretely identified. However, if Gregory defines virginity as "the practical method" by which the soul maintains its upward gaze and resists being dragged down, swinelike, "to the emotions belonging to flesh and blood" (*De virg.* 5), he may also intend that "marriage" be interpreted more metaphorically, as a problem of erotic orientation resulting not from domestic and procreative coupling per se but rather from a failure to remain detached from the painful and distracting trivialities of the "common life."

Reading thus far with Hart, and against the current of a more literalizing interpretive tradition, I do *not*, however, take Gregory's extended lament as ironic or dissimulative, pabulum for the simpleminded. The author of *On Virginity* is, perhaps, both more complicated and less cynical than Hart's ironist. The text seems to intend to immerse the reader in a carnal interpretation of the text of marriage and its troubles, as a necessary first step in the ascent to an understanding of "true virginity."[16] Gregory's rhetoric achieves transcendent height only by first diving into the depths of fleshly pleasure and pain, whence it emerges triumphantly unscathed. Following this logos, the reader must likewise take the plunge if he or indeed she wants eventually to float above the crashing waves of "feelings which his own body gives rise to" (*De virg.* 4). But what might this mean, more concretely? Does Gregory intend his readers to eschew marriage absolutely, or not?

Adding new textual layers to the interpretation of virginity, Gregory now introduces Elijah and John the Baptist as positive biblical models of the single-mindedness of the virginal soul. "It is my belief that they would not have reached to this loftiness of spirit, if marriage had softened them," remarks Gregory, indicating acquiescence to the view that virginity is best (perhaps even necessarily) achieved through a literal abstention from marriage (*De virg.* 6). The theme of single-mindedness is further developed through the image of a stream's flow, which, while referring explicitly to the gush of a mind's creative potency, here also enfolds within its meaning the rush of generative fluids that produce a man's bodily "issues." "We often see water contained in a pipe bursting upwards through this constraining force, which will not let it leak; and this, in spite of its natural gravitation," remarks Gregory. "In the same way, the mind of man, enclosed in the compact channel of a habitual continence, and by not having any side issues, will be raised by virtue of its natural powers of motion to an exalted love" (*De virg*. 7). If this comparison might seem to suggest that spiritual transcendence must be achieved by closing down all other erotic channels, above all the physically sexual, Gregory nevertheless makes it clear that he has no intention of deprecating "marriage as an institution."

Nor, as it turns out, does he intend to present marriage as merely an honorable alternative to virginity for those too weak to abstain from the conveniences and satisfactions of family life. On the contrary, he now audaciously proposes that it is a literalized virginity that is the refuge of the less muscular Christian: "He who is of so weak a character that he cannot make a manful stand against nature's impulse had better keep himself very far away from such temptations, rather than descend into a combat which is above his strength." Another biblical type is placed alongside Elijah and John: Isaac is introduced as the privileged model for the truly virile man who is able both to put "heavenly things" first and to "use the advantages of marriage with sobriety and moderation" in order to fulfill his duty (λειτουργία) to the civic community.[17] The biblical father had intercourse with his wife up to the point that she gave birth, as Gregory tells it; his dimness of sight in old age is taken as a sign that he subsequently shut down "the channels of the senses" and gave himself wholly to the contemplation of the invisible. Here Gregory returns to the example, cited by Hart in the passage quoted above, of the experienced farmer who is able to divert a portion of water and then skillfully redirect it into the main stream, thereby meeting multiple needs without significantly weakening the water's flow (*De virg*. 8). How are we to read this illustration in light of the previous example of "water contained in a pipe bursting upwards" (*De virg*. 7)? Has Isaac simply superseded Elijah and John as the model for Christian manhood?[18] Does the water bursting from a single pipe begin to seem a bit excessive, in comparison with the measured flow of the second farmer's diversified irrigation system? Or might it be that the second farmer's compromise with the fleshly demands of marriage distorts and even parodies the singular heroics of true virginity? Both of these conflicting interpretations are simultaneously supported and undercut by the text, as Gregory draws his readers upward and onward, subverting all temptations to take refuge in the misleading finalities of any dead life.

Having not so much clarified as stabilized the ambiguities of his definitions of virginity and marriage, Gregory now draws on two major textual traditions to refine his argument further—the Platonic myth of ascent and the biblical creation narratives. These converge in the conception of philosophic maternity as the privileged figure of the fertility of a virginal desire that ultimately transcends materiality yet is reached only by ascending through the lower loves of the sensible realm. In a lengthy passage that is among the most overtly platonizing in his works, leaning particularly heavily on the *Symposium*,[19] Gregory notes that, for the "climbing soul," material beauties "will be but the ladder by which he climbs to the prospect of that Intellectual Beauty," or "the hand to lead us to the love of the supernal Beauty." "But how can any one fly up into the heavens, who has not the wings of heaven?" he queries, adding that "there is but one vehicle on which man's soul can mount into the heavens, namely, the self-made likeness in himself to the descending Dove" (*De virg.* 11). Rising heavenward on the wings of the one-and-only bearer of desire, the soul achieves "union" with "the incorruptible Deity" in a match based on sameness. A receptive lover, "she places herself like a mirror beneath the purity of God and molds her own beauty at the touch and sight of the Archetype of all beauty." "The real Virginity, the real zeal for chastity, ends in no other goal than this, namely, the power thereby of seeing God," Gregory concludes (*De virg.* 11).

Sliding from Plato's vision of the end to the Genesis account of the beginning, Gregory notes that the human being in his original creation possessed that untarnished image of the Divine Mind prerequisite for the act of love as the mimetic consummation of likeness. Disruptive "passion" came later, bending free will to the fabrication of evil. Sin thus entered with the force and "fatal quickness" of a bad habit, darkening the soul's mirror with the rust of corruption, smearing the reflective purity of the original creature with a coat of filth, by which it acquired a "resemblance to something else." "Now the putting off of a strange accretion is equivalent to the return to that which is familiar and natural," explains Gregory. The Platonic ascent is thereby scripted as a return to—rather than an Athanasian transcendence of—created nature. Like the woman of Luke's gospel who searches her home for a lost coin, the "widowed soul" need only turn within to recover her lost self, which is also to say to find the divine lover in whose image she is molded. Gregory exhorts the reader to "become that which the First Man was at the moment when he first breathed," stripping off the "dead skins" of sin and death. Innocent of sexual relations with his "helpmeet," the First Man "found in the Lord alone all that was sweet" in those blessed times before marriage was instituted as "the last stage of our separation from the life that was led in Paradise." Marriage's institutionalized heteroeroticism—a concession to the introduction of the taint of difference into love's economy—remains a barrier between humanity and Paradise. Marriage, then, is also "the first thing to be left" on the path back to future bliss. Virginity's salvation is for those who know how to love in a spirit of sameness, its goal the consummating absorption of all sexes in the one (De virg. 12).[20]

Virginity's version of same-sex love cannot possibly have anything to do with fleshly procreation, as Gregory makes clear: "life and immortality instead of children are produced by this latter intercourse." By refusing to perpetuate life's cycles, the virginal body becomes a barrier against mortality; the "virgin mother" conceives only "deathless children" by the Spirit. Having now (with a little help from Paul) wed Plato's concept of philosophic motherhood as a property of men to a biblical notion of a fecund virginity originally Adam's and recovered in Mary, Gregory once again bemoans the "agonies of grief" brought in with marriage, while acknowledging its attractions. Marriage, he here suggests, is like a sword. Its hilt "is smooth and handy, and polished and glittering outside; it seems to grow to the outline [τύπος] of the hand"; "it offers for the grasp of the senses a smooth surface of delights." Gregory will, however, allow our thoughts to linger only so long on the smooth surface and sensual pleasures associated with that swellingly swordlike member that molds itself so delightfully to the contours of a grasping hand. A sword is, after all, more than a friendly hilt: "the other part is steel and the instrument of death, formidable to look at, more formidable still to come across"; it becomes, for man, "the worker of mourning and of loss." The instrument of pleasure is thus also the organ of birth and therefore tainted with the violence of death, the cause—on this reading—of all pain accompanying the loss of children, parents, spouses. For one who would avoid the sword wounds of grief, God is the gentlest Bridegroom, and the virginal soul who becomes his spouse, conceiving with the divine spirit, "brings forth wisdom and righteousness, and sanctification and redemption too." These are children who will never die. To live thus virginally is to anticipate the angelic nature that will belong to humanity once again in Paradise. "In fact, the life of virginity seems to be an actual representation [εἰκών τις] of the blessedness in the world to come," as Gregory remarks (*De virg.* 13).

By this point Gregory has made it abundantly clear that virginity is not a matter of mere abstention from sexual relations. As a psychic condition, it is certainly much more. Remembering Isaac (and also Plato),[21] we might ponder again whether it is not also somewhat less. If the life of true virginity is "an actual representation of the blessedness in the world to come," perhaps carnal celibacy is similarly "an actual representation" of true virginity. Framed thus, the question is one of semiotics, having to do with the status of "representation" or the "image." To what extent does an "image" participate ontologically in what it signifies, from the perspective of this text? Could true virginity's reflection be found in a nonvirginal life, and might the nonvirginal body even (by a strong twist of irony) become the privileged signifier of a transcendent virginity defined in terms of a soul's indifference to merely corporeal conditions? This is possible. And yet, at the same time, Gregory's particular poetic art resists the sharp distinction between literal and figurative language. This is part of what makes his treatise *On Virginity* so difficult to interpret tidily:[22] "virginity" as the sign of the fecundity of desire always means more than it did before; no reader can get to the bottom of it, yet it does not simply mean something *else*, as if the trick of reading lay straightforwardly in the cracking of a code. It may be initially disconcerting to realize that Gregory has placed biblical biographies on the same level of signification as the watery figures of speech that he has concocted out of the materials of a classical literary tradition, by dubbing them all *hypodeigmata*—"signs" or "examples"—of virginity. In his treatise, however, even the farmer's narrowly channeled stream does not remain strictly external to the pent-up flow in the celibate male body that it implicitly depicts. Nor is the silently named (and thereby still more forcefully restrained) erotic energy of that male body merely analogous to the focused potency of the virginally desiring psyche, with which it is likewise drawn into a relation of both close comparison and subtly displaced identification, according to the terms of the same simile.

Thus, even Gregory's most explicit invocations of figurative language to represent virginal desire lapse toward literalism. His biblical exemplars, similarly, resist purely symbolic interpretation, instead continuing to complicate the relation between sign and meaning, literal and figurative virginity, physical and sublimated desire. When Gregory presents Moses as a sign (τύπος) of the Law by which the insightful souls who are dear to God pass unwetted over the sea of life's suffering, he does not explicitly address the matter of the prophet's physical celibacy (*De virg.* 18). It is the figure of Miriam who raises the question, her recounted actions contributing further to his surmisings, as he puts it. Gregory takes Miriam to be "a type of Mary the mother of God," whereas her thoroughly dry "timbrel" (τύμπανον) "may mean to imply virginity." Having been separated from all sources of moisture, as Gregory describes it, the membrane stretched over the vessel of the virginal womb of this first Mary has become as resonant as a drum. "Thus, Miriam's timbrel being a dead thing, and virginity being a deadening of the bodily passions, it is perhaps not very far removed from the bounds of probability that Miriam was a virgin," concludes Gregory. Adding that "we can but guess and surmise, we cannot clearly prove that this was so," he proceeds to discuss the strengths and weaknesses of various arguments from silence that this woman identified as her brother's sister might have been no man's wife. Gregory thus goes out of his way not only to demonstrate the likelihood that Miriam was in fact a virgin but also to show that he is willing to deduce no more than likelihood when arguing backwards from the transcendent virginity signified by the biblical type of Miriam to the sexual status of the woman herself.

By now, Gregory seems a bit deflated by his own act of Marian desiccation, with its withering threat of infertility. Proceeding quickly to cite the examples of Isaiah and Paul, whose self-descriptions privilege a juicier but still spiritualized fecundity, he returns finally to Mary the Godbearer, in whose female body virginity and motherhood coincide despite seeming contradiction. Paul's teaching that each human being is in some sense "doubled," consisting in both an inner and an outer man, leads Gregory to the notion of a doubled marital status, in which the ruling of fidelity dictates that one "self's" virginity must correspond to the other "self's" marriage. "Maybe," he concludes coyly, "if one was to assert boldly that the body's virginity was the co-operator and the agent of the inward marriage, this asser-

tion would not be much beside the probable fact." Thus, for Gregory, the virginal mother becomes not so much a paradoxical conjunction of opposites as an icon of consistency, easily harmonized with a version of the Platonic myth of ascent in which the soul's desire for union with the beautiful moves it ever upward, as virginity gives birth continually to a higher fecundity in the progressive displacements of erotic sublimation (*De virg.* 19).[23]

What does the man want? He wants it all: virginity is the bottomless womb of the self-transcending infinitude of his desire. Isaac models the measured progress of the soul's upward climb, in which each stage prepares the way for the next, youth's passionate rush giving way to a sedate marriage in manhood's full maturity (resulting in a single act of birth), marriage itself giving way to a more divine love and more lasting progeny. Isaac himself is superseded, in Gregory's text, not by Christ but by Mary: what Isaac pursues sequentially, with a fragmented grace, she accomplishes with thrilling integrity, at once virgin and parent, at one in flesh and spirit, salvation's end looping back to creation's beginning. Sometimes inclined to gush, sensitive to the pleasurable touch of a sword's hilt, Gregory reaches for the timbrel's saving aridity: dry now, he leads the dance of the virgins, all the more man in that he is more woman. Icon of "a teleology of reabsorption of fluid in a solidified form," Gregory's text models the congealing of an idealized masculine subjectivity that transcends the "mechanics" of fluids, in Irigaray's phrasing.[24] And yet, startlingly, *On Virginity* does not repress the sticky "reality" of the male body's ebb and flow but rather projects the desire for the reassuring constancy of solid matter onto female form.

Was Gregory married? Have we not here a married Father? Well, in at least one passage subsequent to the reference to Isaac, Gregory does—near the end—try to make an honest man of himself. Establishing an elaborate comparison between bodily and spiritual marriages, which correspond to Paul's "inner" and "outer" men, he represents the inward or spiritual self as a man who courts a bride who is Wisdom herself, in the guise of the good wife of Solomon's Proverbs. The skittish Gregory is seemingly not, however, altogether happy to remain with this "straight" version of the divine union. It is clear, he notes hastily, that the marital metaphor applies to male and female subjects alike; he cites the assurance of Galatians 3:28 that in Christ "there is not male and female," adding the explanatory gloss that "Christ is all things and in all." If Christ can be all things to all people, any gendering of the object of desire will also do: the beloved is equally divine whether figured as the queenly Sophia or the incorruptible Bridegroom, concludes Gregory (*De virg.* 20). Indeed, most of the time Gregory's "inner man" seems happy to play the woman in relation to the "Good Husband" for whom he bears deathless children, protects his chastity (15), and even keeps house (18).

Was Gregory married? Was he a virgin? What counts as marriage, what counts as virginity? If this text insists on putting marriage in question without offering virginity as an easy answer, then it seems to me that one of its perhaps unintended but not accidental jokes is to have been taken almost universally as conclusive evidence that *Gregory was married.* Regarding Gregory's protest that his engagement in the "common life" now separates him irrevocably "from glorious virginity" (*De virg.* 3), Michel Aubineau notes, "One cannot reasonably discount such a categorical disclosure."[25] We have seen, however, that the disclosive logos of this treatise consistently eludes the particular clarities of the categorical. Isaac did, after all, beget in a single birth not one but two sons: Gregory may not be the married Father but the trickster Jacob, who rides in on the heel of his older brother. Wrapped in a deceptively hairy skin, underneath he is actually beardless and smooth—like the hilt of a sword—like a sister or a virginal mother—like Mary. Maybe he was, maybe he was not: a "marriage" that stretches desire across the gulf of sexual difference is truly beside the point, from Gregory's perspective. Mobilizing androgyny's fluidity on behalf of a different love, Gregory's vertically oriented "philosophic logos" does not flow in channels of gendered plurality but begets a singular—and singularly graceful—masculine subjectivity that derives its position of transcendent dominance "from its power to *eradicate the difference between the sexes.*"[26]

The Sword of the Word: 'Against Eunomius' I

> To degrade is to bury, to sow, and to kill simultaneously, in order to bring
> forth something more and better. . . . To degrade an object does not imply
> merely hurling it into the void of nonexistence, into absolute destruction,
> but to hurl it down to the reproductive lower stratum, the zone in which
> conception and a new birth take place. Grotesque realism knows no other
> level; it is the fruitful earth and the womb. It is always conceiving.
>
> —*Mikhail Bakhtin,*
> Rabelais and His World

One can only say that the retention of traditional modes of attack, by a
man who is clearly in many respects a pupil of what he affects to despise,
is a witness to the power of tradition in framing a man's response to
a new situation and a warning about the danger of taking that
sort of argument too seriously.

—*Anthony Meredith,*
"Traditional Apologetic in the *Contra Eunomium* of Gregory of Nyssa"

Soon after his brother Basil's death in 379, Gregory confronted the
"Neoarian" Eunomius's *Apology for the Apology,* a written attack upon
Basil's own defense of Nicene doctrine.[27] Gregory was a man who knew
garbage when he smelled it: "The waste . . . in this pile of words is so enor-
mous, that it makes one think that the residue of facts and real thoughts
in all that he has said is almost nil" (*Eun.* 1.20 [4]).[28] Returning subsequently to the image, he concludes: "It is best to leap over the mass of his
rubbish with as high and as speedy a jump as my thoughts are capable of"
(1.30 [5]). While hinting at a proclivity for intellectual high-jumping, Gregory here demonstrates his expertise in the techniques of degradation. By
way of announcing his own entry onto the battlefield of theological
polemics, he compares his rhetorical task to hurling Eunomius's treatise to
a bloody death. "We are only eager," he enthuses, "now that it has got into
our hands, to take this puling manifesto and dash it on the rock, as if it
were one of the children of Babylon" (1.7 [1]). Anthony Meredith remarks,
with unconcealed regret, that Gregory's penchant for verbal trashing in
this first book, *Against Eunomius,* threatens to drag him down to the level
of those very polemicists whom he "affects to despise." Perhaps the allusion to a transcending leap is indeed no more than an affectation for the
author of a congested text that appears to have retained the sludge of an
ancient rhetorical tradition. On the other hand, the mingling of infantile
with excremental images hints that the tract is after all engaged as much in
reproduction as in an unhealthy retention. If Gregory gets down and dirty,
perhaps he is thereby attempting to plant his rhetoric in the zone "in
which conception and a new birth take place"—to transform the theological dung heap into a compost pile, finding in a corpse the fertile ground
for new life.[29] Reading Gregory's polemics, have we taken that sort of argument seriously *enough?*

Male generativity provides the link between the extravagantly low *ad hominem* attacks that dominate the opening portions of this work and the high theological debate for which Gregory's treatise has traditionally been valued. In each of these modes (to the extent that they turn out to be separable), Gregory reflects with both exuberance and anxiety on the capacity of men to reproduce themselves by generating offspring in their own image and of their own substance. His concept of masculine fecundity here again defines itself implicitly in the sublimated erotic terms of a pedagogical patrilineage; thus the irreducible physicality of sexual generation can be neither openly embraced nor completely ignored. It is along an indirect route, through the figure of the grotesquely carnal heretic, that the generative body is initially invoked, disciplined, and then—by a sleight of hand —translated into the upper region of intellect, where the spiritualized corpus of truth is paradoxically both contained—"a strictly completed, finished product"[30]—and made self-transgressive in its borrowed fecundity. The virginal font of orthodox doctrine "is always conceiving": under the cover of heresiology's negations, the Christian theologian simultaneously staves off sterility and maintains purity. Returning again and again to the compost heap of materiality, "the fruitful earth and the womb," while skillfully masking the traces of the journey down under, he faithfully reproduces the theological truth about the begotten Son's full divinity as proof of his own legitimacy as an orthodox son.

Closely associated with the first book of Gregory's treatise *Against Eunomius* is a brief dedicatory letter addressed to his brother Peter, in which Gregory states that his text represents a son's claim to the patrimony of the recently deceased Basil. There Gregory refers to his own inheritance of the "legacy of the controversy" between Basil and Eunomius, twice designating his brother Basil "our father in God." His status as Basil's son and heir is meant to explain the heat of his polemic against Eunomius in the accompanying treatise. Following Basil's death, "my heart was hot within me with bereavement," he recalls. Offering filial grief as the context for his reading of Eunomius's attack on Basil, he admits that his own rebuttal contains "passages where the flame of my heart-felt indignation burst out against this writer." He hopes that his public will pardon the polemical excesses of his response, "remembering that this display of anger is not on our own behalf, but because of insults leveled against our father in God, . . . a case in which mildness would be more unpardonable than anger" (Epistula 29). Peter's answering letter accepts Gregory's claims, echoing the reference to Basil as "our holy father in God" and conceding that Gregory is "a beautiful example to succeeding times of the way in which good-hearted children should act towards their virtuous fathers" (Epistula 30).[31] Gregory's claim to sonship is made still more explicit in the treatise itself, which accompanies his letter to Peter. Protesting his own inadequacies, he nevertheless affirms that, "both by the written and the natural law, to me more especially belongs this heritage of the departed, and therefore I myself, in preference to others, appropriate the legacy of the controversy" (*Eun.* 1.10 [2]). This treatise will constitute Gregory's formal response in "a case in which mildness would be more unpardonable than anger." In order to locate and interpret the son's passion in the first book *Against Eunomius*, the reader must, however, follow the downward drift of Gregory's degradation. It is above all through his parodic display of Eunomius's grotesque sonship that he attains, by a strategy of negation and displacement, the leaping consummation of his own filial love.

Gregory begins by raising the unexpected question of whether it is wise "to lavish indiscriminately upon the first comer one's own gifts" (*Eun.* 1.1 [1]). Having developed the theme of indiscriminate generosity by means of the figure of the physician who attempts to cure even the terminally ill, he clarifies the significance of this figure. "This thought suggests itself when I think of one who lavishly shared his beauties with others," he notes, immediately specifying that he has in mind "that person of God, that mouth of piety, Basil." Gregory goes on to depict Basil as uncritical and indeed promiscuous in his generosity, "one who from the abundance of his spiritual treasures poured his grace of wisdom into evil souls whom he had never tested"—including most notoriously the soul of Eunomius, here configured as a potential receptacle or "womb" for the seeds of divine wisdom (*Eun.* 1.3 [1]).[32] Eunomius is shown to be nonresponsive as well as unworthy: "pitiable indeed seemed the condition of this poor man." Gregory balances the resulting image of Basil as both an unsuccessful healer and an indiscriminate lover with continued emphasis on his generosity: "Basil alone, from the abiding ardour of his love, was moved to undertake [Eunomius's] cure" (1.4 [1]).

By ironically representing Basil as generous to a fault, Gregory is able to portray Eunomius as irrationally unreceptive of the attentions of the noble teacher. Disrupting expectations established in Gregory's initial scripting of Basil's role, the heretic's recalcitrance threatens to rewrite Basil's therapy as attempted rape, in a topsy-turvy scene in which Gregory depicts Eunomius as one who, "beside himself with fury, resists his doctor; he fights and struggles; he regards as a bitter foe one who only put forth his strength to drag him from the abyss of misbelief." In this protracted turmoil of angry resistance, Eunomius conceives and labors violently to give birth to the "literary monument" of his *Apology for the Apology* against Basil (*Eun.* 1.5 [1]). "When in long years he got the requisite amount of leisure, he was travailling over his work during all that interval with mightier pangs than those of the largest and the bulkiest beasts," Gregory mocks. "His threats of what was coming were dreadful, while he was still secretly molding his conception: but when at last and with great difficulty he brought it to the light, it was a poor little abortion, quite prematurely born" (1.6 [1]). If this is not rape's offspring, then it is the teratism of a parodic parthenogenesis: the heretic produces a bastard text, begotten not through intense intellectual intercourse with a worthy spiritual master but in an unseemly act of rebellion against that noble lover. Shown to have failed to create a text that would establish him as a true intellectual son of Father Basil, Eunomius himself acquires the mark of illegitimate birth.

Plato had famously characterized philosophy as the issue of a (sublimated) man-boy love in which erotic and generative impulses were conflated through a confusion of male and female procreative roles: "begetting [is subsumed] under bearing, as if sperm were a kind of foetus, and orgasm a release from birthpangs."[33] In the Platonic context, the lover begets and gives birth to beauty or goodness in the stimulating presence of the beloved. Insofar as the beloved's soul may be thought of as the womblike receptacle of the lover's seed, begetting-and-bearing occurs in the pedagogical transmission of insight to the beloved, and the beloved not only is the (co-)bearer of the beautiful and the good but also is himself the child, having been begotten spiritually as a son and disciple in the image of a paternal or teacherly lover. The comparison of Eunomius to a laboring woman thus invokes an image long since positively appropriated by male philosophers.[34] For satiric purposes, this image must be grotesquely refeminized by being transferred to the bestial realm of sexual generativity—the bigger, the louder, the more crudely and extravagantly physical the birth, the better for Gregory's purposes.[35] Eunomius is likened to "the largest and bulkiest beasts"; his pregnancy is ridiculously long; his birth pangs are "mighty," his laboring vocal, his delivery traumatic. In the course of this description, Eunomius's physicality becomes disgusting precisely as he is made a spectacle.

Subsequent chapters continue to develop the theme of the spectacular, and at the same time, Eunomius's *specular* function, as a distorted mirror of Gregory's own role, becomes more evident.[36] Showily, Gregory represents Eunomius as an outrageous performer: "He is like those who produce effects upon the stage, adapting his argument to the tune of his rhythmical phrases, as they their song to their castanets. . . . Such, among many other faults, are the trillings of his opening passages, his languid and misenervated Sotadics;[37] and one might fancy him bringing them all out, not with an unimpassioned action, but with stamping of the feet and sharp snapping of the fingers declaiming to the time thus beaten" (*Eun.* 1.16–17 [3]). The feminized figure of the sophist or rhetorician evokes the desired and despised realm of the theater.[38] Like Eunomius himself, the rhetorician's words are cosmetically enhanced, "decked out with all the affectations of style" (1.19 [4]). In Gregory's flamboyant text, Eunomius has become not only an actor but also a carnivalesque reveler—indeed, we are told, his shamelessness is such that he does not even bother with a mask (1.32 [5]). His theologizing is "unmeasured ribaldry" (1.77 [8]; cf. 1.32 [5]) and mere sport, disruptive of the neat linear progression of a carefully built argument: "in this circus of words he drives up and then turns down, over and over again, the same racecourse of insolent abuse" (1.95 [10]). Later Gregory insinuates that Eunomius mistakes theological debate for a drinking bout (1.114, 115, 116 [11]), and in one telling passage the theme of drunken reveling is superimposed upon the figure of the grotesque female. "These low unlovely street-boys' jeers do indeed provoke disgust rather than anger," notes Gregory. "They are not a whit better than some old woman who is quite drunk grunting through her teeth" [γραός τινος διακωθωνιζομένης καὶ ὑπ᾽ ὀδόντα γρυζούσης]" (1.96 [10]).

It is finally Eunomius's inferior literary output—the birth of a text that is little more than "grunting through his teeth"—that makes him a ridiculous parent and returns the reader to the opening image of the laboring woman. Although "he has spent no small portion of his life on the composition of this treatise" (*Eun.* 1.12 [3]), as Gregory puts it, his "laborious care in writing" (1.13 [3]) has begotten words as overwrought as they are empty: a "fussy conceit" and a "conceited fussiness" (1.15 [3]). Gregory suggests that Eunomius's child is a prematurely born weakling, despite the great length of the pregnancy (1.6 [1]). Subsequently he implies that Eunomius has given birth not to a lean and articulate son but rather to a "twaddling story" (1.28 [4]), a fat text that must surely bore even its author, "although a strong natural affection for his offspring does possess every father" (1.29 [4]). Only parental affection would seem to account for the fact that Eunomius and his followers "nurse and coddle" the work. Gregory, however, claiming critical distance, has no trouble imagining a more appropriate response to the misbegotten child: this is the context of his enthusiastic vow to "take this puling manifesto and dash it on the rock, as if it were one of the children of Babylon" (1.7 [1]).

The script of Eunomius's failed sonship gives rise to Gregory's contrasting role as Basil's truly beloved son. Whereas the gross Eunomius "was perfectly insensible" to Basil's gifts (Eun. 1.3 [1]), Gregory is able to recognize in Basil a "godlike and saintly soul" whose "divine trumpet-voice would drown any word that could be uttered," were he still on earth (1.8 [2]). "Rising up to speak" in the silence left by Basil's death, Gregory takes on the "laborious task" of refuting Eunomius by writing his own treatise (1.9, 10 [2]). It is not merely conventional modesty when Gregory protests that neither "superior powers of argument" nor "gift of philosophic skill" distinguish him as Basil's heir (1.10 [2]). Rather, he is marked as a true son by the very quality of his devotion; the seemly ardor of his love for Basil is evidenced in the manifest fertility of a soul that gives birth—even as we read!—to a filial text "fair in the beauty of truth" (1.19 [4]). Unlike Eunomius, Gregory knows just how female to make himself in order to conceive in his mind's womb the theological word that will win him full manhood. Whereas Eunomius's overdone, grunting travail has pushed out a fatherless, puny son whose elaborate ornamentation scarcely masks his effeminate weakness, the stronger, nobler issue of Gregory's more efficient and seemly gestation and labor—comprising a mere seventeen days, as he tells us elsewhere (Epistula 29)—can claim the "natural beauty" of a "simple truth" worthy of a father's admiration (*Eun.* 1.19 [4]). On this reading,

Gregory's implicitly maternalized masculine self-representation is crucial to the filial authority of his text; yet the indirect strategy by which he constructs his own authorial fertility is equally significant. Only by standing at several removes from the body can Gregory here suggest the unspeakable paradox of a silent and invisible generativity in language. As if passing through a prism in reverse, his deflected gaze transforms the vivid and varied hues of the grotesquely feminized heretic into the clear, focused beam of a sublimated and finally sexless masculine fecundity.

By ironically casting Basil in the role of generous lover, Gregory is able not only to contrast Eunomius's resistance with his own filial compliance but also to venture a gentle critique of Basil's indiscriminate sowing of seed. As he claims his own manhood in relation to his spiritual father, Gregory also distances himself from the paternal style he has constructed for Basil at the outset of this work. It is not in the guise of a lover that Gregory approaches Eunomius in this text, for "to lavish indiscriminately upon the first comer one's own gifts" appears after all "not a thing altogether commendable, or even free from reproach in the eyes of the many" (*Eun.* 1.1 [1]). A competing image of Basil as phallic physician seems to match Gregory's own self-presentation more closely: "That genuine emulator of Phineas' zeal, destroying as he does with the sword of the Word every spiritual fornicator, dealt . . . a sword-thrust that was calculated at once to heal a soul and to destroy a heresy" (1.87 [9]). The depiction of Basil as swordsman is echoed in Peter's enthusiastic letter of response to Gregory's treatise, which underlines the comparison of Basil—who "pierced with one stroke of his Answer both master and pupil"—to the Israelite priest who killed an Israelite man and his Midianite woman lover with a single thrust of the spear (Numbers 25). With boyish excitement, Peter encourages his brother to imitate both Basil and Phineas in his swordsmanship. Peter urges Gregory to a task of double slaughter, enjoining him to add to his refutation of Eunomius's first book (which Peter now has in hand) a second volume refuting Eunomius' own second round of attack: "with your intellectual arm plunge the sword of the Spirit through both these heretical pamphlets, lest, though broken on the head, the serpent frighten the simpler sort by still quivering in the tail" (Epistula 30).

If the manly grapplings depicted in this treatise are largely affairs of the

written word, that word is once again represented, and indeed partly produced, by the indirect techniques of rhetorical degradation. Gregory has
begun by invoking a traditional image of Basil as orator: "If indeed that
godlike and saintly soul were still in the flesh looking out upon human affairs, if those lofty tones were still heard with all their peculiar grace and all
their resistless utterance, who could arrive at such a pitch of audacity, as to
attempt to speak one word upon this subject? That divine trumpet-voice
would drown out any word that could be uttered" (*Eun.* 1.8 [2]). It is by
way of unflattering contrast that the déclassé Eunomius is depicted as
a *writer* from the start—albeit one easily compared with a flashy, foot-
stamping, finger-snapping rhetorician (1.16–17 [3]). Having learned to
form the alphabet from his peasant father, who whittled letters in his off
time, as Gregory reports contemptuously (1.49 [6]), Eunomius subsequently studied shorthand and earned his living by plying the scribe's trade
in a servant's role, after leaving the farm with the ambition of becoming an
orator (1.50 [6]). Oratory is more than Gregory is willing to grant his rival:
if Eunomius's recent text has told the tale of a trial at which his first *Apology* was delivered orally,[39] Gregory will now express disbelief in the event
(1.61–90 [7–9]), preferring to confine Eunomius to his notebooks. Responding to Eunomius as a text-monger, Gregory quotes extensively from
his *Apology for the Apology*—even as he also loftily protests his unwilling-
ness to "write down, taking word by word, an explanation of that mad
story of his," "to follow step by step each detail of his twaddling story"
(*Eun.* 1.27, 28 [4]).[40] Despite such disavowals, Gregory's textual cross-ex-
aminations do in fact most frequently proceed "word by word," since any
turn of phrase—once fixed via a literal, written citation—may be made
witness to Eunomius's guilt. Thus, already in the introduction, Gregory
quotes Eunomius's criticism of Basil's text: "he called me a Galatian,
though I am a Cappadocian." While seeming to present himself as dismis-
sive of such quibbling distinctions, geographic as well as textual, Gregory
nevertheless is not above casting aspersions on the accuracy of Eunomius's
citational remappings, thereby shifting an appeal to truth to a questioning
of the authenticity of a text: "Supposing, that is, that it is proved that he
[Basil] said this. I have not found it in my copies; but grant it" (*Eun.* 1.105
[10]). In refuting another polemical citation of a Basilian passage subsequently, Gregory again clings to the language of his rival, just as Euno-

mius's text has built its argument on Basil's use of a particular word. Eunomius has made much of Basil's concession that Eunomius's winning the episcopacy of Cyzicus was "the prize of his blasphemy," notes Gregory. "If [Eunomius] insists on our own words against ourselves," Gregory counters, "he must accept both these consequences or neither"—that is, that Eunomius's "prize" is the "prize of his blasphemy" and that he incriminates himself when he willingly receives it as such (*Eun.* 1.111–18 [11]). In degrading Eunomius as a mere scribbler, Gregory has not only virtually reproduced his opponent's text but also made it the matrix of his own, partly *dis*owned identity as a Christian writer.[41]

Gregory concludes the introduction to his refutation of Eunomius's text with a rousing representation of Basil as a heroic warrior engaged in a "new combat" (*Eun.* 1.130 [12]). This image both displaces the ink-stained Eunomius's now parodied self-representation as "truth's champion" and transfers Basil's own struggles from the petty realm of "sophistic juggles, where victory is no glory and defeat is harmless" to the serious realities of imperial politics (1.22 [4], 122 [12]). "The adversary whom he had to combat was no less a person than the Emperor himself," Gregory announces grandly (1.126 [12]). "No one could describe his contempt of danger, so as to bring before the reader's eyes this new combat, which one might justly say was waged not between man and man [οὔτε παρὰ ἀνθρώπων οὔτε πρὸς ἀνθρώπους], but between a Christian's firmness and courage [ἀρετήν καὶ παρρησίαν] on the one side, and a blood-stained power [δυναστείαν φονῶσαν] on the other" (1.130 [12]). In this contest that is not so much "between man and man" as between competing styles of manhood, virility's virtue and fearless power of speech is on the side of the true Christian, now divorced from the naked violence of coercive power. A martyr, Gregory's Basil need not die in order to prevail over his imperial persecutors. But neither, as it happens, is the *spoken word* at the center of his defiant witness: the confession having already been written, the *text* is what must now be preserved. As the "imposing power" "turned with all its threats into flattery," offering peace "if only one little word in the written creed is erased, that of *homoousios,*" Basil "would not change even the order of the written words," as Gregory relates it (1.136, 137 [12]).[42] By this refusal to shift the language of a written text, Basil may be seen to have "stemmed in his own person this imperial torrent of ruin that was rushing on the churches, and turned it aside; he in himself was a match for this attack, like a grand immovable rock in the sea, breaking the huge and surging billow of that terrible onset" (1.138 [12]).

When at last Gregory shifts attention to the theological content of Eunomius's blasphemous treatise, he registers outrage that his opponent "will not make use of the words by which our Lord in perfecting our faith conveyed that mystery to us" but instead "suppresses the names of Father, Son and Holy Ghost" in his teachings about God (*Eun.* 1.156 [13]). "Everyone, when the words father and son are spoken, at once recognizes the proper and natural relationship [σχέσιν] to one another which they imply," asserts Gregory; the scandal is that Eunomius "robs us of this idea of relationship which enters the ear along with the words" (1.159–60 [14]). But exactly what is it that "everyone recognizes"? Subsequently Gregory expresses himself more cautiously: "conjecturing about the transcendent from lower existences would not be altogether sound" (1.213 [18]); it would be wrong to imagine that a process similar to animal generation "is going on also among pure existences" (1.215 [18]). Nevertheless, if one were to draw some such analogy—exploiting the possibilities of degradation once again—it would be necessary to admit that "if anything is produced by mutual transmission, such as the race of animals, not even here does one produce another, for nature runs on through each generation"; "productions are of the same type as their progenitors" (1.215 [18]). On the basis of this assertion that biological generation reproduces the one as the same, Gregory argues that Eunomius, with his suggestion that "one is produced from another," abandons the metaphor of paternal generation, insisting on the *difference* between divine parent and child and thereby "exhibiting the Son as a bastard when compared with his Father's nature" (1.216 [18]). Eunomius's Son "creeps like a bastard into relationship with the Father," repeats Gregory; similarly, his Spirit "is from a lineage of unrealities" (1.248, 259 [20]). Horrifyingly, Eunomius seeks "to establish that there is no connection between the Father and the Son, or between the Son and the Holy Ghost, but that these Beings are sundered from each other, and possess natures foreign and unfamiliar to each other" (1.224 [19]).

His opponent's alienating theology threatens Gregory's own conception of divine relationality. While he grants that the title "Father" signifies his status as the "unbegotten" source of all, Gregory refuses the substitution of terms proposed by Eunomius. Unlike the title "Unbegotten," "Father" *also* signifies "begetter" and therefore necessarily implies both a "begotten" and a process of begetting that is proper to Deity. "Let us manfully [ἀνδρικῶς] own our belief," urges Gregory: "the word 'Father' introduces with itself the notion of the Only-begotten, as a relative bound to it [συνημμένως διὰ τῆς σχέσεως μεθ ἑαυτοῦ]" (*Eun.* 1.557 [38]). Thus, for Gregory, divine Father-hood cannot represent the singular "unbegotten" nature of Deity itself (as Eunomius would have it) but is rather a term of purely relational distinc-tion *within* Deity. Indeed, "Fatherhood" is the conceptual font of godly multiplication, begetting and binding the Son and thereby also produc-ing—by means yet more mysterious—the Holy Spirit as well (e.g., 1.280–81 [22]). At stake is not only the capacity of the divine Father to duplicate himself exactly in his equally divine Son, but also—and perhaps even more importantly—the imagining of Deity as the site of holy relations between "individuals" who are equal and also profoundly akin. Gregory has been easy to charge with "tritheism" because of his quickness to compare divine plurality to the plurality of human beings—"for instance, Peter, James, and John" (1.227 [19])—yet he could almost equally well be charged with "mono-anthropism." Without dissolving the difference between created and un-created being, Gregory presses the analogy between humanity and God to produce a model of erotic and procreative relationality that is based on the unity of sameness.[43]

Gregory's insistence on trinitarian nomenclature, however continuous with his preoccupation with male generativity and relationality, may seem to sit oddly alongside his emphasis on the unknowability of God and the limits of language. He mockingly represents Eunomius—with his categor-ical proclamation that God is Unbegotten Being itself—as one "versed in the contemplation of that which eludes thought" (*Eun.* 1.575 [38]). Gre-gory, in contrast, claims merely to comprehend incomprehensibility, as-serting that God is "incapable of being grasped by any term, or any idea, or any other device of our apprehension, remaining beyond the reach not only of the human but of the angelic and of all supramundane intelligence, unthinkable, unutterable, above all expression in words" (1.683 [42]). "No one gives more emphatic expression to this religiously attractive insistence on the mystery of God's being than Gregory of Nyssa," as Maurice Wiles notes. "But such a radical stress on transcendence raises a serious problem," Wiles adds; "we seem to be in danger of falling into a Feuerbachian abyss, in which we discover that not only is our language a matter of human invention but so is that to which we believed it to refer."[44] However, to the extent that language does indeed appear groundless in Gregory's account, the "abyss" may be construed not as a "danger" for theological discourse but rather as its generative source, the material of an endless inventiveness: bottomless, language can mirror the infinite elusiveness of God.[45] On this reading, the problem is not that Gregory has cut *logos* loose from *theos* but that—in such an endlessly expansive economy of word and desire—he has inscribed "Father, Son, and Spirit" as theology's eternal bottom line. The mystagogue's foreclosure on the pursuit of God's unfolding depths and heights—rather than his assertion of divinity's mystery itself— underwrites what Richard Lim describes so compellingly as the foreclosure, through ideological mystification, of an ancient tradition of discursive reasoning and public debate.[46] If Gregory wants to privilege particular "names" of God, is this, as has frequently been suggested, because he is simply seeking a healthy balance between "apophatic" and "kataphatic" ways of knowing?[47] Or is it because he is claiming the right to the inconsistency of an arbitrary authority on behalf of some version of "patriarchy"? More persuasive than either of these possibilities is an interpretation that acknowledges both the complex consistency and the consistent complexity of the writings of this ethereal lover and filial Father. Perhaps Gregory so emphatically and indeed excessively privileges these particular "names"— "Father," "Son," and "Spirit"—because he is convinced that they uniquely contain language's uncontainability, by enfolding, womblike, the abysmal depths and infinitely receding heights of the very God.[48]

Gregory is, at any rate, always poised to dive into the abysmal depths of rhetorical degradation in this self-consciously naughty text. His first book ends, as it has begun, on a distinctly trashy note. Representing himself as outraged by a passage in which Eunomius challenges the theological terminology of sameness, he observes scornfully, "The formidable two-edged sword which he has sharpened is feebler than a make-believe in a scene-painting" (*Eun.* 1.478 [34]). Make-believe manhood makes itself up like a woman, as Gregory remarks prissily—"such a glitter of style," "this elaborate prettiness," "flowers of the old Attic" (1.481–82 [34]). A self-professed mudslinger, Gregory once again refuses to recognize the dirt as his own: "it is easy also to find mud in his words . . . to cast upon this execrable teaching" (1.492 [34]). Entering into what purports to be the dizzyingly alien thought-world of the heretic, in which "one is begotten by oneself, having oneself for father, and becoming one's own son," Gregory mimes a drunkard's reeling: "it is like the mental state of one with his senses stupefied with drink, who shouts out persistently that the ground does not stand still beneath, and that the walls are disappearing, and that everything he sees is whirling round and will not keep still" (1.493 [34]). Eunomius is likened to a brawling youth: "When striplings challenge to a fight, men get more blame for pugnaciousness in closing with such foes, than honor for their show of victory." Gregory, however, admits that he cannot resist joining the fray. Bestial imagery resurfaces: "As the cattle that run blindfolded round to turn the mill remain with all their travel in the same spot, so does he go round and round the same topic and never leaves it" (1.601 [38]). Gregory's text has, of course, followed the same monotonous course. Eunomius's logic is "vomit," to which he returns incessantly. Gregory himself seems to repeat his invectives incessantly: "Directly he repeats the logic so often vomited. . . . How often he returns to his vomit; how often he blurts it out again!" "It would perhaps be more decent to be silent in a case like this," observes Gregory civilly, only immediately to transgress the bounds of decency (1.602–3 [38]). Imitation is irresistible: "Now I broach these ridiculously childish suggestions as to children sitting in the marketplace and playing; for when one looks into the groveling earthliness of their heretical teaching it is impossible to help falling into a sort of sportive childishness" (1.675 [42]). Still simmering, he instructs Eunomius sternly: "Let him however cool his combative heart" (1.689 [42]).

Warm with the passion of both combat and love, Gregory's first book, *Against Eunomius*, mobilizes *ad hominem* attacks as well as theological polemics to mount a contest of masculinities initially represented by competing figures of the birthing male. The grotesquely feminized heretic seems to boast the capacity to give birth to a textual child who will in turn mark him as the true son of Basil. However, it is of course not the oversized, gruntingly maternal Eunomius but the elegant Gregory who finally lays claim to the status of sonship in relation to his famous brother, through the production of a superior theological progeny. Fittingly, Eunomius's duplicitous writings can produce only a fake or bastard Son spawned from "another," while Gregory authors a transparent theological discourse on the truly divine Son who is the spitting image of his Father. If "one might be able to interpret the fact of being deprived of a womb as the most intolerable deprivation of man," suggests Irigaray, then one might also "understand quite a few . . . cultural products" as results of the search for an equivalent to motherhood. "And the desire that man here displays . . . eternally and ever to reproduce him (as) self, is a far from negligible indication of the same thing."[49] "Equivalence," however, gains much in the translation across sexual difference, and the fecund Father—who is also a son—might himself be envied for his immaculate womb.

Following the relational logic of Platonism's spiritualized homoerotic economy, Gregory—unlike the Eunomius of his text—thus exalts and masculinizes the degraded female reproductive body. Yet "masculinity" remains a usefully slippery category, and Gregory's maleness is defined as much by its opposition to a hypermasculine subjectivity as by its rejection of the excessive "femininity" of a grotesquely maternalized male. Indeed, for Gregory, there can be no simple identification of the feminine with the grotesque, for masculinity must also be degraded in order to be exploited and transformed. Although willing to derive strategic advantage by feminizing his opponent, Gregory more often prefers to position himself as superior to a grotesquely masculinized rival by claiming a feminized transcendence of the very competitive struggle in which he is engaged. In a text that opens with the hint of rape and the explicit evocation of the slaughter of an infant, Gregory models a manly aggression, while yet claiming to rise above such violent tactics. Openly accepting the phallic sword his brother Peter offers, he nevertheless insists that the blade is "curative" and that he, like Basil, is in the end no swordsman but a physician (*Eun.* 1.87 [9]). In a second book written against Eunomius, composed soon after the first, Gregory plays beardless David to Eunomius's gigantic Goliath. Here the sword with which he vanquishes his enemy proves not to have been inherited from his father but rather stolen from the enemy (*Eun.* 2.4–6 [12B/13]). As Peter articulates Gregory's disavowal of violence, it is really the enemy who has "whetted the sword against himself" (Epistula 30). In contrast, Gregory is all responsive receptivity: his rousing discourse, sweetened by the mysteries of God's word, is the child born of a desiring soul moved by the spirit of truth. Gregory's text—and thus also its author—becomes a mirror of the divine Son, who is both the only-begotten and beloved child of the Father and his most ardent lover, joined to the Father in an inexpressibly intimate and exact cooperation coalescing in the coessentiality of absolute equality and oneness.

In a Different Voice: 'On the Soul and the Resurrection'

Why is Diotima a woman? Why did Plato select a woman to initiate
Socrates into the mysteries of a male homoerotic desire? . . . Diotima
has turned out to be not so much a woman as a "woman," a necessary
female absence—occupied by a male signifier—against which Plato
defines his new erotic philosophy. And my own interpretation of Plato
has exemplified the same strategy, insofar as it has appropriated a
feminist perspective for the purpose of legitimating its own
discourse about the erotics of male culture.

—David Halperin,
"Why Is Diotima a Woman? Platonic Erōs
and the Figuration of Gender"

I would suggest that [a view similar to Halperin's interpretation of
Plato's Diotima] might apply to Gregory of Nyssa's portrayal of Macrina
in his two treatises concerning her. In this light, Macrina is not
herself a teacher of wisdom, but a trope for Gregory: he is, in
contemporary parlance, "writing like a woman." Gregory has
appropriated woman's voice.

—Elizabeth Clark,
"Holy Women, Holy Words: Early Christian Women,
Social History, and the 'Linguistic Turn'"

Gregory of Nyssa's dialogue *On the Soul and the Resurrection* was not the first Christian takeoff on Plato's *Symposium*: Methodius of Olympus had already written a more overt and heavily allegorical revision that recast the original all-male drinking party held in Eros's honor—where the prophetess Diotima was present only *in absentia*—as a female gathering at which the famous virgin Thecla delivered the winning speech in honor of virginity. Gregory, however, who scripted his own dialogue on desire as a private conversation between himself and his dying sister, Macrina (whose "secret name" was Thecla, as he tells us elsewhere), does distinguish his work, not least by transgressing the homosocial worlds of gender kept intact by both Plato and Methodius. He dares to represent a direct and indeed purportedly "historical" exchange between a man and a woman on the topic of love. Or does he? Momigliano remarks, "Macrina is here Socrates to her brother."[50] Making the Macrina of Gregory's dialogue male, Momigliano seems to anticipate David Halperin's cue to hear in Diotima's speech mere "Sokratic ventriloquism,"[51] so that Macrina as Diotima is really Socrates in drag—a "woman" but not a woman, as Elizabeth Clark suggests. Of course, Momigliano only *seems* to anticipate such a reading, for his remark in its context refers fairly straightforwardly to the strong allusions in Gregory's text to Socrates' deathbed discourse in the *Phaedo*.[52] Nevertheless, such a suppression of the *Symposium's* influence may amount to much the same thing as Halperin's spookily mimetic encrypting of the woman within "scare quotes." If, as Catherine Roth notes in reference to Gregory's dialogue, "there are not only many parallels with Plato's *Phaedo*" but "also a relationship with Plato's *Symposium*, where Socrates becomes the not-so-apt pupil of the wise woman teacher Diotima,"[53] why has this relationship so rarely been commented on?[54] And if we choose to comment now, what might we—whether feminist or "feminist" or otherwise oriented—make of Gregory's choice not only to write like Plato but also to write like a woman? His choice, that is, to employ a literary format that advertises that he is creating his own role and "hers," that both voices are his own, and that neither is simply and singularly proper to him?

The dramatic occasion for the conversation between Gregory and Macrina is Gregory's overweening grief at Basil's death. Gregory explicitly casts Macrina as "the Teacher" (ἡ διδάσκαλος), whose task is to school her overwrought brother in the proper management of his passion. This displaced self-critique stands in marked contrast to Gregory's self-presentation in his letter to his brother Peter, which (as we have seen) creates the expectation that Peter will excuse—perhaps even applaud—the bereaved Gregory's unchecked rage (Epistula 29). In his own voice (and by return post), Peter yields to the flow of Gregory's feeling (Epistula 30); but in Gregory's scripting of an exchange that may or may not ever have taken place, Macrina resists. Although she initially gives way to Gregory's grief ("like a skilled

horseman," as he puts it), Macrina moves subsequently to curb the galloping excesses of his sorrow (*Anim. et res.* 12A).[55] She addresses her younger
brother in a gently chiding and distinctly maternal tone from the privileged vantage point of her own deathbed. ("Those who look on a deathbed can hardly bear the sight!" he protests [13A]). Having hoped for a
soothing sibling empathy, as he represents it, Gregory instead encounters
in his sister both fresh cause for mourning—Macrina's unexpected ill-
ness—and a stern exhortation to pull himself together. Macrina delivers
her loving admonitions in the form of a discourse on the passions, in which
grief is subsumed within the Platonic duo of anger (θυμός) and desire
(ἐπιθυμία): of the other passions, "each of them seems akin to the principle of desire or to that of anger," as she remarks (56B).

Already it becomes evident that the links between Gregory's dialogue
and the Platonic corpus are multiple and complexly intertwined: as Rowan
Williams has suggested, the *Phaedrus's* metaphor of the soul's charioteer
and his yoked horses (θυμός, ἐπιθυμία) may be almost as important to the
allusive construction of this text as the *Phaedo* or the *Symposium*. The figure of the chariot is initially introduced by Gregory in the narrator's voice,
with Macrina in the driver's seat and Gregory on the side of the horses.
Subsequently Macrina herself explicitly rejects the Platonic passage in favor of a scriptural guide (*Anim. et res.* 49C); yet still later it apparently offers her just the resolution she seeks to her psychological dilemma (61B–
C). The charioteer and his bestial team thus haunt the text with ambivalence.[56] Williams suggests that "the *Phaedrus* analogy is evoked at this
early stage to pre-empt any undialectical reading of Macrina's apparent critique of the passions wholesale." We are to understand that throughout
the dialogue Macrina will both give rein to Gregory's passions and—allowing him to be carried by their horsepower—eventually lead him where
she wants him to go; through a similar pattern of give and take, the
Teacher will also draw the acute reader along the path of psychological insight and health. Williams notes further, "The dialogue form not only en-
acts what it discusses (the protracted exploration of an emotion) but, later
on, allows Macrina to modify her initial rigorism in response to Gregory's
objections in behalf of emotions."[57] If, however, as Warren Smith argues,
Gregory's initial analogy refers either to the "breaking" of a young horse
not yet used to the bit and bridle or to the similar technique of allowing

an excited horse to run until it has exhausted itself, Williams's conflation of this analogy with the later invocation of the Platonic chariot may falsely confuse "the relationship between Macrina's initial indulgence of Gregory's sorrow and her pedagogical method."[58] Whether Macrina is merely taming or also already instructing her brother in the opening lines of the dialogue, the roles seem familiar enough: here (as in *On Virginity*) "Gregory" overflows with the passion of his grief in the face of life's transience, while the maternalized virgin—someone's sister, a "woman"—is left high and dry(-eyed). But if it appears easy to place the *characters*, where, or who, is the *author* of the text? Does he simply identify with Macrina, as the stern discipliner of passion's horses? Is he instead more ambiguously allied with the younger brother's cautious support for the value of a little emotional laxity? Or does he not rather locate himself elsewhere, beyond compromise or synthesis, as both "Macrina" and "Gregory," driver and horse, and also neither, also *more*? If so, how does he get there? How does he come to have it all?

One of the central questions to be pursued in the course of the dialogue is, as Macrina formulates it, "what we are to think of the principle of desire and the principle of anger within us." Are desire and anger "consubstantial with the soul, inherent in the soul's very self," or not? (*Anim. et res.* 49B). Macrina's initial answer is that they are not, and this is the context for her rejection of "the Platonic chariot and the pair of horses of dissimilar forces yoked to it, and their driver, whereby the philosopher allegorizes these facts about the soul" (49B–52A). The passions are "only like warts growing out of the soul's thinking part, which are reckoned as parts of it because they adhere to it, and yet are not that actual thing which the soul is in its essence" (56C). "Accretions from without," they nevertheless lie close "on the border-land" of the soul (57C), representing the effects or "touch" of "the other things which are knit up with" the soul in its divine creation (61A). Acknowledging the "deep-rootedness" of the passions in created human nature (61A), Macrina absolves the Creator of any authorship of evil (or even "warts") by returning to the metaphor of the charioteer, now in a positive vein. The emotions of the soul, divinely implanted, can "become the instruments of virtue or of vice," according to her now partly revised account; when properly governed by reason's driver, anger generates fortitude, and "the instinct of desire will procure for us the delight that is Divine and perfect" (61B). Rejecting the "dissimilarity" built into a tripartite model of a composite soul that seems to grant each part too much independence, Macrina nevertheless seems to concede that a unitive psychological theory might after all be propelled by the figure of a skillfully guided chariot.[59]

The fault lines of incipient contradiction running through Macrina's position offer Gregory an opportunity to pose a question and Macrina the occasion to clarify. In the process, attention is shifted from the original constitution of the soul's "nature" to its final purpose. Is the *telos* of human perfection the proper direction of the emotions or their eventual eradication (*Anim. et res.* 88C–89A)? The latter, Macrina answers swiftly, seeming at first to reaffirm that passion is external to the nature of a soul defined exclusively by its rationality. The soul purified of vice will ultimately transcend "the need of the impulse of desire to lead the way to the beautiful," she states. Anger now drops out of the discussion, and the focus remains solely on desire. "Whoever passes his time in darkness, he it is who will be under the influence of a desire for the light; but whenever he comes into that light, then enjoyment [ἀπόλαυσις] takes the place of desire, and the power to enjoy renders desire useless and out of date" (89C). "Desire" (ἐπιθυμία) will be reconfigured as "love" (ἀγάπη), as the yearning for what is lacking gives way to the enjoyment of what has been found. Indeed all other movements of the soul will cease except the movement of love. She adds, "love alone finds no limit" (96A). "When the thing hoped for actually comes, then all other faculties are reduced to quiescence, and love alone remains active, finding nothing to succeed itself" (96B). Passion has not been eradicated but transformed, the horse not so much "tamed" or even "trained" by means of bit and bridle as given its own head, when logos and love melt into one.

At this point, it becomes clear that Gregory is citing not just the role but also the words of Diotima in his Macrinan dialogue.[60] Diotima's speech in the *Symposium* (203c–e) offers a startling depiction of Eros as a "needy" god, standing on the borderlands of poverty and resourcefulness, ignorance and wisdom, embodying the productive longing for the beautiful that he himself lacks. Love for the beautiful, she clarifies, is not so much "for the beautiful itself, but for the conception and generation that the beautiful effects [τῆς γεννήσεως καὶ τοῦ τόκου ἐν τῷ καλῷ]." "Those whose procreancy is of the spirit [ψυχή] rather than of the flesh—and they are not unknown, Socrates—," she confides, "conceive and bear the things of the spirit," thereby winning a kind of immortality (*Symposium* 206e–209a). Diotima closes with a famous description of the "heavenly ladder," which we have already seen alluded to in Gregory's *On Virginity*. The soul ascends this "ladder" rung by rung, "starting from individual beauties" and moving from there to "*every* lovely body," thence to the "beauty of institutions, from institutions to learning, and from learning in general to the special lore that pertains to nothing but the beautiful itself—until at last he comes to know what beauty is." Through the drive of eros (in the guise of an awareness of lack), the ever-conceiving soul moves up toward the ultimate *telos* of desire, which is represented as "an everlasting loveliness which neither comes nor goes, which neither flowers nor fades, for such beauty is the same on every hand, the same then as now, here as there, this way as that way, the same to every worshiper as it is to every other" (*Symposium* 210e–211c).

In the setting of the *Symposium*, this speech is reported by Socrates, who introduces it by informing his audience: "I want to talk about some lessons I was given, once upon a time, by a Mantinean woman called Diotima—a woman who was deeply versed in this and many other fields of knowledge. It was she who brought about a ten years' postponement of the great plague of Athens on the occasion of a certain sacrifice, and it was she who taught me the philosophy of Love [τὰ ἐρωτικὰ]. . . . And I think the easiest way will be to adopt Diotima's own method of inquiry by question and answer" (*Symposium* 201d–e). Gregory seems to find this "the easiest way" as well. His own dialogue is not so much a rescripting of the *Symposium* itself as a rescripting—in question and answer format—of the prior, offstage conversation between Diotima and Socrates. In Plato's dialogue, Socrates reports this conversation to a gathering of somewhat dubious fellow philosophers; in Gregory's dialogue, the readers themselves are the guests at the party at which Gregory relates his exchange with Macrina, transmitting what she taught him of the philosophy of Love.

Halperin argues that the Diotima of Plato's *Symposium* articulates a specular femininity that is finally reabsorbed by the male subject, who is himself thereby transformed. Plato, he suggests, is engaged in a radical contestation and reinscription of classical pederastic love that strategically borrows from two culturally available (and also contradictory) conceptualizations of women as desiring subjects: first, women as excessively responsive to the tug of sexual desire, and second, women as drawn solely to procreate. By introducing these representations of female desire through the figure of Diotima, Plato is able to construct a new theory of male erotics that, according to Halperin, highlights the sublimated procreative potentialities of mutual or reciprocal relations between men within a strictly homosocial community. In the end, then, the absent figure of Diotima functions to erase the "feminine" via male appropriation, a strategy furthered by Plato's subtle hints that "she" is a fictive construction from the start, a mask for a Socratic performance of "mimetic transvestitism."[61]

As Clark notes, this interpretation of Diotima "provides sobering food for thought" for historians who have wanted to mine not only Plato's but also Gregory's dialogue for social-historical data on gender roles and relations.[62] Before sobering up entirely, however, I would like to return briefly to the raucous scene of Plato's dialogue, not to quibble with the charge of appropriationism (or even fictionalism) but rather to complicate our sense of its dynamics and structure. One of the first decisive actions taken by the group of assembled men on the legendary evening of the symposium on love was, we are told, the agreement not to become excessively drunk, and to "dispense with the services of the flute girl" who had just come in. "Let her go and play to herself or to the women inside there, whichever she prefers, while we spend our evening in discussion," the host proclaims (Symposium 176e). The excluded flute girl (αὐλητρίς) thus stands in rather explicitly for what is excessive in relation to the form of rational discourse to be fostered on this occasion, yet her banishment from the symposium still seems to locate her, along with "the women" more generally, in the inner courtyard (αὐλή) of the men's talk. Nor does she remain safely roped off from the party. For just as Socrates finishes delivering his own suspiciously cross-dressed Diotima speech, the flute girl herself intrudes again, accompanying a drunken, ribbon-bedecked Alcibiades (Symposium 212d). Alcibiades crowns Socrates with his ribbons, calls for more wine, and proposes that it is Socrates himself, so lately self-presented in verbal drag as Diotima and now dripping with ribbons, who is to be configured as Eros, whose eulogy (offered by Alcibiades) will finally displace and thereby reinterpret the previous eulogies of Love. It is, however, no simple or sober text, warns Alcibiades—the eulogy of Socrates whose satyric pipings and

Bacchic performances incite others with "this philosophical frenzy, this sacred rage," while he himself "spends his whole life playing a little game of irony, and laughing up his sleeve at all the world." As Alcibiades reinscribes Socrates as a Dionysiac text of Love, the party dissolves into a drunken revel (*Symposium* 212e–223d). The flute girl is back—indeed perhaps she never really quite left—and the Platonic dialogue seems to construct her as a catachrestic figure for those excesses on whose imperfect exclusion the masculine symbolic order is founded. Transgressively identified with Socrates through the mediation of Alcibiades, the flute girl also puts into question the extent to which the figure of Diotima is controlled by the specular economy of a male subjectivity. Has the masculine subject simply absorbed the feminine element, or does she not also partly displace *him*, disrupting his singularity by miming her role as "object" excessively, even parodically, while "also remaining elsewhere"?[63] And does the excess that remains "elsewhere" in relation to discourse not benefit the male subject as well, offering impurity's antidote to the sterility threatened by the closure of a perfect mimetic circulation? Insofar as she practices a "different" dialectic, Diotima introduces an "other" love, suggests Irigaray: "Its fecundity is *mediumlike, daimonic*, the guarantee for all, male and female, of the immortal becoming of the living. . . . Love's aim is to realize the immortal in the mortal between lovers."[64]

Returning to Gregory's dialogue, we can now ask: Why is *Macrina* a "woman"? She is a "woman" in part for reasons similar to those diagnosed by Halperin in the case of Diotima's "womanhood." Gregory is indeed repeating, and also exaggerating, the gestures of Plato's own sublimating restructuring of pederastic love. A "dry" female virgin embodies most eloquently, for the gushy son, the elusive goal of an absolutely transcendentalized erotic desire, while the maternalized body serves as a particularly fertile site for the forced conflation of erotic and procreative urges, effectively "sealed" by one thin (and resonant) membrane. Macrina is a "woman," then, because she both is and is not a wife and also because she both is and is not a mother. In the dialogue, her positioning as a virginal lover and a spiritual mother is subtle but pervasive. Gregory's biography of his sister is more explicit. We learn from the *Life of Macrina* that the beautiful girl, much sought after as a bride, was widowed before consummating her marriage and was thus (on her own interpretation) both wife and virgin (*V. Macr.* 4–5); dying, she becomes the virginal bride of Christ himself (22).[65] The *Life* also identifies Macrina extremely closely with her own (and Gregory's) mother, Emmelia, to whom she chose to be in effect wed—as if she had never left the womb, as Emmelia is said to have described the bond (5). Although her daughter's ascetic achievements are foreseen by Emmelia, who grants her the "secret name" of Thecla during childbirth (2), Macrina is later presented, in a reversal of roles, as mother to her own mother, Emmelia's "guide toward the philosophical and unworldly way of life"—an "existence [that] bordered on both the human and the incorporeal nature," as Gregory puts it (11). With unwavering firmness she sees her mother through the death of a favored son—Naucratius—and takes over for her in the nurturance and education of another—Peter (10, 12). Following the deaths of Emmelia and Basil, Macrina "remained like an undefeated athlete" (14).

Macrina then, not unlike Diotima, is the reflection of a masculine erotics—initially displaced or masked via its feminized representation—that is marked by both a sublimated and maternalized fecundity and a radical transcendentalization of erotic passion via its transformation into an agapic love. To adapt (and appropriate) Halperin's words: Macrina is a woman because Gregory's philosophy must borrow her femininity in order to seem to leave nothing out and thus to ensure the success of its own procreative enterprise, namely, the continual reproduction of its universalizing discourse in the male culture of late-ancient orthodox Christianity.[66] As I have already suggested, however, the "borrowing" involved in "appropriation" produces an inherently shifty and unstable structuring of gender.

Gregory's *Life of Macrina*, when read alongside the dialogue, illumines the ways in which the "woman" enters disruptively into the terrain of Gregory's speech in the dialogue as well, even as he depicts himself as intruding into "her" space. His account of Macrina's funeral in the *Life* portrays the virgins of his sister's community as flamboyant in their expressions of grief. Like Plato's flute girl, these women embody a transgressive potentiality that cannot be completely excluded from the discursive space of the carefully crafted texts they inhabit, that is even constitutive of those texts. "My soul was disquieted for two reasons," Gregory relates in his report of the funeral: "because of what I saw and because I heard the weeping of the virgins." Although, as he tells it, they had "kept in check the grief in their souls and they had choked down the impulse to cry out in fear of her, as if they were afraid of the reproach of her voice already grown silent," subsequently their voices burst through the disciplined silence. "A bitter, unrestrained cry broke forth," writes Gregory, "so that my reason no longer maintained itself but, like a mountain stream overflowing, it was overwhelmed below the surface by my suffering and, disregarding the tasks at hand, I gave myself over wholly to lamentation." Gregory here quite explicitly "borrows" the explosive subterranean voice of the virgins, but its liquidities subsequently possess *him*. He records their lament that "the bond of our union [with Macrina] has been demolished" by her physical death, remarking that "the ones who called her mother and nurse were more seriously distraught than the rest" (*V. Macr.* 26). Dragging his soul from the abyss of his own grief, he attempts to reassert the control of rationality's word, "shouting at the virgins in a loud voice" intended to drown out their wailings, commanding (in Macrina's name) that they should not lament but sing psalms (27). Temporarily sent back to their quarters, the irrepressible virgins later reappear: "the maidens' psalm-singing, mingled with lamentation, resounded through the place," drawing a huge crowd from the surrounding area. Out of the virgins' hybrid voice of psalm and lamentation, now swollen with the wails of the country folk, Gregory eventually achieves a suitable effect by "separating the flow of people according to sex": "I arranged for the singing to come rhythmically and harmoniously from the group, blended well as in choral singing with the common responses of all" (33). But control by sexual segregation is tenuous at best. During the burial, as Gregory reports it, one virgin cried out, and "the rest of the maidens joined her in her outburst and confusion drowned out the orderly and sacred singing." Soon everyone was weeping. As the habitual prayers were intoned by the persistent clergy, the people only gradually returned their attention to the liturgy (34).[67]

By giving voice to Macrina's preference for praise over grief, Gregory is able to make himself once again a man.[68] But his "identity" is barely contained by his masculine logos, for Gregory's Macrinan texts also invoke and recall, sloshingly, seductively, "what milk and tears have in common," in the language of Julia Kristeva: "they are the metaphors of non-speech, of a 'semiotics' that linguistic communication does not account for." The liquid laments of the virgins seek convergence with the expressive body of the maternal Macrina. To the extent that it is women (or rather "women"?) who "reproduce among themselves the strange gamut of forgotten body relationships with their mothers," Gregory both does and does not want to be one of the girls, like a mountain stream flowing beyond the limits of language, searching for that "complicity in the unspoken, connivance of the inexpressible, of a wink, a tone of voice, a gesture, a tinge, a scent," the enjoyment of a love without limit.[69]

In Gregory's Macrinan dialogue, as in the funeral scenes at the end of the *Life of Macrina*, the flute girl is always in the act of breaking in—or rather "she" is always *coming out* into the company of men, as Gregory himself opens the door on the inner space where he and his sister are closeted. But who is "she"? If the arid Macrina comes out in Gregory's texts, it is only so as to bring with her that soggy boy whose emotions *will* run away with him: the tearful Gregory comes out too, like one of Macrina's wailing virgins spilling onto the public landscape of his sister's funeral. If Macrina is Diotima, then Gregory is Socrates; if Gregory is the weeping virgin, then Macrina must be Socrates after all. The "woman" is everywhere and nowhere, and the transgressive element of excess produced by "her" exclusion from discourse is for Gregory the necessary source of his own transcendence. The potentially static *telos* envisioned by Macrina's ambivalently cited "Platonism"[70] is overtaken and transformed in the stampede of a desire not limited by logos: Gregory's womanish *agape* does not so much tame Plato's eros as drive it over the edge.[71] As Irigaray paraphrases Diotima's message, she repeats Gregory's act of retrieval: "Everything is always in movement, in a state of becoming. And the mediator of all this is, among other things, or exemplarily, *love*. Never fulfilled, always becoming."[72]

Momigliano observes, "Gregory and Macrina did speak to each other; but if Basil spoke to Gregory, I am not sure that Gregory ever answered Basil."[73] In fact, as we have seen, when Basil speaks, Gregory stands and ultimately delivers, thereby winning the right to supersede his brother—who is most safely "answered" when safely dead. But Gregory and Macrina *must* be seen talking to each other, face to face, lip to lip. Their words, mingled on Macrina's deathbed, will continue to mesh dialogically in the complex, harmonic tones of Gregory's many-voiced speech.

Love Without Limit: 'The Life of Moses'

The womb must be denied, or converted, before one can honorably return to it. But no conversion converts without remainder, without creating fresh opportunities and needs for further conversion. . . . The womb is converted by being naturalized. But it is naturalized by being masculinized, which is to say, unnaturalized. The natural form of the cave is made available for human purposes by being routed through the masculine, a two-stage conversion that renders the cave an object of desire, an object to desire instead of the womb: one lives in a cave instead of with a woman. This is, to the ascetic, a natural desire that takes natural form, the form of the cave. . . . But life in a cave also represents a renunciation of natural desire, a will to desire the nonnatural, the unnatural, to have an unnatural desire, the very type of which is anal intercourse. The cave—or anus—is the natural and human site of gender conversion or transformation.

—*Geoffrey Galt Harpham,*
"Asceticism and the Compensations of Art"

The third theophany is the most extensively treated of the three, and its discussion clearly constitutes the climax of Gregory's presentation about the knowledge of God and eternal progress. We refer to the story in Exodus 33:17 ff. where Moses asked to see God's glory and was told he could not see God's face. Instead he was placed in the cleft of a rock and permitted to see the "back parts" of God as he passed by. Here we get one of Gregory's most original interpretations of the Biblical text as he applies it to the theoretical basis for and content of the spiritual life. . . . Gregory explains that Moses' request to see God is both granted and denied. Indeed it was granted in what was denied. God fulfilled Moses' desire, but did not promise any cessation or satiety of the desire. God would not have granted the request if it would have ended Moses' desire.

—*Everett Ferguson,*
"Progress in Perfection: Gregory of Nyssa's Vita Moysis"

If Gregory's biography of his sister gives us Macrina as she might have been, his explicitly allegorical *Life of Moses* gives us Moses as he surely never was. Perhaps this is because manhood, like the sun, cannot be gazed at directly.

The view of Moses is screened not only by the original biblical text of which he is both subject and (presumed) author but also by the added layers of Gregory's narrative simplifications and theoretical expansions. Inscribed, reduced, sublimated—in the end, Moses is made as fine and light "as the thread of a spider web," enveloped in a tunic the color of air (*V. Mos.* 2.191).[74] One begins to suspect that what "has been both granted and denied" is Gregory's request to see this man: following in the footsteps of Moses, he finds himself suddenly staring straight into the cleft of the unrepresentable. The scholarly temptation to categorize this subtle text as the fruit of old age and a contemplative, even "mystical" lifestyle is not hard to understand, though it may be difficult to defend historically.[75] On the one hand, there *is* something consummative about the work; on the other hand, unfurling seamlessly, it moves beyond even consummation's finality. For the author of the *Life of Moses*, there can only be multiple climaxes on the never-ending ascent of the ever-receding peak, where satisfaction always opens out into the desire for something even better. Slipping into the hole in the rock is not a regress to the smug stasis of the maternal womb but rather a conversion of the womb's abysmal potentiality into the expansive site of a man's absolute transformability: pursuing Moses, Gregory surges forward toward masculinity's perfection, his only goal to make the chase last forever.

The work opens to the pounding hooves of racehorses. Acquiescing to a friend's request that he offer some advice on the "perfect life," Gregory represents himself playfully as one of the spectators who shout encouragement "even though the horses are eager to run." Introducing a treatise that will argue for the importance of *theoria*, or visual contemplation, and the imitation of divine perfection, he here gently mocks those who rivet their gaze upon the charioteers and mime their gestures, "leaning forward and flailing the air with their outstretched hands instead of with a whip," as if they might help speed the teams along. The joke (once again) is perhaps on his own initially misplaced Platonic identification with the charioteer of the soul rather than the horses of passion. Moreover, by agreeing merely to instruct a younger man who is himself already "light-footedly leaping and straining constantly for the 'prize of the heavenly calling,'" Gregory may appear to be taking himself out of the race (*V. Mos.* 1.1). In reality he is setting the pace in a race that all may hope to win, a "father" who models obedience for the son (1.2). Galloping smoothly by now, he warns his disciple that this course has no end: "The one limit of virtue is the absence of a limit. How then would one arrive at the sought-for boundary when he can find no boundary?" (1.7). The joy is in the running itself.

Gregory's concern in this *Life* is "not with logical connection but with progress, not with chronology but with sequence," as Everett Ferguson notes.[76] The main thing is that the quest for perfect virtue must go on. Or, to borrow Ronald Heine's words, "each [event] represents another upward step, and in this sense all are of equal importance in showing that Moses never stopped on the course of virtue."[77] Gregory's account moves both forward and upward. He formalizes the two-dimensionality of his analysis by dividing his text into two parts, the first a paraphrase of the biblical narrative, the second a "theoretical" interpretation of that narrative. This device exaggerates almost to the point of parody the parallel and interrelated sublimations of exegetical and ascetic practices.[78] Under Gregory's penetrating gaze, the truth that begins with Moses' birth unfolds. This birth is first and foremost the birth of a male, or perhaps rather more abstractly of the principle of maleness, marked by "austerity and intensity of virtue" and shaped by ongoing resistance to the "tyrant" who favors "the female form of life" (*V. Mos.* 2.2). As mutable creatures, human beings are constantly giving birth to themselves, remarks Gregory, and gender is a matter of choice: "we are in some manner our own parents, giving birth to ourselves by our own free choice in accordance with whatever we wish to be, whether male or female, molding ourselves to the teaching of virtue or vice" (2.3). Free will assists in the begetting and delivery of virtuous male selves, protected by the ark of education from "the stream made turbulent by the successive waves of passion" in which the less well endowed children drown (2.5–7). Fruitful Christianity is the "natural" mother to whom the male child must return for milky nurturance, while a secular education, "which is always in labor but never gives birth," may serve as an adequate, if temporary, foster mother (2.10–12).

To the one who has given birth to himself as male, the truth which is God comes, illumining his soul with its flame. If Christ is the flaming truth, the Virgin is the thorny bush that is miraculously not consumed by the fire. (Once again, Gregory's Mariology engulfs his incarnational Christology.) In order to get close enough to see the light shining through the womblike container within the bush, the man Moses removes the coverings of skins—materiality itself—from the feet of his soul. Stripped naked, he finally perceives the difference between being and nonbeing, between the "transcendent essence and cause of the universe" and the created order that exists only by participation in true being (*V. Mos.* 2.19–26).

One of the first miracles to occur following this theophany, continues Gregory, is "the rod's changing into a snake" (*V. Mos.* 2.26). However, Gregory assures his readers that "the change from a rod [βακτηρία] into a snake should not trouble the lovers of Christ" (2.31). "For our sakes [the Lord] became a serpent that he might devour and consume the Egyptian serpents produced by the sorcerers. . . . This done, the serpent changed back into a rod" (2.33–34). In a seeming association of philosophy with the serpent of sorcery, he adds that circumcision is necessary to "cut off everything that is hurtful and impure" as is the case with "philosophy's generative faculty [γονή]" (2.38–39). Its fleshy excesses sheered away, the snake is once again refashioned as a sleek rod. Although admitting that "we have probably already sufficiently interpreted the rod [ῥάβδος]" (2.63), Gregory cannot resist elaborating his account of the marvels of "that invincible rod of virtue which consumes the rods of magic" (2.64). Vanquishing the serpentine forces of a hypermasculinity, the rod also purifies the man of the swampy mire of a "frog-like life" (2.77). However, when struck against the dry rock that is Christ, the rod "dissolves hardness into the softness of water," so that the rock "flows into those who receive him" (2.136).

Heine's insistence that the events "all are of equal importance" in this ongoing narrative disrupts a scholarly obsession with its theophanic moments, which have, following the influential work of Jean Daniélou,[79] been invoked to support a reductive and anachronistic reading of Gregory's *Life* as descriptive of a tidy, three-stage "mystical" ascent.[80] Heine urges us to attend, instead, to the continuous flow of the text—to listen (as it were) for the relentless pounding of the hooves of horses that never stop in the race for perfection. Heine's interpretation is compelling, yet it might be admitted that Gregory himself does demarcate the three "theophanies" in a way suggesting that they are privileged purveyors of the message of eternal progress,[81] even if they are not ends—or indeed quite climaxes—in themselves. Discussing what Moses saw on Sinai, Gregory explicitly relates this vision to his hero's earlier glimpse into the virginal bush: "What is now recounted seems somehow to be contradictory to the first theophany, for then the Divine was beheld in light but now he is seen in darkness" (*V. Mos.* 2.162). Having passed through a period of spiritual adolescence— all that preoccupation with the contest of rods!—Moses reaches a higher level of erotic knowledge. True sight now turns out to be partly a matter of blind touch, as the mind pushes ever deeper into the "luminous darkness," yearning to understand that which exceeds understanding (2.163). Within this account of penetration, the movement of Moses' ascent keeps repeating itself: it is "as though he were passing from one peak to another." Ascending beyond the base of the mountain, he hears the trumpetlike cry of a God who is at this point apparently beyond words; next, "he slips into the inner sanctuary" where divinity is to be found; finally he reaches "the tabernacle not made with hands" (2.167)—a "limit" that itself quickly expands into the all-encompassing (2.177). If the clarity of light has been converted to the mystery of darkness, the ascent of the peak has been transformed into a dive into the bottomless deep. In the process, Moses himself has also been entered and changed: "It was not marriage which produced for him his 'God-receiving' flesh, but he became the stonecutter of his own flesh, which was carved by the divine finger, for 'the Holy Spirit came upon the virgin and the power of the Most High overshadowed her'" (2.216). God's own finger having written on his body, impregnating him with its word, Moses is still a virgin after Sinai.

But there is more, always more. Seemingly not satisfied with the limits of his own historical retelling, Gregory deepens his interpretation with a supplemental theophany not mentioned in the initial recounting of events. Pulled out of sequence from an earlier chapter in the biblical text, the episode is refashioned into a divine encore whose structural excessiveness merely underlines the point that even expansion into the all-encompassing "tabernacle" is not the end of knowing God. "He still thirsts for that with which he constantly filled himself to capacity, and he asks to attain as if he had never partaken" (*V. Mos.* 2.230). If Moses has now asked to see God "face to face, as a man speaks with his friend" (or his sister!) (2.219), God both satisfies his desire and leaves him in an eternal state of frustrated excitement. What he wants exceeds his human capacity, he is told. "Still," reports Gregory, "God says there is 'a place with himself' where there is a 'rock with a hole in it' into which he commands Moses to enter." Entering, Moses cannot see, for God has placed his hand over the mouth of the hole, but Moses hears God call out to him. Coming out of the hole, he sees "the back of the One who called him" (2.220). The reader, it would seem, is, like Moses, invited both to see and not to see what is being described in such charged passages. "These sentences raise mystery to sublimity, so that my understanding rests in a state of quiet apprehension of something beyond my powers to decipher. I am confused, I do not understand . . . unless—I do. But if I do, I perform a rapid, even instantaneous gesture of cancellation." In these terms, Geoffrey Harpham describes his own reading of another ascetic text. Gregory, for his part, admonishes the reader to perform just such a "cancellation" as is depicted by Harpham, explaining, "If these things are looked at literally, their concept of [God] will be inappropriate" (*V. Mos.* 2.221). Harpham, however, continues to peek behind the veil of his own reluctance: "the conjunction between the mysteries of faith and the groaning, heaving processes of homosexual fornication is so grotesque, impossible, ridiculous that it could not be admitted." Indeed, it is as Gregory has predicted: "If therefore one should think of the back of God in a literal fashion, he will necessarily be carried to such an absurd conclusion" (*V. Mos.* 2.222). "Thus the homoerotic serves as an explanatory model in the material world of desire for faith," theorizes Harpham, "one that illuminates without defiling because it is so altogether defiled that its function is never actually admitted."[82] Gregory seems to offer elusive agreement: "All of this would more fittingly be contemplated in its spiritual sense" (*V. Mos.* 2.223).

Perhaps because his confidence in theory's sublimating power is so strong, Gregory does not attempt to cancel the impulse of desire itself but only to reorient it—indeed, there is no other horse for the race! If bodies have a "downward thrust," he admits readily that the soul is not so different but simply "moves in the opposite direction." "Once it is released from its earthly attachment, it becomes light and swift for its movement upward, soaring from below up to the heights" (*V. Mos.* 2.224). It does not just soar, it expands: "Activity directed toward virtue causes its capacity to grow through exertion; this kind of activity alone does not slacken its intensity by the effort, but increases it" (2.226). No longer bound to a fleshly cycle of filling and emptying (cf. 2.61), the soul's longing for God swells ever larger. Engorged with an endlessly expansive desire, it can only rise, paradoxically, "by means of the standing": "I mean by this," clarifies Gregory, "that the firmer and more immovable one remains in the Good, the more he progresses in the course of virtue" (2.243). The place of stasis is the rock, repeats Gregory, and the hole in the rock where God directs him to take his stand turns out to be . . . the heavenly tabernacle (2.245). It is also the place where the race is run (2.246). And so goes the progression of conversions: through the virginal bush into the all-encompassing tabernacle of darkness, thence via the naturalized topography of the cave to the masculinized backside of the Supernatural himself. Face-to-face is not after all the best position for love: "for good does not look good in the face, but follows it," and Moses is "the man who has learned to follow behind God" (2.253–55).

And still (as Heine points out) the story is not finished, however much we may be tempted to rest with the satisfying finality of a seemingly climactic moment. "Let us proceed," Gregory urges briskly (*V. Mos.* 2.264). The last episode before Gregory's tumbling recapitulation of the route of continuous perfectibility (2.305–18) involves the same Phineas whom we have already seen referred to in the first book *Against Eunomius*. Here, as at the beginning of the *Life*, Gregory underlines both the gendered structure of erotic sublimation and the violence inherent in the renunciations demanded. Captured by lust for foreign women, the Israelites "were themselves wounded by feminine darts of pleasure," as Gregory tells it in his most sternly moralizing voice; "as soon as the women appeared to them, showing off comeliness instead of weapons, they forgot their manly strength and dissipated their vigor in pleasure" (*V. Mos.* 2.298). It was Phineas who reestablished the order of virility. Piercing a mixed couple with a single thrust of his spear, "he did the work of a priest by purging the sin with blood" (2.300). Thus did Phineas defeat Pleasure herself, "who makes men beasts." Gregory amplifies his own disgust at manhood's disgrace through this contamination with the female and the foreign: "they did not hide their excess but adorned themselves with the dishonor of passion and beautified themselves with the stain of shame as they wallowed, like pigs [or frogs!], in the slimy mire of uncleanness, openly for everyone to see" (2.302).

"After all these things," continues Gregory (*V. Mos.* 2.313), Moses—forgoing the finality of arrival in the promised land—did not so much stop his race toward perfection as pass beyond our sight. His is a "living death, which is not followed by the grave, or fills the tomb, or brings dimness to the eyes and aging to the person" (2.314). Imitating him, his followers will prolong the tale of true perfection, which emplots the unfolding desire of ageless, bright-eyed men "to be known by God and to become his friend" (2.320).

Reading this as a "late" work, it is tempting to conclude that Gregory has at last grown into his manhood—indeed, *how* he has grown! If dry Miriam was the star of *On Virginity*, in this text she makes only a brief appearance as a degraded symbol of "female" envy (*V. Mos.* 1.62, 2.260), while Moses controls the ground of dryness (1.31, 2.311). No longer content with the desire either to "have" or to "be" the woman, Gregory, standing tall with Moses on the rock of Christ, seems to have achieved the pinnacle of an active virility in and through his imitative desire for God. Perfectly self-disciplined, the horse of his passion no longer even requires a driver.

And yet, to reach any conclusion, in relation to this work in particular, would perhaps be a mistake. Master of style, and never at rest, this fluid author is always giving birth to himself anew. In another work generally assigned to Gregory's last years,[83] "he" is the bride of the Song of Songs, "constantly making progress and never stopping at any stage of perfection." The bride's lover is compared to an "apple tree" whose shadowy house she enters. Wounded by the lover's dart, "then she herself becomes the arrow in the hands of the archer, who with right hand draws the arrow near and with left directs its head toward the heavenly goal." Called to leave the shadow, the bride rests "in the cleft of the rock." Finally coming to bed, thinking to achieve "that more perfect participation" in her union with the divine Spouse, she finds herself, "just as Moses" did, suddenly enveloped in the inner space of a secret, sacred darkness. In the encounter with her ambiguously feminized divine Partner, who is all fruit and shadow and cleft, the bride transforms the potential emptiness of mutual receptivity into a swollen plenitude of eros that knows no end: "far from attaining perfection, she has not even begun to approach it" on her wedding night.[84] "Are we unsatisfied?" she might (he might), with Irigaray, query rhetorically. "Yes, if that means we are never finished. If our pleasure consists in moving, being moved, endlessly."[85]

Sexing the Son

Stripping humanity of essential difference, Gregory of Nyssa reconstructs a lost paradise in which the logic of desire produces neither "sex" nor "sexuality." Indeed, sexual difference is itself an unnatural perversion, according to Gregory, manifested most dramatically in the institution of marriage as the fall's primary effect. However, reknitting a fractured humanity into a single sex paradoxically leads Gregory to confront the seemingly irreducible particularity of maleness and femaleness. One might propose, then, that he posits an androgynous rather than a sexless self—yet there is nothing of the composite in his idealizing construal of human subjectivity. Gregory's texts suggest that a man must make himself virginally female in order, as a woman, to restore humanity's created nature by making himself wholly male. Gregory shows us, in Cixous's words, "a man beginning to be a woman in order to be a man." Here, "woman" is the object not so much of desire as of envy; this is the case above all because she has the capacity to *conceive man*. The "conception" that interests Gregory is spiritual rather than fleshly, as he might put it; it is a matter of cultural rather than biological reproduction, as we might say. What provokes his envy is a woman's capacity to conceive *herself* as "man." Women are exalted as icons of an admired aridity, within the terms of a medical tradition that identifies the male as dry, the female as wet. Still wet behind the ears himself, Gregory will become a man by imitating virginal mothers like Miriam, Mary, and Macrina. In the process of projecting an achieved masculinity onto heroic women, Gregory scripts his own "natural" maleness as more stereotypically "female"—damp, weepy, emotional, excessive. He thereby reimagines the body of man as both penetrable and overflowing, alternately empty and full, hard and soft. This imaginary body is pressed firmly into the service of sublimation's symbolics: ascent by the progressive conversion of fleshly desire (the "female form of life") into spiritualized *agape* (the "male") is, finally, the making of Gregory's manhood and the making of man according to Gregory. Conversion differs, however, from the negation of a more absolute repression, and Gregory retains positive traces of the appropriated "woman" as well as of the emotive body, even as he follows "her" lead in making himself male by shedding the weight of carnal passions. Impregnated with the female, Gregory has actually conceived "woman." "She," in turn, becomes the womb of his maleness.

For Gregory, the distinction between the Creator and the created overshadows the (now internalized) distinction between the male and the female. Desire is the force that keeps man in motion, drawing him ever upward toward God, as the limitlessness of human longing meets its match in the infinitude of the Divine object's transcendence. The originary distinction between the Creator and the created—protected by the limit of limit itself—proliferates an endless series of less stable distinctions within the realm of manhood's sameness, while thereby also holding open space for desire between men. In Gregory's ontology, the vertical fluidity and erotic dynamism of an earlier Christian Platonism's multilayered cosmology is thus retrieved and retuned to a later antiquity's higher key. Despite his resistance to Eunomian christological subordinationism, Gregory provisionally projects a hierarchical distinction onto the Uncreated's differentiation as Father and Son, who set the standards for an intergenerational and successional manly love. At the same time, divinity's sharply asserted unity of essence restructures the society of virginal men according to a counterlogic of equality and mutuality. Thus, if a Platonic pederasty still establishes the terms for the structuring of desire within a single-sexed economy, its hierarchies continue to be significantly destabilized. Feminized as "soul," the filial Gregory is God's receptive beloved—as a Platonist might expect. As he rides the horse of his passion for Christ right up to the abysmal edge of knowledge's consummation (where he glimpses the divine backside!), he is also, however, the aggressive lover in pursuit of the infinitely desired Son, the Son in pursuit of the Father. In divine love's unendingly expansive relational economy, a man can have it all ways.[86]

Given his biographical habit, it is odd to discover how little we learn of Gregory's own history. His is the one life he has chosen not to write. Ever elusive, never hemmed in by any identity, Gregory leaves space for a man to gather together the seeming contradictions of his roles as "son" of Basil and Emmelia, of that other Basil and his sister Macrina, of town and church, of monastery and perhaps also marriage—while still also "remaining elsewhere." It is the particular convergence, in that "remainder," of both a soaringly masculine transcendence and an abysmally feminine excessiveness that is the distinctive mark of Gregory's remaking of man.

Is Gregory not only "a man beginning to be a woman" but also "a woman ending"? Is he the ending of the woman whom he has made his own? I have found that I can neither stop asking nor make an end of answering this question. Reading Gregory as a woman, "what grips me," as Cixous writes of Tancredi, is not so much the beginnings and endings as "the *movement* of love." "It is a question of the grace of genders instead of the law of genders, it is a question of dancing, of the aerial crossing of continents."[87]

"I should also say that in order to know him better internally, I close my eyes, I avoid looking her straight in the face because it is not impossible that at first sight she may look a little like one of these men who are not at all feminine, but who are capable of this slow inner dance, who have a loving, elastic rapport with the earth and are thus a bit f ... thus in short a bit m ... and thus ...

"And then I feel her so clearly and again I know without any doubt how lightly powerful she is like a man who is powerful lightly like a woman who is powerfully light like a man who is gently powerfully powerful like a woman of powerful tenderness. . . .

"And all I wanted to try to say is that she is so infinite."[88]

CHAPTER 3

Spirited Advocacy

Ambrose of Milan

The notion of an original or primary gender identity is often parodied
within the cultural practices of drag, cross-dressing, and the sexual
stylization of butch/femme identities. . . . *In imitating gender, drag implicitly
reveals the imitative structure of gender itself—as well as its contingency. . . .*
Consider gender . . . as *a corporeal style*, an "act," as it were, which is
both intentional and performative, where *"performative"* suggests a
dramatic and contingent construction of meaning.

—*Judith Butler,*
Gender Trouble

I n a late-Roman "age of ceremony,"[1] when appeals to decorum constituted an elite class's best strategy for mitigating the arbitrary violence of autocratic rule, Bishop Ambrose—famous for bringing the emperor Theodosius to his knees—presented himself as a master of the
ceremonial style. Indeed, as Neil McLynn reads him, Ambrose was *all* style
and stratagems: his literary oeuvre, although betraying signs of hasty construction, is nonetheless so "carefully controlled" in its effects as to be most
safely interpreted on "the tactical level."[2] Traces of tactics may be all that
remains of a man who steadfastly refused to personalize his self-image,
with whom the irascible Jerome could scarcely pick a fight, to whom Augustine himself failed to attribute a fully engaging interiority in his well-
known portrait of the bishop in the pose of the silent reader.[3] When, in the
later books of his *Confessions,* the eagerly imitative (and newly ordained)
Augustine subsequently strikes a similar pose, the excesses of his readerly
meditations starkly contrast with all that we do not know—more significantly, to all that we, like Augustine, do not even dare to ask—about the
thoughts and emotions that may have stirred behind the facade of Ambrose's indefatigable poise. Ambrose's own writings, for their part, collude
with Augustine's portrait, firmly reminding us that the inner life is terrain

to be carefully guarded, sealed against the penetrating eyes of inquisitive spectators. A diagnosis of "self-control" or even "repression" does not, therefore, so much crack the deep meaning of Ambrose's texts as bounce off their shiny surfaces: the author of this literary corpus fully intends to be viewed as a man virginally self-possessed. Modeling a public role rather than revealing a private life, the statuesque bishop sets himself apart from his more sloppily self-expressive peers—of whom "biographies" might more plausibly be written, suggests McLynn—while also emerging as a quintessentially late-antique man, icon of the spirit of a theatricalized culture in which the line between "person" and "impersonation" quickly blurs and superficiality styles itself the bearer of hidden depths.[4]

The stage for Ambrose's polished performance was the imperial capital of Milan—a center for self-fashioning, then as now. Having become the seat of an emperor's court, the northern Italian city had molded the relative docility of its municipal notables into a "conduit" (as McLynn puts it) for interactions between the court and Rome's senatorial aristocracy.[5] By the same token, Milan served as an arena for the mediation of relations of alliance and opposition, tangled collaboration and carefully maintained disengagement, between imperial and ecclesiastical functionaries and factions. If, in Milan, a distinctive civic receptivity thus fostered nuanced renegotiations of power between elite men in the late Roman empire, what might it mean to say that Ambrose appears altogether at home in such a milieu? Or, to put the question slightly differently: does the city make the man or the man the city? Easily represented as a vigorous Father to whom the matrix of a Christianized empire owed its very existence, the "Saint Ambrose" of Christian scholarly record is also the Roman historian's "Ambrose of Milan," a suspiciously adaptable son who is himself largely the shrewd product of circumstance. It is, however, perhaps most tellingly in the guise of a holy spouse that the ascetic Ambrose embraces the city: his episcopacy emerges from such an intricate cooperation with situation and locale that the distinction between the individual and his context begins to dissolve, even as the worlds of "church and court"[6] partly overlap. Partnered, and laboring together with a seemingly effortless grace, Ambrose and Christian Milan are the making of each other.

Cultivating a reputation for "unflinching public action,"[7] Ambrose the bishop left an impression of "immense energy"[8] while (partly paradoxically) appearing unwavering to the point of immobility. Despite significant opposition to his leadership, he remained firmly ensconced in the episcopal chair of Milan from 374, when he was dramatically summoned from his post as provincial governor, until his death, in 397. Ambrose initially signaled his determination to occupy what remained contested territory with an impromptu rite of quasi-imperial *adventus*.[9] Ecclesial edifices erected with admirable alacrity concretized his elevated position as bishop, and a tight liturgical weave of hymns and showily erudite sermons further sealed the boundaries of Ambrose's Milan. From his much-admired rhetorical performances—some of which he took care to circulate in written form—emerged the ideal of a church embodied as a virginal female, besieged yet nevertheless still intact, swollen with potent fecundity yet unmarked by the wound of procreative loss. Extravagantly exploiting the potentialities of a Marian ecclesiology, Ambrose, with mirror in hand, rhetorically transformed the miraculously whole and stiffly upright body of the mother of God—unmoved and unchanged even by the ripping pains of childbirth, as he insisted—into a fertile site for his own conception of the Christian community.

If for Ambrose the church was Mary, his Mary was all surface and border, defense and containment; in abbreviated form, she "was" her eternally unruptured hymen. By reshaping an intricately folded anatomy into a simple, taut boundary separating "them" from "us," Ambrose conformed the church of his imagination to the contours of Mary's modesty. "Arian" was the name he gave to the enemy against whom he defended his alluringly vulnerable and reassuringly resistant lady. This chronologically and geographically remote "scare figure" distracted attention from ongoing local disputes and their political and theological niceties. There remained many in Milan who, like Ambrose's predecessor Auxentius, preferred to describe the divine Son as "similar" to the Father, thereby rejecting the uncompromisingly essentialized "sameness" guarded by Nicaea's watchword *homoousios*. In Ambrose's own time, bishops of the homoian (or "similarity") camp circulated within Milan, and the ardently anti-Nicene empress Justina made the city the home of her court. From the liminal provinces that had become the center of a besieged empire's military preoccupations, homoian preachers tickled the emperor's ears with their theological discussions and disputes. Yet Ambrose himself "belonged to a younger genera-

tion of militant upholders of the Nicene Creed," as Brown puts it suc-
cinctly:[10] the adherent of a Western theological party already habituated to
battle, he was not inclined to accommodate theological pluralism or even
to debate doctrinal positions, preferring simply to hold the line. The basic
elements of catholic trinitarian theology already having been established,
as he saw it, Ambrose, heroically humble, was merely their translator and
advocate. While Basil and the Gregories were developing and securing the
Athanasian legacy for the Greek-speaking East, their Milanese colleague—
a virtual plagiarist, frequently proceeding quite directly from both Alexandrian and Cappadocian sources—positioned himself as extending the victory of Nicaea to the Latin-speaking world.[11] He could thus eventually be
seen to have brought an "end" to the complex theological controversies
that would henceforth be known simply as "the Arian-Nicene conflicts"—
as Daniel Williams aptly frames the achievement.[12] While withdrawing
from overt competition with the newly announced ecumenical Council at
Constantinople, Ambrose, ever the adept stage manager and star in his
own dramas, pointedly conducted his own local show in 381 at the Council of Aquileia in defense of the Nicene cause in the West. When his homoian opponents complained that the outcome had been fixed in advance,
he was seemingly not fazed: how else was a council to be staged?

Ambrose not only resisted the "Arian" but also, simultaneously, defended the church against the world: the intimately familiar enemy was the
saeculum as well as the "heretic" for this most secular of episcopal perform-
ers. In uniting his advocacy of a Nicene orthodoxy with his emergent zeal
for a Christianized empire, Ambrose instinctively grasped the principle of
upward mobility at work in the erecting of an "other world" atop the structures of an existing order. He neatly directed man's traditional *cursus* onto a
higher plane, while vigorously recruiting new members for God's elite
corps. With a few uplifting adjustments, Cicero might still instruct in the
arts of self-made manhood, even after the "revolution of late antiquity"[13]
was well under way. However, such acts of sustained elevation—if they
were not to collapse back into mere accommodation—required both the
discipline of an austere asceticism and the stimulus of threatened victimization, with its accompanying thrill of defiance. Though undoubtedly under direct and severe attack at several dramatic moments in his episcopacy,
Ambrose seems nevertheless to have relished and therefore amplified his

claims to the time-honored role of the suffering witness. The stance of the martyr became one of his habitual poses, as he recounted the scintillatingly gruesome tales and flourished the oversized bones of the Christian heroes of a bygone day. The same defiance in the face of threat that had characterized his entry into the episcopacy reappears at every turn: even as his claims grow ever more confident, his cries of alarm remain shrill. In an era of imperial patronage, "the Catholic congregations that he exhorted were still encouraged by him to think of themselves as on the defensive, and as hedged around with inflexible boundaries," as Brown notes.[14] It is revealing that Ambrose's earliest showcased alter egos are world-rending girls who face the executioner's knife with a focused ferocity and an uncanny feel for the dangerous and exhilarating power of a repressed sexuality. There is, finally, something of the hysterical (as well as the histrionic) in Ambrose's act: the man who, like Mary, so carefully guarded his own inner space seems beset by a version of the malady the ancients attributed to the displacement of an empty and hungering womb.

Brown remarks that the "studied vehemence" of the Ambrosian style betrays not only the vigor of a "man of action" but also a certain "feminine intensity."[15] Like Gregory of Nyssa, the bishop of Milan chooses to wrap himself in the protective cloak of his sister's virginal authority. When musing about swords, he seems to be as preoccupied with girls and marriages as with men and war; "the inner bedroom of the well-to-do Christian house"[16] is the landscape of Ambrose's ascesis. The hymn-writer's musical tastes and poetic proclivities further mark him as seductively womanish. What are we to make of such a "sexual stylization," which appears by turns exaggeratedly virile and affectedly "femme"? At first glance, Ambrose seems to project an interiorized femininity contrasting with the public man's hypermasculine exterior. And yet such an "inner woman" is perhaps after all just another surface display and indeed itself a mark of Ambrose's attentiveness to appearances. In other words, to read Ambrose, with Brown, as harboring a feminine aspect might not be to drift down the "false trail" of an elusive or even nonexistent "inner life"—as McLynn interprets it[17]—but to begin to comment on the bishop's theatricality. "How does a body figure on its surface the very invisibility of its hidden depths?" is a version of "the question"[18] raised by this man and his avant-garde act of self-enclosure. One possible answer is: by wearing nothing but borrowed clothes. In a culture where dissimulation was itself already marked as a feminine trait and transvestitism was "the *norm*, not the aberration" in theatrical representation,[19] "playing the other"[20] might very well mean "playing the woman" and thereby also both interrogating and reinserting the "inner *man*." When Ambrose adopts a female role, he does not intend to "pass" any more than did Aristophanes' bristly Mnesilochos (who wore a dress yet was still clearly "male from top to toe") but rather means to hint at the suggestive bulges lying just below the surface of the act.[21] To the extent that his appropriations of the quasi-hysterical stances of girl martyrs and other ostensibly besieged virgins smack of contrivance, his penchant for rhetorically dressing himself up like a woman only serves to set off the fact that he has still got the requisite equipment for manhood. Ever competitive, he scrutinizes the performances of the other players, alert to those moments when the outward act gives way to reveal not virtue's contrasting hardness but the slippery softness of the truly effeminate male—from which he intends to distance himself at all costs. "A man may hold femininity in contempt at the same time that he appropriates it," as Tania Modleski remarks.[22] On this reading, Ambrose's "feminine intensity" is all on the surface, enveloping the not-so-secret depths of his manhood.

But Ambrose's girlish act did more than accentuate his masculinity by creating a titillating contrast between the seeming and the real. Ambrose *needed* this virgin's part if he was to restyle the philosopher's worn and faded mantle and claim the full power of plain speech:[23] without a little help from some other wardrobe and a different script, he might not have pulled off the rhetorical act of transcending imperial manhood itself, representing himself in ascetic sternness as tutoring one emperor and repeatedly rebuking another. If clothes—or roles—largely make the man, then Ambrose is a partly *re*made, "femminized" man.[24] To the extent that he succeeds in refashioning manhood, the spectator begins to suspect that even classical masculinity is just another "butch" act that Ambrose intends to upstage via parodic citation of some of its most aggressive moves. The sustained ambiguity of Ambrose's womanish act is finally hugely productive, yielding much more than the sum of its apparent inconsistencies. Dressed like a virgin, he coyly veils his virile member, thereby putting into question not only the cultural power of a nakedly phallic masculinity but also the very significance of merely fleshly markers of sex. If femininity is invoked on the side of "the figurative, the body's transcendence," linked with "impersonation, performance, masquerade, rhetoric," and the realm of the superficial,[25] the shroud of womanhood is nonetheless a surface that re-creates its own depths: by purporting to cover *something*, it becomes the matrix of manhood's unearthly rebirth. Having made himself virginal and thereby posited *an essentially veiled virility*, Ambrose creates a chain of inferences—"it" is never what you *see* but always something *more*—along which manhood is transported upwards, as if on a dove's borrowed wings, into the invisible domain of divinity.

Borrowed wings? The Holy Spirit itself is appropriated for manhood's flight, in the linguistic slide west from the Semitic feminine to the Greek neuter to the Latin masculine of grammatical gender, and it is Ambrose who (at a sword-wielding emperor's request) plays a crucial role in this translation. In the texts of Ambrose, "a man of the spirit,"[26] the ever-copulating third person is pressed more firmly than ever into the role of the divine inseminator who embodies the principle of disembodiment itself. The Holy Spirit—like Ambrose—remains nevertheless airily elusive in "his" gendering, as if constantly on the verge of sliding across even the most strongly drawn boundaries. As Mary's more transcendent double—and also her partner in the salvific crime of dispassion that breaches the boundaries of heaven and earth—the Spirit slips into the body of the Virgin mother's anatomical literalism even as she appears in danger of vaporizing altogether. If in that transaction Ambrose's otherworldly manhood seems to steal far too much of both woman's spirit and her flesh for the good of this world, we may at least hope to catch him *in flagrante delicto*, in the midst of an act in which repeated costume changes finally also produce "an internal subversion in which the binary is both presupposed and proliferated to the point where it no longer makes sense."[27]

The Daughter's Seduction: 'On Virgins'

Those wonderful hysterics, who subjected Freud to so many voluptuous moments too shameful to mention, bombarding his mosaic statue / law of Moses with their carnal, passionate, body-words, haunting him with their inaudible thundering denunciations, were more than just naked beneath their seven veils of modesty—they were dazzling. . . . Yes, the hysteric, with

her way of questioning others (because if she succeeds in bringing down the
men who surround her, it is by questioning them, by ceaselessly reflecting
to them the image that truly castrates them, to the extent that the power
they have wished to impose is an illegitimate power of rape and violence).—
The hysteric is, to my eyes, the typical woman in all her force.

—*Hélène Cixous,*
The Newly Born Woman

Ambrose remembered one Roman girl who had rushed up to the altar and,
in front of the bishop, wrapped the altar-cloth around her head as a veil,
pleading for protection through consecration as a virgin of the church.
In the stunned silence that followed, a relative shouted out: "'Do you think
that if your father was alive, he would have allowed you to remain
unmarried?' 'Maybe he died,' the girl snapped back, 'so that no one should
stand in my way'" [*Virg.* 1.11.65–66]. . . . No Latin writer saw the
implications of this new situation more clearly than did Ambrose.
The notion of virginity served him as a sounding board.

—*Peter Brown,*
The Body and Society

It took Ambrose more than two years to find his voice as an episcopal
writer, and even then he required the amplification of a "sounding board."
In *On Virgins*, a text pieced together out of passages borrowed not only
from the treatises of Cyprian and Athanasius but also from his own spoken
sermons,[28] Ambrose represents himself as struggling to emerge from an extended silence. His mouth, like Zacharias's, has been "long dumb" (*Virg.*
1.1.2).[29] He fears the Lord will accuse him of burying his small measure of
talent, yet he fears even more imperiling his modesty by talking out of turn
(1.1.1). The womb of his speech remains closed: if he does speak, it will be
a miracle on the order of the scriptural accounts of talking asses and
bushes, the budding of sterile rods and barren fig trees (1.1.2–3). Beginning
to despair—although he "ought not"—Ambrose seems to be choking on
his own words. "There is something which the voice cannot explain," he
blurts out. Fortunately, mute Zacharias, the biblical cipher of his predicament, also offers him a clue to its resolution by scratching his son's name
on a tablet (1.1.4). "I determined to write something," recounts Ambrose.
"A book has no feeling of modesty" (1.1.1), he adds, deeming that what a

modest bishop hesitates to utter out loud "the pen can write" (1.1.4). Ambrose will, then, "venture to compose an address" to be read, not heard (1.1.2). He will write of Christ's generation; he will "announce the family of the Lord" (1.1.4).

No sooner has Ambrose sealed his virtue within the silence of the written word than a virgin breaks startlingly through the veils of his thundering inaudibility. The bishop, for his part, indeed seems to grasp "the implications of this new situation" quite quickly. Having just begun to write, like Zacharias he suddenly finds his voice. Or perhaps it is rather the other way around: by speaking boldly about a brash-tongued girl, he gives birth to his own chaste authorship. Representing himself as preaching on the anniversary of the death and rebirth of Agnes, Ambrose turns his own reported talk of a martyr—the discourse itself a sacrificial offering, as he puts it— into the seed of a text on virgins (*Virg.* 1.2.5). Despite his initial appeal to the modesty of a written text, this swift invocation of an oral performance suggests that it is not possible after all that a brother "who cannot speak" should "venture to write" (1.1.4): rather, speaking and writing, boldness and modesty, man and virgin, must proceed hand-in-hand. Furthermore, the virgin's entrance disrupts the expectation that Christ's "generation" will be the sole or primary focus of the treatise. If Ambrose is to deal with divine family affairs, he will begin not with the conventional topics of Christ's ancestry or birth but rather with his *bride*. And, oh, how she dazzles!

Agnes is a mere girl, we quickly learn, only twelve years old when delivered up to the persecutor's sword—"not of fit age . . . , but already ripe" (*Virg.* 1.2.8). "Was there room for a wound in that body?" Ambrose wonders rhetorically.[30] The answer is no, and yet the innocent maid is more than a match for the blood-stained steel, he assures his audience, his words highlighting the thin line of a potent present that joins the child she has been to the woman she will soon become. She "offer[s] her whole body to the sword of the raging soldier, as yet ignorant of death, but ready for it" (1.2.7). Agnes's martyrdom thereby takes the place of a bride's bed, Ambrose suggests (1.2.8). The seal of her virginity, her death is also the consummation of her marriage to Christ, a spouse parodied by the figure of a trembling executioner who cannot quite bring himself to plunge his sword into the body of the fearless girl, though she declares herself more than ready. At this near-climactic moment, Ambrose suddenly speaks out directly in Agnes's voice. "He who chose me first for Himself shall receive me. Why are you delaying, executioner?" cries the eager virgin to her wilting stand-in groom (1.2.9).

Having virtually equated virginity with martyrdom by means of a starkly eroticized death that makes a girl of the world into a wife of Christ, Ambrose is in danger of seeming to urge his audience of female ascetics on toward a very bad end. He backs out of this awkward corner by addressing his "holy sister"—who is herself in the habit of keeping silence (*Virg.* 1.3.10). (Modesty runs in the family, it seems, and lineage counts for much, whether a man is a God or a bishop.) Now Ambrose sings the praises of a delicately personified "virginity," "who has found herself a spouse in heaven," a husband none other than "the Word of God," whom she "has drawn . . . into herself with her whole heart" (1.3.11). Voluptuous virginity, represented typologically in the Hebrew scriptures and imperfectly in pagan practice, first came fully when Christ planted himself in the flesh, as Ambrose explains (1.3.12–13). Exploring the topic of the inadequacy of pagan virgins, he cannot resist reintroducing the Christian Agnes to compete with the famously aphasiac Pythagorean who "bit off her tongue and spat it in the tyrant's face" (1.4.17). In Ambrose's view, there is really no contest: Agnes "did not destroy her tongue through fear, but kept it for a trophy," he brags (1.4.19). Holding her tongue and thereby preserving her integrity, the virginal Christian—bearing witness with her "carnal, passionate, body-words"—is thus fetishized as a silent icon of voice. A slim figure of speech, with scarcely room for a wound, she nevertheless encloses an Ambrosian preface of immodest proportions: "all that was still only a prelude."[31] Meanwhile, the bishop has made off with the trophy. Wagging his newly loosed tongue, Ambrose will finally begin to write his encomium of virginity.

Obedient to the dictates of rhetorical custom after all, he begins by lauding the birthplace and ancestry of his newly defined subject. Virginity is swiftly identified as a citizen of heaven (*Virg.* 1.5.20), but her family relations prove a bit more difficult to specify. Although from one perspective the "immaculate Son of God" who first implanted purity in the flesh can be identified as virginity's "author," with only a slight shift in the angle of vision "virginity" becomes the "Virgin," and she appears not as daughter but rather as mother to this twice-born child. As Ambrose expresses it paradoxically: "Christ was before the Virgin, Christ was of the Virgin; begotten indeed of the Father before the ages, but born of the Virgin for the ages" (1.5.21). Furthermore, the bishop continues serenely, "Christ is the spouse of the Virgin." Christ makes of Mary simultaneously a daughter, a mother, and a wife. Similarly, Mary makes of Christ a father, a son, and a husband. Thus, the singularly promiscuous Virgin, by repeatedly coupling with the divine Man (but never in the same position!), miraculously gives birth to the triune God of Nicene faith. With an allusion to Jeremiah's "virgin of Israel" (Jer. 18:13–14) and a neat redistribution of that biblical text's double streams of water into triple channels, Ambrose queries in disarming wonderment, "Who is this virgin that is watered with the streams of the Trinity?" And who, we might ask as well, is this many-masked Man who is also a streaming Trinity? The bishop's images slide as easily as the Virgin's relations with Christ. Initially he extracts from the prophetic text a rock (to which he appends breasts), the rock's yield of milky snow, and a tumble of fast-flowing waters "borne by the strong wind." Immediately, however, the trinitarian boulder begins to leak in the even more distinctly feminine flavors of a baptismal Eucharist—water, milk, and honey. At the next turn, the rock is reserved for designating a well-endowed Christ, whose "teats fail not," while God sheds brightness like the sun and the Spirit produces a river's rush. On the verge of lapsing into metaphoric incoherence, Ambrose quickly brings his account of divine family relations to an end:[32] "This is the Trinity which waters their Church, the Father, Christ, and the Spirit" (*Virg.* 1.5.22).

Descending abruptly from such spinning heights, he leaves the topic of the well-watered heavenly "mother" and turns instead to the more mundane praise of her virginal "daughters" (*Virg.* 1.5.23). As Yves-Marie Duval points out, this is not the only abrupt transition in the first installment of the three-book treatise *On Virginity*, into which Ambrose braids the strands of his sources, creating periodic interruptions that proliferate repetitions in incantational patterns of three: "Book I entwines . . . praise of virginity and response to objections in a balanced triple movement, as if the author started the same subject over again three times, at different levels and in different tones."[33] The theme of divine espousal is picked up and woven in again subsequently, as Ambrose notes that the church is a Virgin who painlessly "bears us her children, not by a human father, but by the Spirit." Alternatively, the Virgin's lover may appear in the guise of the Son: "she has not a husband but she has a Bridegroom"; "she weds the Word of God as her eternal Spouse" (1.6.31). Elsewhere, as we have seen, as the Son's mother, the Virgin is symmetrically—if distantly—partnered with the ever-begetting Father.

Not only the bride of this shifty Trinity but also the mother of His children, Ambrose's Virgin is nevertheless feeling no birth pangs, because her vaporous progeny never leave the paradisal womb. "A garden enclosed is my sister, my spouse, a garden enclosed, a fountain sealed (Song of Songs 4.12)," quotes Ambrose. Glossing the biblical text, he notes that virginal modesty, "fenced in by the wall of the Spirit, is enclosed lest it should lie open to be plundered"; it is "inaccessible from without" (*Virg.* 1.9.45). The church is a maternal fortress virginally intact, he continues, sheltering her children "as a wall with breasts as many towers" (1.9.49). A mother erected from pneumatic defenses, the impenetrable Virgin may indeed have concocted her pregnancy out of thin air. As if to allay such suspicions of a false conception, a rustling of feathers and a burst of applause break suddenly into Ambrose's text, announcing the stirrings of life after all, as he proclaims that another virgin has been "surrounded with a chaste band of modesty" and, having been made "forgetful of her father's house," has entered the "fenced-in home of chastity" enclosed by the wall of the bishop's own breezy discourse (1.11.61). This new arrival is the same girl whom Brown imagines to have "snapped back" at the male relative who questioned whether her deceased father would have approved her vow. Her defiant words, giving birth to her own profession, prove fatal to those who obstruct her desire: the one who has spoken in the name of the father is himself quickly stricken with a death that forcefully exposes the divine agency at work in the conception of virgins. "You see, maidens, the reward of devotion, and do you, parents, be warned by the example of transgression," Ambrose concludes his first book threateningly (1.12.66).

Ambrose's second book of *On Virgins* is both more direct in its message and simpler in its triadic structuring than the first. Even the opening performance of blushing authorial modesty proceeds relatively briskly. As praise gives way to instruction, the issue is now less the audacity of public speech per se than the inadequacy of Ambrose's topical knowledge and experience—"for he who teaches ought to excel the one who is taught" (*Virg.* 2.1.2). Agreeing to instruct them because "the virgins ask it" of him, Ambrose professes himself willing to endanger his own modesty in order to avoid disappointing the girls (2.1.3). Writing, however, is here presented more as a matter of convenience than as a necessary veil for immodest desire, and the author's eros is blatantly displaced onto the virgins: "Because many who were absent desired to have the use of my discourse, I compiled this book, so that they who hold the offering of my voice—which has set out towards them—might not think that he whom they were holding was failing them [*quo profectae ad se vocis meae munus tenentes, deesse non crederent, quem tenerent*]" (2.1.5). Indeed, Ambrose now seems to be feeling remarkably cocky. He perceives himself to be, unfailingly, a man who can offer even his absent readers something that they can cling to: he assures them that when they hold the gift of his inscribed voice (which is always reaching out, searchingly), they hold *him*—no one need find him lacking. Furthermore, although he may not have long familiarity with the life of Christian asceticism, he comes of good stock and is an eminently reflective man. When reflecting, the trick is all in the angles, as he well understands: instructing by example, he borrows his models from his pupils (who may after all excel their teacher); having been shaped in virginity's image, his own discourse thus merely returns the virgins' likeness to them, allowing them to see what they "have to correct, to effect, and to hold fast" (2.2.6).

The "life of Mary"—lauded by Charles Neumann as "the most beautiful picture of the Virgin Mary that Ambrose or for that matter any Father painted"[34]—is the first panel in the second book's specular triptych of virginal representations. The peerless Mother of God is extolled for her modesty, "companion" of all her many virtues (*Virg.* 2.2.14). If Mary's soul was utterly pure, her "outward being" was "the image of her soul": "There was nothing gloomy in her eyes, nothing forward in her words, nothing unseemly in her acts, there was not a silly movement, nor unrestrained step, nor was her voice petulant" (2.2.7). Her physical bearing thus signaled her deep-seated modesty. Indeed, the more constrained her shuffling gait, the more quickly and nimbly she seemed to advance her career: "she did not so much raise her foot in stepping as elevate the level of her virtue [*non tam vestigium pedis tolleret, quam gradum virtutis attolleret*]" (2.2.9). Small wonder her parents were able to marry her into such a fine family! (2.2.10). "Mary was such that her example alone is a lesson for all," proclaims Ambrose (2.2.15)—even as he reaches to supplement the singular image.

Mary models the perfect virginal life, but it is Thecla who teaches "how to be sacrificed," Ambrose now explains (*Virg.* 2.3.19). His meaning is not immediately clear, since an ancient reader would almost certainly know that Thecla—the well-tried heroine of apocryphal legend—does not, strictly speaking, ever achieve the exalted status of victim. The phrase does, however, recall the economy of exchange at work in Ambrose's own "sacrifice" of the virgin Agnes, whose tongue he won in the telling of her death. Thecla, while she may survive her ordeal with the beast in the arena, is, like Agnes, heavily marked in this text by the rake of the bishop's acquisitive gaze. It is, nevertheless, a mark with a difference. Where Ambrose implies that Agnes's trembling executioner eventually rises to the occasion and makes a real martyr of her, Thecla's ferocious lion becomes a virgin, and the girl—though polite enough to offer her very "vital parts" (*Virg.* 2.3.19) —is after all preserved intact. Reinterpreting tradition, Ambrose has already converted the upstart Thecla to modesty, but it is by playing fast and loose with the lions in her tale that he has put the transformation of masculinity at the center of the story. Where the second-century *Acts of Paul and Thecla* tells of a lioness martyred in the arena while successfully defending the plucky girl from an attacking male lion, Ambrose's revision introduces a single leonine adversary who learns from Thecla's melting example how to make himself virtually female according to the model of modesty. The lion's feminizing conversion to virginity proves infectious, in Ambrose's account: virility is universally tamed, as all the male beasts— most notably the human spectators—immediately drop their eyes to the ground, shrinking from the heat of Thecla's dazzling nakedness. The angle of the mirror has shifted: it is now not the female virgin but the male lions who "set an example of piety when reverencing the martyr." Thecla, it would appear, has little choice but to follow suit. They "gave a lesson in favor of chastity when they did nothing but kiss the virgin's feet, with their eyes turned to the ground, as though through modesty, fearing that any male, even a beast, should see the virgin naked" (*Virg.* 2.3.20). Performing his own act of reverence for the martyr's virginal purity, the ostensibly imitative Ambrose likewise pushes through the veils of his borrowed virtue and makes himself a model for the virgins—and indeed for us all.

But Ambrose is not yet done with teaching by example in this second book of *On Virgins*. Indeed, while seeming to proceed from the highest to the lowest,[35] he has perhaps rather saved the best for last—although hier-archical distinctions tend to be leveled, as his trinitarian structures work off the interpretive principle of forced interchangeability to achieve a maximal sharing of characteristics between persons. Whereas the bishop acknowl-edges that both Mary "the Lord's mother" and the apostolically trained Thecla may seem dauntingly distant models for some of his listeners, he promises that "a more recent example" will prove universally accessible. In-deed, his final narrative of chastity threatened and defended will leave no doubt that the apostle Paul's message concerning the value of virginity is intended not for only one sex but for all (*Virg.* 2.3.21). The virgin of this tale is unnamed but by no means undistinguished: a maiden of Antioch, her beauty was so potent that it had to be hidden, and because hidden it grew all the more potent. The fires of masculine desire fueled by her elu-sive charm could only be quenched by the rage that overtook love when she declared herself permanently off-limits by dedicating herself to an as-cetic life. "So a persecution arose," continues Ambrose, introducing a nar-rative episode that will again conflate sexual aggression with the domina-tive violence of imperial rule. Arrested, and refusing to sacrifice to the pagan gods, the virgin faces a sentence not of death but of prostitution. Playing up the thrilling horror of her impossible choice—should she tar-nish her vow to Christ by adultery of body or faithlessness in religious rite?—Ambrose puts his audience through the rhetorical paces of a mimed aural fidelity. "Close your ears, ye virgins! The Virgin of God is taken to a house of shame." Ears are closed tight and the door is shut on the virgin. "But now unclose your ears, ye virgins," Ambrose continues, anticipating miraculous encounters to come. "The Virgin of Christ can be exposed to shame, but cannot be contaminated" (*Virg.* 2.4.26). If the place still sounds all wrong, "forget the name of the place," commands Ambrose, extending the power of selective aural resistance into memory itself. Having brought his readers to a state of focused receptivity, Ambrose once again makes so bold as to speak directly in the virgin's voice. Praying, and thereby overrid-ing other named realities, the girl's speech remakes the house of prostitu-tion into a temple; she ends with an appeal that "I, who came here for shame, may go away a virgin!" (2.4.27).

The girl's triumph of transformative invocation is, however, quickly jeopardized. "Scarcely had she finished her prayer, when lo!, a man with the aspect of a terrible warrior burst in." Whereas Agnes's executioner was a bit unsteady, now it is the virgin who trembles before the swordsman. She continues, however, to invoke the magic of an optimistic renaming: "A sheep may be hidden in the shape of this wolf. Christ has His soldiers also. . . . Or, perchance, an executioner has come in" (*Virg.* 2.4.28). In a dramatic denouement, the man reveals himself to be, if not a liberating executioner like the one who finally satisfied Agnes, then a protector as eagerly imitative as Thecla's sheepish lion. "I, a brother, am come hither to save life, not to destroy it," he declares. In this tale, the desired exchange of gendered identities hinted at in the account of Thecla (who might have been known to readers of the *Acts of Paul and Thecla* as herself an occasional transvestite) is made both explicit and complete: "Let us change our attire, mine will fit you, and yours will fit me, and each for Christ," suggests the improbable lady's man (*Virg.* 2.4.29). Veiled like a virgin, the terrifying soldier will make himself nakedly vulnerable to the persecutor's sword; playing the woman, he hopes to enact martyrdom's heroics. Cloaked as a military man also suspected of being "a persecutor and adulterer," the gentle virgin will gain her freedom so as to defend her modesty; making herself male, she will rise above the ignominy of sexual shame. "Having changed her garment, the maiden flies from the snare," recounts Ambrose, "not now with wings of her own, seeing she was borne on spiritual wings" (2.4.30). Only the cross-dressed soldier remains behind in the brothel, and from the perspective of the onlookers, soldier and virgin are not two but one. "This is . . . in truth a virgin become a soldier," reports one man who is bold enough to enter the place for a peek at the girl. "Christ changed water into wine; now He has begun also to change the sexes. Let us depart hence while we still are what we were." The scene is comical and the joke is on the gullible gawker. And yet he is also a privileged witness whose testimony finally touches on the truth of the matter. The miracle is not so much that a virgin has become a soldier as that a soldier has become a virgin. "Am I too changed who see things differently from what I believe them to be?" the witness queries. "I go out chaste who came in unchaste," he concludes (2.4.31): like the soldier, he has been sexually transported.

The soldier is sentenced to die in place of the girl, sealing their exchange of identity. But the tale is not yet complete. "It is reported," adds

Ambrose ambiguously, "that the maiden ran to the place of punishment, and that they both contended for death." Deprived of the opportunity for martyrdom through the loss of the appearance of maidenhood, the virgin recognizes that she has given up too much in the trading of clothing that has allowed her to save her hymenal skin. She demands her death back from the soldier who has taken away her very capacity for a more consummating fidelity to Christ. "Beware, pray, of resisting, beware of venturing to contend with me," she warns (*Virg.* 2.4.32). Competing against each other for one victory, both virgin and soldier are winners in the end: "the crown was not divided but became two" (2.4.33). What began as a swapping of sexes has become rather a fertile proliferation of feminized virtue and its concomitant satisfactions. Ambrose seems to assure readers that, although all his own examples are admittedly "taken from virgins" (2.6.39), appropriation need not be confused with theft, when there are more than enough veils to go around.

Commencing a third book, Ambrose makes a show of finally addressing his sister directly, after having so long "digressed." He recalls the day of her profession of virginity, which was signified by a "change of attire." Having decked himself out in the instructive examples of virgins in book 2, the mute and modest bishop now seizes the opportunity to appropriate the "precepts" of Liberius, formerly bishop of Rome, as preached on the occasion of Marcellina's "espousal" to Christ. Borrowing Liberius' words, he is also laying claim to Marcellina's memory, for the sermon which Ambrose now represents himself as repeating back to her he knows from her own report (*Virg.* 3.1.1). Once again, the bishop would like to be seen as the mirror of a virgin. In this he is apparently not unlike the divine Father Himself, according to the faith confessed in the borrowed report of Liberius' discourse (3.1.4). If Christ is the Virgin's single Son, being thus "only-begotten on earth," he is likewise "only-begotten in heaven" (3.1.2). So carefully constructed is the symmetry of Christ's parentage that it becomes impossible to say who is modeling the pattern of the eternally faithful womb for whom: "He it is whom the Father begat before the morning star, as being eternal, He brought Him forth from the womb as the Son; He uttered him from His heart as the Word . . . , for He proceeded from the mouth of God" (3.1.3).

After duly dispensing Liberius's motherly advice on the chaste upbringing of maidens, Ambrose once again defers to a woman's desires. "As I am drawing near the close of my address, you make a good suggestion, holy sister," he remarks, elaborately performing his compliance with Marcellina's request that he consider the possible merits of a literal self-sacrifice. From Ambrose's perspective, where martyrdom is discussed, the topic is still virginity, and "as regards virgins placed in the necessity of preserving their purity" the answer appears "plain" (*Virg.* 3.7.32). The tale of Pelagia leaves little doubt, he is certain, as to the virtue of self-immolation in the event of imperiled virginity—and when is virginity *not* at risk? This fifteen-year-old maiden, "seeing herself surrounded by those who would rob her of her faith and purity," took the matter of martyrdom into her own hands, not awaiting the help of an executioner where seemingly none was forthcoming. "I can die by my own weapons," she proclaimed, deeming even a sword's thrust a nonviolent act of self-care because entirely voluntary (3.7.33). If all of Ambrose's bridal *exempla* derive much of their power from proximity to the parodic, here (in conclusion) he draws closer than ever to a crudely literalizing enactment of a complex metaphor, once again resorting to a change in clothes to make his point. "She is said to have adorned her head and to have put on a bridal dress; one might therefore say that she was going to a bridegroom, not to death," he relates (3.7.34). Where Agnes was suggestively positioned as both like and unlike a bride, acquiescing eagerly to a death by the sword that was nevertheless delivered at least partly against her will, Pelagia, dressed to kill, leaves little to the imagination and nothing to chance, having explicitly taken on the roles of both the bride and her phallic executioner. And since, as Ambrose reminds her, his sister is not merely the disciple but—as descendent of one "holy Sotheris," another virginal martyr—the *heir* of girls like this (3.7.38–39), is the legacy not also his?

Only so long as he dresses like a virgin. In a treatise entitled *On Widows*, written soon after the three books of *On Virgins*, Ambrose makes it clear how different are his views of *men* who voluntarily "use the sword against themselves." Involuntary eunuchs may achieve the neutrality of sexual irrelevance: escaping the sin of unchastity, they are nevertheless denied the virtue of chastity. *Self*-castration, however, is another matter, seeming to broadcast "a declaration of weakness rather than a reputation of strength." Ambrose notes with dismay that "on this principle no one should fight, lest he be overcome, nor make use of his feet, fearing the danger of stumbling,

nor let his eyes do their office because he fears a fall through lust," concluding that "it becomes us to be chaste, not weak, to have our eyes modest, not
feeble" (*Vid.* 76). Having reached this point of clarity, the bishop's rhetoric
gains momentum: "No one then ought . . . to mutilate himself, but rather
gain the victory; for the Church gathers in those who conquer, not those
who are defeated" (*Vid.* 77). The troubling energies of a violent and uncon-
trolled sexuality cannot be confined to the male genitalia and then simply
pared away: "what does it profit to cut the flesh, when there may be guilt
even in a look?" (*Vid.* 76). Yet it would seem that a Christian's virile strength
cannot be altogether dissociated from the male organ, either. "For why
should the means of gaining a crown and of the practice of virtue be lost to
a man who is born to honour, equipped for victory?" queries Ambrose.
"How can he through courage of soul mutilate himself?" (*Vid.* 77). The resonance of the image of a sword turned against the self hints at a parallel positioning of the figures of the self-martyred virgin and the self-castrated eunuch. Ambrose, however, raises the possibility only to reject it sharply: by
refusing the analogy, he both protects the hierarchy of gender established by
relations of penetration and heightens the eroticism of an ascetic body that
transforms a negation into an affirmation—indeed a consummation—of
desire.[36] For the virgin martyr, "no" means "yes."

In the treatise *On Virgins* Ambrose appropriates the figure of the martyred virgin, who maintains the integrity of her body and faith by welcoming the plunge of the executioner's sword that makes her a bride of
Christ. However, the bishop's superficially feminized preoccupation with
intactness veils, and also reveals, the contours of an underlying masculinity,
which resists "mutilation" and indeed configures itself as the precondition
for a manly "victory." Ambrose's fascination with the dazzling daughters of
virginity—those typical women in all their force—thus constitutes a will-
ful act of seduction that, through a trick of refractive circulation, owns and
thereby also *dis*owns the accusatory image of the hysteric's sexual panic.

Reproducing Orthodoxy: 'On the Faith' and 'On the Spirit'

Two petals which meet and embrace endlessly: movement-trace of the
copula? the engendering, metastable, of one petal by the other, the
engorging of the petal, at the same time for both. Not the outpouring

from the one to the other, nor even from the one into the other. The
mysterious energy of the copula, rediscovering a buried source.
Hidden before the separation of the elements? Before hatred?

—*Luce Irigaray,*
Elemental Passions

The importance of Ambrose as a theologian has not hitherto been
adequately realized. He has been thrown into the shade by Augustine.
The lesser genius has been absorbed by the greater. Yet this Doctor may
claim a distinguished place in the history of Western theology. He was the
mediator between Eastern and Western theological speculations; he was the
ancestor of the Western mystics; he was, in many respects, the anticipator
of medieval Catholicism. He was also . . . an Augustine before Augustine.
Possibly his significance in the history of theology lies principally in this,
that he was by far the richest and greatest of the tributaries which fed that
mighty river of Augustinian thought and teaching which for so many
centuries fertilized the intellect of the Western world.

—*F. Homes Dudden,*
The Life and Times of Saint Ambrose

At best, Ambrose's dissemination of the trinitarian theology of the East
wins him a condescending appreciation, allowing his notorious sloppiness
and apparent lack of creativity to be excused as the result of a hectic sched-
ule. At worst, he is depicted as a vulgar plagiarizer incapable of grasping the
profundity of the Greek sources from which he snuck his lines. As Christoph Markschies comments wryly, "The current widespread depiction of
the trinitarian theological work of the Milanese bishop can scarcely be described as particularly friendly."[37] Even so sympathetic a biographer as
F. Homes Dudden, who highlights Ambrose's crucial influence "in deter-
mining Western belief with regard to the Person and Work of the Holy
Ghost," nevertheless suggests that his treatise *On the Holy Spirit* "has little
claim to originality" beyond its mere Latinity. The same scholar represents
Ambrose as a "mediator" between East and West and a "great tributary" to
the oceanic genius of Augustine. While protesting loudly that there is "no
excuse for the rudeness of Jerome," Homes Dudden makes sure that his
readers do not miss Jerome's caustic critique: Ambrose, we are to know, was
"described . . . as a jackdaw tricked out with other birds' plumage and

charged . . . with spoiling the good things which he had pilfered from the Greeks."[38]

Reading Ambrose the theologian as anything other than derivative or contributory is, evidently, not easy. The challenge lies, perhaps, in comprehending "the mysterious energy of the copula." Like the Virgin Mother or the Holy Ghost, the Milanese bishop is evocatively positioned as "a 'bond,' a 'middle' or an 'interval.'"[39] If, however, Ambrose's "middling" theologizing is not adequately captured in the metaphor of "the outpouring from the one to the other, nor even from the one into the other," how *are* we to give substance to this conjunctive third, whose "importance . . . has not hitherto been adequately realized"? Although a seemingly ineluctable historiographic tradition destines him to mediate between the Greek Fathers and a filially self-positioned Augustine, Ambrose cannot be reduced to a mere conduit, if we adhere to even the weakest logic of personhood. As Markschies has argued, the act of translating the evolving technical terminology of Greek trinitarian thought into Latin vocabulary, while also drawing on the existing linguistic resources of the Western Christian tradition, required considerable "creativity" on Ambrose's part and resulted in the emergence of a distinctive Latin Neo-Nicene theology partly shared with men like Marius Victorinus and Augustine.[40] Perhaps we should therefore attempt to search out the textual traces of the Latin lover of God *in his very linguistic particularity*, taking the hint from the patternings of his own trinitarian thought as we read this Doctor of the Western Spirit. We may then find that Ambrose's polemically pro-Nicene writings, studded with the stolen trophies of a triumphalistic faith in the patrilineal production of the same, *also* betray a subtly different copulation: one in which like engenders like, originality is beside the point, and divinity itself—now laid flat—thickens with the excitement of an expanding mutuality of exchange, within and between the one that is manifold and the many enfolded as one.

Ambrose's major doctrinal works are apologetic tracts written relatively early in his career, which skillfully exceed—and thus partly reverse—their own ostensibly modest objectives of compliance and self-defense, as the bishop seizes a time of trial as a moment for witness. "It is the Augustus, ruler of the whole world, that has commanded the setting forth of the faith in a book, not for your instruction, but for your approval," Ambrose ac-

knowledges, in an address to the emperor Gratian penned sometime between late 378 and mid 380 (and thus no more than about two years later
than *On Virgins*) (*Fid.* 1.prol.1).[41] Having been commanded, Ambrose has
no choice but to give an account of his belief, in a context in which his homoian rivals are accusing him of heresy; he writes not for Gratian's instruction, but for his approval, as he says. Yet by a trick of negation, he
insinuates himself rhetorically into the very role he claims to disavow,
emerging as an authoritatively orthodox teacher who can be judged by
God alone. The writing of the first two books of the treatise *On the Faith*
"marked a turning-point in Ambrose's career," as Daniel Williams observes.[42] It is no accident, but rather a tribute to his skills of persuasion,
that an author for whom humility is a favorite pose has here been routinely
mistaken as falsely modest, to the great benefit of his episcopal fame: "Gratian's instruction that Ambrose write 'something about the faith' has traditionally been regarded as a straightforward request from a zealously orthodox but theologically untutored youth, to a bishop whose reputation was
already established."[43] Compelled by a skeptical emperor to defend his
own orthodoxy, as he himself admits, Ambrose—following a most un-
straightforward rhetorical route—tricks his readers into perceiving him as
championing Nicaea before a hostile world at the invitation of an upright
youth. Submitting reluctantly to a ruler's demands, he delivers his own
risky opinions on the proper comportment of a Christian prince, opinions
successfully dressed up as the welcomed advice of an esteemed mentor.

To pull off this act—dubbed by McLynn as "misrepresentation on a
heroic scale"[44]—Ambrose must remain rhetorically nimble, to say the least:
in relation to Gratian, he will prove a distinctly shifty subject. Having first
carefully marked his subordinate status as one "commanded," the bishop
adjusts his position subtly in order to address the emperor man-to-man.
Gratian is about to go to war; Ambrose is about to write a book; and both
are equipping themselves for victories that are to be "gained more by faith
in the commander than by valour in the soldiers," as he argues. Indeed,
their roles are practically identical, Ambrose now audaciously proposes,
performing a rhetorical *communicatio idiomatum*: the emperor setting out
to fight the Goths is addressed as one who "worships Christ" and "defends
the faith" (*Fid.* 1.prol.3), while the bishop embarking upon a theological
campaign is aligned with the Nicene Fathers, who (by establishing a creed)

raised a "trophy" announcing their victory over the faithless "throughout the world" (1.prol.5). Enclosed within this enacted exchange that casts the two men as equals as well as allies in war is, however, yet another self-depiction of the bishop, in which we may observe a seeming hesitancy serving the still more immodest purposes of one-upmanship. Although he has agreed to write, Ambrose here pauses momentarily to showcase an inner reluctance: "truly, I would rather take upon me the duty of exhortation to keep the Faith, than that of disputing thereon." Worried about falling into "rash presumption," he implies that he is even more anxious about seeming to shirk his "duty of loyalty" to the emperor. Thus, as requested, he "will take in hand a bold enterprise"—but he will do so "modestly," he adds. Ambrose immediately spells out what this compromise with modesty entails: eschewing the conventions of dialectical argument, he will instead "gather together a multitude of witnesses" (1.prol.4). The chaste manhood that leads a Christianized empire to victory will rise above even rhetorical swordplay, Ambrose suggests; he prefers to intimidate by a forceful show of numbers rather than submit to the uncertainties of close combat. And where does this restyling of male supremacy leave the swashbuckling emperor? He remains exactly where Ambrose has placed him in the very first sentence: "The Queen of the South, as we read in the book of Kings, came to hear the wisdom of Solomon" (*Fid.* 1.prol.1). In fact, we read in the book of Kings that the queen came to *test* the wisdom of Solomon with hard questions—but by the end of the visit, the tables had been turned (1 Kings 10). Gratian, the Sheba in this text, faces some hard questions about his manhood.[45]

At this point, Ambrose moves briskly to satisfy the emperor's request by proclaiming his faith in the triune God (*Fid.* 1.1.6–1.4.33). A mere profession is, however, not nearly enough to satisfy Ambrose himself, who will after all take a stab at "dialectical disputation" with those whom he boldly labels "Arians," while claiming merely to mirror the wrangling style and blasphemous theological platform of the very men who have cast aspersions on his own orthodoxy (1.5.42). Ambrose's reluctance to engage his opponents is clearly feigned. Accuracy, consistency, or the construction of a sustained argument will, however, prove irrelevant to his polemical purposes. If Ambrose jumbles the names and doctrinal positions of various anti-Nicene theologians, this only serves to heighten the dizzying (even

nauseating) chaos by which he produces the disgust of heresy in his text.[46]
He makes a show of fussing and fretting: "But why they will not agree with
one another, I do not understand" (1.6.44). Dissension, we comprehend, is
beyond the comprehension of a tidily orthodox mind. Ambrose's accusers
"do not agree among themselves." However, to impose order, he will address them "by the common name of heretics." Thus through a trick of la-
beling, heresy finally emerges into view as a single entity, and when it does,
it appears as unstable and monstrously multiple as the legendary hydra,
whose heads, if severed, increase exponentially in number. As if that sight
were not enough to make a man sheath his sword, Ambrose introduces a
second many-headed mythological *exemplum*: "like some dread and monstrous Scylla, divided into many shapes of unbelief, she displays, as a mask
to her guile, the pretense of being a Christian sect." From Scylla's "cruel
fang," Ambrose's gaze drifts downward to her fantastic belt of bestial unchastity and thence to "the monster's cave"—"thick laid, as seafaring men
do say it is, with hidden lairs." By this point, he scarcely needs to voice his
warnings to steer clear of such treacherous waters. The text echoes with the
fearsome howling of Scylla's black dogs (1.6.46–47). Being "willing to exhibit" the abysmal horrors of heresy, Ambrose can almost dispense with
verbal debate (1.9.58). Indeed, it seems he will have to: before the mysteries of divine generation that are at the heart of the theological dispute, "the
mind fails, the voice is dumb" (1.10.64).

Ambrose will continue, then, to tell by showing, as he moves from
these specters of heresy to the wonders of orthodox faith. The central ex-
hibits, however, remain veiled, with the viewers' cooperation. "Do thou,
then (like the angels), cover thy face with thy hands, for it is not given thee
to look into surpassing mysteries!" (*Fid.* 1.10.65). What is required is a trick
of speculation, some fancy work with the mirrors of imagination, that will
allow his readers a glimpse of the scene of primal begetting without risking
the potentially devastating disillusionment of a full exposure. Here is what
we might—but ought not to—suppose, "borrowing from the custom of
human generation": "that the Father bare the Son in a bodily womb, and
laboured under the burden while ten months sped their courses." The
problem is obvious enough to the clear-sighted and commonsensical Ambrose: generation "as it commonly takes place" requires "difference of sex"
(1.11.72); "surely the common order is determined by difference of sex"

(1.12.78). "Cease, then, to apply to the Godhead what is proper only to created existences," Ambrose commands his constructed audience of would-be reconstructed heretics. "Or, if you insist upon forcing the comparison" —a tantalizing thought!—"bethink you whither your wickedness leads" (1.12.74). Ambrose directs the eyes of his listeners' imagination away from the Father's lack and instead toward the Virgin's womb: the miracle of "birth without the seed of a man" stands as a guarantee of the wonder of Christ's generation from the wombless Father (1.12.77). Indeed, it is a match made in heaven, as far as the Ambrosian aesthetic is concerned: the perfectly balanced symmetry of parentage that produces the intimate and delicate conjunction of a two-natured Christ in effect restores the aspect of "sexual difference" that so preoccupies Ambrose in its lack. It is, however, sexual difference of an uncommon order, producing mutual autonomies that result in an abstracted act of intercourse occurring in no time and space. The primal scene cannot be seen.

Only the "Arians" try to put false color on all that near-invisibility by imagining an all-too-human Father who preceded his Son (*Fid.* 1.18.119). Such fatal vulgarities of theological output are matched by the grotesque image of Arius, "wallowing amid the outgush of his very bowels," "burst asunder in the midst, falling headlong, and besmirching [his] foul lips." Ambrose would rather throw in his lot with "St. John, who lay on Christ's bosom," his lips close to the source of the purifying drink pressed from the crucified body that hung like a cluster of grapes on a vine (1.19.123–24, 1.20.135). Here sexual difference once again seems to layer itself across the male body, and—despite his rejection of "Arian" literalism—Ambrose cannot resist another peek at "the womb of the Father," the "Father's inmost, unapproachable sanctuary," an organ of generation borrowed from the Virgin for the veiling of a mystery (1.19.126). The enacted banishing-and-summoning of his imperious discourse—now you see it, now you don't, but *what* and *whose* is "it"?—seems intended to draw our gaze "past the mother's presence, in the mother, beyond-veil, to the presence of God, beyond the sky, beyond the visual horizon." If *something* of the Mother is being sent beyond, "with the help of a more or less white, more or less transparent veil," it is not after all "some phallus she guards jealously—even if this is a condition he depends on—but rather the mystery of a first crypt, a first and longed-for dwelling place."[47] The Father's secret is his stolen womb.

Acknowledging that what he has already written in response to Gratian's request is "plentiful even to overflowing," Ambrose seems nevertheless to hope to drown out all opposition by composing another book (*Fid.* 2.prol.2). He begins this second volume with a glistening display of finery, arranging the crystalline terms of his discussion in symmetrical patterns—three groups of four, "close joined and fitting one into another" like the tribes of Israel, "woven into the robe of holy Aaron" like so many gleaming jewels, "sardius, jasper, smaragd, chrysolite, and the rest" (2.prol.2–4). Decked out in such exotic vestments, the episcopal discourse proceeds ceremoniously to celebrate the scripturally recorded manifestations of the goodness and power of the fully divine Son. Those adversaries who have not been healed by the kindness of Ambrose's persuasive word (2.11.89–90) are, finally, summoned to be judged for dishonoring God's noble offspring (2.12.100), in a mock trial in which the sentence has been pronounced in advance (2.14.123). Descending from the seat of judgment, Ambrose recalls momentarily who is actually being interrogated by whom: "These arguments, your Majesty, I have set forth, briefly and summarily, in the rough. . . . If indeed the Arians regard them as imperfect and unfinished, I indeed confess that they are scarce even begun" (2.15.129). With this gentle threat to reopen the floodgates of the language of faith, should his accusers (or his emperor) not find his defense sufficient, Ambrose feigns sudden recollection of Gratian's urgent military task: "I must no further detain your Majesty, in this season of preparation for war, and the achievement of victory over the Barbarians. Go forth, sheltered, indeed, under the shield of faith, and girt with the sword of the Spirit" (2.16.136). Once again, the roles of emperor and bishop are knit tightly together within the weave of military metaphors. Ambrose, who lends Gratian the weapons of faith in the battle with the Goths, expresses confidence that he can expect in exchange the emperor's support in his own "contest with unbelief" (2.16.139). The homoian Christians—displaced in Ambrose's rhetoric from Milan to the borderlands where Gratian is campaigning[48]—cannot be counted on to defend the Roman state against barbarians from whose babbling their mingled blasphemies can scarcely be distinguished (2.16.140). Gratian should rather align himself with the core of Italy's upright and articulate manhood; *thus* will he demonstrate that there is after all "no wavering mind [*mens lubrica*] in our emperor, but faith firm fixed [*fides fixa*]" (2.16.142).[49]

In the event, the anti-Nicene Christians whom Ambrose had at-tempted to push beyond the margins of an imperial orthodoxy were not in the least satisfied with his profession of faith. The fierce attack led by the elderly Illyrican bishop Palladius seems to have resulted not only in Ambrose's rapid addition of three more books to his apologetic *On the Faith* but also in a request from Gratian that he expand his statement to address the difficult and apparently unresolved question of whether the Spirit was God. By spring of 381, Ambrose had responded to this request with the three books of *On the Holy Spirit*.[50] Seemingly somewhat more secure and optimistic in his political positioning—and thus less stridently defen-sive—he writes with the confidence of the well-read scholar in tackling a notoriously controversial topic. Deftly invoking the traditional spectrum of prophetic, christological, and eschatological activities of the Spirit, Am-brose begins by nudging these scattered fragments into coherence under the mythically masculine metaphors of the shower of rain and the sprin-kling of dew by which the earth is made fertile. Shifting fluidly from the Old Testament to the New, he evokes the more complex image of foot-washing. Not only the feet of the body but also "the feet of our minds" and "the footsteps of the soul" are cleansed and enlivened by the Holy Spirit, as Ambrose phrases it fancifully (*Spir.* 1.prol.1–18).[51] The skin-drenching Spirit of God, penetrating down to the very soles of humanity's physical *and* psychic feet, may seem in danger of being reduced to a principle of di-vine immanence and thereby consigned to a mediatory ontological sta-tus—as, indeed, a homoian perspective might have it. Ambrose, however, insists firmly and repeatedly that "the Holy Spirit . . . is not among but above all things" (1.1.19); "the Holy Spirit is not . . . of the substance of things corporeal, for He sheds incorporeal grace on corporeal things; nor, again, is He of the substance of invisible creatures, for they receive His sanctification" (1.5.62). Far from being degraded to quasi-materiality, the Spirit is privileged as the marker of the divinity's absolute *transcendence* of materiality. As proof that the Holy Spirit "is not among but above," Am-brose cleverly recounts Gratian's recent and unexpected restoration of a formerly "sequestered" basilica to the Nicene party of Milan—an imperial fiat explainable (or so he implies) as nothing less than an irruption of tran-scendent power, a divine "gift" from outside the very order of creation. Once again, emperor and bishop are as one through a conjunction of word and deed: the Holy Spirit "was at that time preached by us, but was working in you" (1.1.20–21).

Ambrose's discussion of foot-washing has baptismal overtones—and indeed his words suggest that Christ's cleansing of the disciple's feet may have been reperformed by the bishop himself in the contemporary Milanese rite. The sanctifying act thus calls to mind the Scripture's most quotable trinitarian formula, a favored prooftext for the Spirit's divinity: "Go and teach all nations, baptizing them in the name of the Father and of the Son and of the Holy Ghost" (Matt. 28:19).[52] As Ambrose frames the matter, it was—scripturally—in "the sacrament of baptism" that the Spirit "was joined to the Father and the Son" (*Spir.* 1.4.55). He refrains, however, from *explicitly* invoking the crucial Matthean passage in his introduction and in the immediately subsequent analysis of the biblical language of baptism—although the verse almost breaks the surface of citationality several times, as in the statement that "baptism is complete if one confess the Father, the Son, and the Holy Spirit" (1.3.42). This reticence is not accidental. The uncited text of triune naming stands in for a discourse both complete and unitive that *need not* be named in so many words; it is most frequently "left . . . to be understood" (1.3.32). For Ambrose, the metonymic slide of trinitarian truth is automatic and indeed irresistible: in theological language, any part attracts the whole, and fullness can always be abbreviated without loss, even as one partial naming can be swapped for another. "He who is blessed in Christ is blessed in the Name of the Father, and of the Son, and of the Holy Spirit, because the Name is one and the Power one; so, too, when any divine operation, whether of the Father, or of the Son, or of the Holy Spirit, is treated of, it is not referred only to the Holy Spirit, but also to the Father and the Son, and not only to the Father, but also to the Son and the Spirit" (1.3.40). Ambrose's method of trinitarian exegesis is thus already in full circulation early in the first book. Later, when he does directly cite the Matthean commissioning, he will not linger over the tripartite formula itself. Rather, he suppresses any Origenian troping of the fracturing nature of linguistic expression—in which God's begetting of the Word is also the proliferation of divine "names"—in favor of emphasizing the "oneness" or "unity of Name" (1.13.132). "There is no difference of Name in the Father, the Son, and the Holy Spirit; and that which is the Name of the Father is also the Name of the Son, and likewise that which is the Name of the Son is also that of the Holy Spirit, when the Son also is called Paraclete, as is the Holy Spirit" (1.13.156). This principle of promiscuous substitutability is both derived from Scripture and immediately folded back into the interpretation of the text. Studying the writings with an eye for pattern, Ambrose extrapolates *identity* from syntactic and semantic *similarity* by reading the trace of difference as an encrypting of sameness. With the code cracked, words are released into the dynamic —but still highly controlled—flow of linguistic decomposition and recombination, by which the one multiplies and the many unite as one. "We have said that the Father is Light, the Son is Light, and the Holy Spirit is Light; let us also learn that the Father is Life, the Son Life, and the Holy Spirit Life" (1.15.171).

But what of the Spirit's unique personhood? Pursuing the Holy Ghost, Ambrose puts a distinctive spin on his Trinity without quite succeeding in delineating the Spirit's difference. Indeed, at times the specifiability of this Third as "person" seems almost beside the point; rather, its *im*personality functions both to enhance and to complicate the personhood of Father and Son. Producer and sustainer of the fertile interrelations of theological titles and names, the mediating Spirit prevents the Father-Son dyad from being either dissolved into a modalistic monism or separated by a static subordinationism. "God, then, sheds forth of the Spirit, and the love of God is also shed abroad through the Spirit," quotes Ambrose (*Spir.* 1.8.94; cf. Rom. 5:5). The Spirit is the copulative energy shining out from the Father, "shedding" his love, "poured forth from the mouth of God" (*Spir.* 1.8.97), begetting the born-again Son as the Virgin's offspring (2.5.43). The Spirit is also the undying seed of divinity perduring in Christ, the enfleshed presence of the only-begotten Logos himself. "So, then, both the Father is Spirit and Christ is Spirit . . . , but the Holy Spirit is not commingled with the Father and the Son, but is distinct from the Father and from the Son" (1.9.106). Distinct from the persons of Father and Son but seemingly inconceivable without them, the Spirit enables *both* the unconfused particularity of Father and Son in relation to one another *and* their subtle, interpenetrating continuity. Like "a cord, a placental-veil, a womb-bed,"[53] Ambrose's partially transparent Ghost of Holiness is suspended across every site of separateness and interchange, between divine Parent and Son, between heavenly Father and virginal Mother, between God and creation's flesh, measuring the interval that is the condition of an interrelatedness grounded in both multiplicity and unity, difference and identity.

In a surprising cameo appearance at the beginning of book 2, Samson fleetingly brings the Spirit of copulation down to earth in a crudely phallic guise—indeed, he seems to bring it very low indeed. Ambrose's cue is the cited word of Scripture: "the Spirit of the Lord began to be with him in the camp [Judg. 13:25]." "Foreshadowing the future mystery [*sacramentum*]," as he puts it, the sturdy hero, under divine inspiration, "demanded a wife from the aliens." But precisely what sacrament of conjunctive desire is here foreshadowed? Even as we are led to wonder, the text begins to proliferate new sacraments, mysteries, and questions, layering them onto the initial enigma. "As he was going to his marriage [*mysterium nuptiarum*], a roaring lion met him." No blushing Thecla, brawny Samson bare-handedly rips into the beast, "in whose body, when about to enjoy the wished-for wedlock, he found a swarm of bees, and took honey from its mouth." So we have it: as he was going to his marriage, about to enjoy the wished-for wedlock, Samson discovered in the sundered leonine body of his hypermasculine desire a habitation for bees and a receptacle for honey's yielding sweetness. "And it does not seem to have been without purpose," Ambrose intones purposefully. It seems that Samson, as the Spirit's newest strongman, is after all yet another lion converted by virginity's feminizing love. If the lion is already familiar from *On Virgins* as a metaphor for the conversion of manhood, so too is the purportedly parthenogenic bee as a sign for the converted virginal soul who drinks in the divine dew and gives forth her honey: "Virginity is fit to be compared to bees, so laborious is it, so modest, so continent. The bee feeds on dew, it knows no marriage couch, it makes honey" (*Virg.* 1.8.40). Confronted with the mystery of his own experience, Samson poses it as a riddle for his friends: "out of the eater came forth meat, and out of the strong came forth sweetness." They answer with a question: "what is sweeter than honey, and what is stronger than a lion?" The knowing query betrays the secret of Samson's companions' illicit collusion with his carnal bride, as he acknowledges with yet more encoded speech: "if you had not farmed with my heifer, you would not have found out my riddle." What *is* the riddle's secret, who interprets it rightly, and why is Ambrose so giddy with delight? "O divine mystery! O manifest sacrament!" At this point in the bishop's narration, the Spirit comes again upon Samson, and he kills his erstwhile companions, his inspired victory represented as a mark of the sharpness of his insight, as well as wisdom's reward. Such feats of wondrous strength have nothing to do with literal hairstyles, as the bishop remarks scornfully, but are characteristic of the man who has not yet "fallen from his virtue on the knees of a woman, caressed, captivated," and thereby "shorn" of his manhood (*Spir.* 2.prol.1–16). The Holy Spirit is, evidently, a terrible thing to waste on a wife.

"So much concerning the mystery [*de mysterio*]," concludes Ambrose. "Let us now consider the order of the passage [*lectionis seriem*]," he proposes, veering back into the more sober domain of linguistic analysis, without altogether abandoning either the text or the topic of its nuptial mystery. The interchangeable use of the terms "Lord" (by which Ambrose understands the Son), "Spirit," and "Spirit of the Lord" indicates again the oneness of substance and name in the Godhead (*Spir.* 2.1.17–18). "And what wonder is it that the Spirit works Life, Who quickens as does the Father and as does the Son? . . . The Spirit quickens," the bishop repeats (2.4.29–30). The impregnating powers of the Holy Spirit are easily exemplified in the virgin birth: "The fruit of the womb is the work of the Spirit." A fruit, Christ is also a flower. Mary is thereby no longer merely a womb but also a rod (*virga*). "The root of Jesse the patriarch is the family of the Jews, Mary is the rod, Christ the flower of Mary" (2.5.38). The tireless Holy Spirit—seemingly displaced by Mary's swelling *virga*, the rod bridging the gap between paternal root and filial bud—returns nevertheless to rest on Christ her feminized flower, who is no less fragrant and lovely after having been pierced by the lance (2.5.39). "So then we cannot doubt that the Spirit is Creator, whom we know as the author of the Lord's incarnation" (2.5.41). "How, then was Mary with child of the Holy Spirit? If, as it were, of substance, was the Spirit, then, changed into flesh and bones?" queries Ambrose. "Certainly not! But if the Virgin conceived of His operation and power, who can deny that the Holy Spirit is Creator?" (2.5.43). Perhaps now we have reached the heart of the mystery foreshadowed in Samson's spiritual desire for a wife.

Spiritual conception turns out to be very much a product of a literal (as well as a strongly intertextual) reading of Scripture. Ambrose worries about "variations in the Latin codices, some of which heretics have falsified" and recommends consultation of the Greek, where the command to "serve the

Spirit of God [Phil. 3:3]," neatly aligning with the implied admonition not "to serve the creature rather than the Creator [Rom. 1:25]," is made clear (*Spir.* 2.5.44–47). The argument frequently turns not only on words but on mere syllables (2.8.70). While following his Greek precursors in demonstrating the interchangeability of prepositions in Scripture (by which Basil, for example, deconstructs the hierarchy potentially inscribed by the liturgy's doxological text, in his own treatise *On the Spirit*), Ambrose moves more quickly to put the *copulative* function of such particles at the symbolic center of the scriptural grammar that produces the Spirit's divinity. If "the Apostle" apparently makes little distinction between prepositional particles, this is because such syllabic units are already terms of conjunction, he suggests somewhat airily; "and conjunction does not cause separation, for if it divided it would not be called a conjunction" (2.8.77). His confidence in the completeness of Scripture's capacity to embrace trinitarian theology is finally greater than Basil's: whereas the Cappadocian Father had marked the limits of the written word for delineating an explicitly trinitarian doctrine of the Spirit (*On the Spirit* 27.66–67), Ambrose seems to find an excess of Spirit in the text. The Spirit becomes intimately associated not only with the briefest connective particles of speech but finally with the fecundity of the letter itself.

This theme continues in the more overtly polemical third book. If the Son is the hand of God, the Spirit is the divine finger, argues Ambrose. "With this finger, as we read, God wrote on those tables of stone which Moses received." Although citing Paul in his interpretation of Moses, Ambrose does not seek so much to separate as to *conjoin* the written "letter" and the sublime "spirit" of the law (cf. 2 Cor. 3:6): "For the law is spiritual, which, indeed, is written not with ink, but with the Spirit of the living God; not in tables of stone, but on fleshy tables of the heart [2 Cor. 3:3]," he quotes. As author of Scripture, God inscribes his letters simultaneously on the page and on the human being, body and soul; writing carnally with the finger of his Spirit, he does not stain but illumines the "secret places of our minds and hearts," insists Ambrose. If Moses' tablets were broken, the divine letters were not thereby lost (*Spir.* 3.3.11–14). Nor can the "heretics"—through an attempted erasure of the letters of Scripture—blot out the Spirit of God, planted in the flesh of human memory and history (and preserved in more authentic copies of the text!) (3.10.59–

60). To read spiritually is therefore also to read carnally: only a close pe-
rusal of the letter of God's Word reproduces the Spirit of his law. The
Holy Ghost is the divine copula, the finger of God by which the sublime
Word is sunk into both flesh and text. In affirming the palpable power of
the Spirit lodged in the Scripture, Ambrose says simply: "I lean on what is
written" (2.10.64).

Leaning on what Ambrose himself has written, Christoph Markschies
has suggested that we view the Milanese theologian not as "an Augustine
before Augustine" but rather as the author of a distinctive form of "Latin
Neo-Nicenism": mining the resources of a traditional Latin theological vocabulary, Ambrose fashioned a remarkably simple and elegant container for
Greek trinitarian truths, thereby freeing them of the sometimes jargonistic
complexities generated by theologians like Gregory of Nyssa.[54] However, it
is possible that Ambrose's originality lies as much in the complexity of his
figures as in the simplicity of his terminology, and that in this respect his
theology is no more (if also no less) "Cappadocian" than it is "Augustinian." The arresting characters that Ambrose has placed on his doctrinal
page frequently waver and shift, fracture and merge in turn. At first glance,
his trinitarian personae may appear all to be cut of the same masculine
cloth—like identical triplets. And yet, under closer inspection, that very
cloth of manhood begins to look suspiciously like a virgin's veil. Indeed,
neither Father, Son, nor Spirit can stop playing the virgin in Ambrose's
texts, and this may be in part because they depend on the currency of a
"fem(m)inized" virginity to secure their distinct positions and relations
within a "hom(m)o-sexual" economy of mutual exchange.[55] Where the
ghostly Virgin is the signifier of the womb that the heavenly Father both
does and does not have or need, she can also be offered as an eternally un-
touched bride for his divinely motherless Son—even as she materializes to
give birth to the Son's humanity. It is, however, the conjunction of the Virgin and the Spirit under the sign of holiness that makes *almost* visible the
copulative act that continually generates a sameness always marked by difference, in a trinitarian God whose most telling issue is the irreducibly hybrid figure of the two-natured Christ. If the Virgin is the receptacle of the
seed of the Spirit, she is also the honey bee contained within his leonine
skin, and how is one finally to decide *who* is borrowing *whose* clothes in
such a spectacle of sexual exchange? For the "Neo-Nicene" Ambrose, the

shimmeringly cross-dressed Spirit of Virginity betrays the "mysterious energy of the copula" that may finally produce a God that is not one.

Making Modest Men: 'On the Duties'

A history of "codes" would analyze the different systems of rules and values
that are operative in a given society or group. . . . A history of the way in
which individuals are urged to constitute themselves as subjects of moral
conduct would be concerned with the models proposed for setting up and
developing relationships with the self, for self-reflection, self-knowledge,
self-examination, for the decipherment of the self by oneself, for the
transformations one seeks to accomplish with oneself as object. This . . .
is what might be called a history of "ethics" and "ascetics," understood
as a history of the forms of moral subjectivation and of the practices
of self that are meant to ensure it.

—*Michel Foucault,*
The Use of Pleasure

Ambrose, in his *De officiis,* expressly acknowledges that Cicero's *De officiis* is
his model, which gives a ready-made basis for comparison [of their ethics].
One of the issues I want to consider is how faithful Ambrose actually was to
his announced model. . . . Ambrose makes two general points about
virtue. . . . First, he remarks, following Panaetius, in discriminating among
the duties the individual should consider his age, situation, and talents. Like
Cicero, he omits the factor of sex, but for practical, not for conventional or
sexist reasons: his book is for priests, an exclusively masculine occupational
group. Second, Ambrose's Stoicism is susceptible of permeation by other
philosophical traditions. He counsels *decorum* in the exercise of all the
virtues, a wholly Stoic idea. At the same time, he interprets *decorum* in
the light of the Aristotelian golden mean: "hold to the mean in all
things" (*modum tenere in omnibus*), he counsels; and he describes
virtue as an Aristotelian *habitus* that curbs nature, rather than
following the Stoic definition of virtue as *naturam sequi.*

—*Marcia L. Colish,*
"Cicero, Ambrose, and Stoic Ethics:
Transmission or Transformation?"

Skilled in the art of turning used words into new texts, Ambrose was not generally inclined to call attention to his own writerly acts of appropriative recycling. His silence might bespeak not embarrassment but a lofty indifference: where all authorship ultimately derives from one Spirit, only the letter of Scripture, bearing the original traces of God's holy finger, is really quotable. Reluctant to identify even his Christian sources by name, Ambrose also learned to substitute biblical references for allusions to such classical mythological figures as Hydra and Scylla (*Fid.* 3.1.3–4). It is thus striking that the bishop of Milan "expressly acknowledges that Cicero's *De officiis* is his model" when he sets out in the late 380s to compile his own treatise, *On the Ministerial Duties.*[56] He seems thereby to invite comparison with this pagan classic and indeed to encourage the question of his fidelity to his "announced model," as Marcia Colish comments. "As Cicero wrote for the instruction of his son, so I, too, write to teach you, my sons," Ambrose states forthrightly in his prologue. "For I love you, whom I have begotten in the Gospel, no less than if I had received you in marriage [*quam si conjugio suscepissem*]." Curbing the claims of nature with the ease of long habit—"for nature does not make us love more ardently than grace," as he puts it (*Off.* 1.7.24)—Ambrose, "like Cicero, omits the factor of sex," as Colish also notes. Such an omission is surely strategic for one whose professed task is the reproduction of manhood through the education of sons who are all the more beloved for having been begotten by adoption into an "exclusively masculine occupational group," rather than conceived with a wife. Leaving aside the question of the possible "sexism" inhering in such an exclusive masculinity, we may yet productively interrogate the "conventionality" of Ambrose's pedagogical endeavor—which, being without precedent or parallel in Christian literature, may seem all the more comfortably "Roman." Yet how faithful *is* Ambrose even to Cicero's ethics when he reshuffles the order of the cardinal virtues so as to place modesty (*verecundia*) ahead of wisdom, justice, and courage? And what might this promotion of modesty have to do with his competitive privileging of grace over nature in the molding of man?

While loyally transmitting the moral codes catalogued in Cicero's text, the ever decorous Ambrose also silently interrupts the flow of ethical discourse at the site of what Michel Foucault describes as "the forms of moral subjectivation." Foucault himself draws a line between "Roman" and

"Christian" stylings of the ethical subject, making Christianization the harbinger of both a chastened docility and an intensified introversion. Replacing an earlier Roman emphasis on the necessity to care for a self construed as vulnerable or sickly, ethics in later antiquity comes to define its subject matter in relation to fleshly "finitude, the Fall, and evil," he suggests. The self emerges not by subjecting itself to the rules of its own carefully discerned "nature" but through "obedience to a general law that is at the same time the will of a personal god." The work of self-formation shifts away from diagnostic and therapeutic regimens toward "decipherment of the soul and a purificatory hermeneutics of desire," while the goal of such ethical practices "tends toward self-renunciation" and deferred heavenly bliss, rather than the present pleasures of an austere self-delight.[57] Like Cicero and Ambrose, Foucault himself "omits the factor of sex" by virtually banishing woman (as well as pathic men) from his text and thereby repeating the erasure of sexual difference from the domain of subjectivity. There is, however, an implicit history of masculinity inscribed in his account of the transformation of the desiring subject. As Elizabeth Clark points out,[58] Foucault hints that the coming of Christianity spelled danger for classical manhood in its Roman as well as Greek variations: "the day would come when the paradigm most often used for illustrating sexual virtue would be that of the woman, or the girl," notes Foucault; "the exercise of a virile type of activity" in self-rule would give way to striving for "a purity whose model was to be sought in virginity."[59] *Vir* begins to mimic *virgo*, as Foucault describes it, and man is reformed as a maid, when the well-tended fragility of the flesh is allowed to slide toward corruption, adaptive obedience is preferred to stern self-rule, and the naked desire for truth is transformed into a veiled truth about desire that creates puzzles and ambiguities, digressions and deferrals, and never really seems to get to the bottom of things. This not altogether unfamiliar account of Christianization as the feminization of Roman manhood, however evocative, is also problematic, as Clark goes on to argue. Reading the texts of Egyptian asceticism, she suggests that the data do not by and large "bear out Foucault's claim that the monks manifest a 'feminine' desire for 'intactness'"; on the contrary, the combative desert monks seem considerably more virile—and therefore more Greek, in Foucault's terms—than the hypochondriac Romans.[60] Reading the urbane Ambrose's ascetical ethics, however, we may conclude that both Foucault and Clark have it right: while Foucault's account highlights the feminized self-styling of the late-antique man, Clark's gloss points up his thinly veiled masculinized aggression. Ambrose's move on Cicero's text is not, after all, a completely friendly takeover. Self-avowedly equipped for victory, as we have seen, and now resting on the laurels of his triumphs not only at the Council of Aquileia but also within the basilicae of a Milan occupied by a homoian court, Bishop Ambrose—who (like Cicero) sometimes decked himself out in borrowed Greek plumes—will claim to supersede even the virtuous Tully as the Latin authority on duty and decorum. Modeling himself not only on the Greek but also on the woman (or the girl), he will prove the most manly of all contenders for the honor of representing *Romanitas*.

The bishop begins his treatise paradoxically—and not for the first time—with a sermonic discourse on silence. As in the earlier text *On Virgins*, he represents himself as attempting to avoid the burden of teaching, yet finally having no choice but to yield to the call of both desire and duty (*Off.* 1.1.1–2), a far cry from Cicero's calm assertion of professional competence (Cicero, *De officiis* 1.1.2). A reluctant guide, Ambrose will modestly narrow his focus to the interpretation of Scripture, the least of the spiritual gifts (*Off.* 1.1.3). He warns his readers not to expect too much from one who was still a novice when promoted to the episcopacy; but as he does so, he invokes the image of his own renounced authority as well as his present office. "I was carried off from the judgment seat, and the garb of office, to enter on the priesthood, and have begun to teach you, what I myself have not yet learnt," he reminisces, memorably (1.1.4). Snatched from the tribunal, Ambrose was not just carried off, but also carried along on the wave of the success of his past performance, into a priestly authority that seemed only natural for one accustomed to rule: indeed, he barely had time to change his costume as he shifted his role. And yet, always an apt pupil, Ambrose dons the new robes of his humility swiftly enough in this text: untaught in Christian doctrine, he at least knows enough to keep quiet, he suggests. Carrying to its extreme the conventional admonition to exercise self-control in one's speech, he effectively negates the authoritative figure of the elite male as public speaker. "How many have I seen to fall into sin by speaking, but scarcely one by keeping silent" (1.2.5). The Psalmist is the model of how to hold one's tongue: "I said, I will take heed to my ways, that I offend not in my tongue [Ps. 39:1]," he quotes (*Off.* 1.2.6). Susanna's tale offers a more vivid representation of an assertive silence: she "did more by keeping silence than if she had spoken" (1.3.9). Ambrose may still have this striking heroine in mind when he subsequently invokes the image of the "inner self" as a garden to be carefully fenced in (cf. *Virg.* 1.9.45). "A pure inner life is a valuable possession"; "hedge in, then, this possession of thine, enclose' it with thought, guard it with thorns"; "guard thy inner self, . . . for its fruit is not perishable and only for a time"; "cultivate, therefore, thy possession, and let it be thy tilling ground" (*Off.* 1.3.11). The mouth, gateway to the garden of the mind, should not gape open, he concludes, returning to the theme of silence: "Let there be a door to thy mouth, that it may be shut when need arises and let it be carefully barred" (1.3.13). In Ambrose's text, silence thus becomes a metonym for a larger complex of virtues joined under the virginalized image of the ideal self as an enclosed garden.[61] "In guarding his mouth and restraining his tongue," a man "certainly is practicing moderation, gentleness, patience [*exercet modestiam, ac mansuetudinem, et patientiam*]," the bishop assures us. By controlling not just what comes *into* but above all what comes *out* of the mouth—and thus keeping the force of desire (*libido*) and anger (*iracundia*) under wraps—one also protects the purity of the interior life (1.4.14). Implicit in the image of the mouth as the entrance to the inner self, therefore, is the acknowledgment of the self-censorship accomplished by silence and the central role of the suppression of the passions in ethical formation.

Having already used the example of Susanna to argue for a silence that is not idle but productive, Ambrose is now at pains to represent a silence that is not passive but active in relation to external opposition. If the Christian is not to be ashamed of his silence (*Off.* 1.5.17), that is because silence is an instrument of victory. Silent responses to insult—even from his social inferiors—"are the weapons of the just man, so that he may conquer by giving way, as those skilled in throwing the javelin are wont to conquer by giving way, and in flight to wound their pursuers with severer blows" (1.5.20). His meditations on the exhortation of Psalm 39 to watch one's tongue have convinced Ambrose not only that silence has virtues but also that silence is the basis of all virtues (*Off.* 1.7.23). Thus it is that the psalm that has left him tongue-tied has also led him to write *On the Duties*, following the model of Cicero, for the instruction of his chosen sons (*Off.* 1.7.23–24).

Ambrose's endeavor to Christianize the genre of philosophical ethics is further legitimated, in his text, by the gospel reading at hand—none other than the account of Zacharias being struck dumb in the temple, in which the word *officium* conveniently appears (*Off.* 1.8.26). As Maurice Testard points out, Ambrose often proceeds by a method of "verbal composition,"[62] weaving Scripture onto the loom of Cicero's work at the points of literal terminological correspondence. Here, however, the bishop also engages Cicero's compositional framework itself, which separates into three books the discussions of virtue (*honestum*), expediency (*utilitas*), and the work of both in defining moral obligation or duty. Ambrose will follow Cicero's outline, yet that does not render his work merely redundant or apologetic on Cicero's behalf: he makes clear from the start that, from the perspective of Christian eschatology, the question of even an *apparent* conflict between virtue and expediency never arises, since virtue is always on the side of expediency where heavenly rewards are the only advantages worth measuring. "This work of ours is not superfluous," he concludes, "seeing that we and they regard duty in quite different ways" (*Off.* 1.9.29). Ambrose is not, however, quite done with justifying either his borrowings from Cicero or the unconventional attitude of silence with which he approaches his topic. David, understood to be the author of the psalm, antedates not only Cicero but even the Greek philosophers as a moralist with a sound respect for silence, Ambrose points out (*Off.* 1.10.31). Nor was David either advocating or practicing an absolute dumbness but rather exhorting "due measure in keeping silence and also in speaking," as Ambrose now clarifies (1.10.34–35). At this point, Ambrose veers back to hint at further inadequacies in Cicero's account, arguing at length that what expands and perfects "ordinary" duty is mercy (1.11.37–64).

It is only after this extended and digressive series of preparatory gestures that Ambrose finally turns to a discussion that is distinctly "Ciceronian in tone,"[63] addressing the topic of modesty (*verecundia*) and its accompanying virtues (*Off.* 1.17.65–24.114). Ciceronian in tone and indeed in much of its content, this section is also notably out of order according to the sequence of Cicero's text.[64] Cicero expounds upon *verecundia*, along with its close allies—temperance (*temperantia*), moderation or restraint (*modestia*), and propriety (*decorum*)—only after completing his discussions of wisdom, justice, and courage (Cicero, *De officiis* 1.27.93–42.151). Ambrose, for his part, has shifted much of this material to the front of his text, where it is packaged as a more generalized discussion of virtue that founds the exploration of the four cardinal virtues in their specificity—leaving the fourth, which he names temperance and moderation (*temperantia ac modestia*) (*Off.* 1.43.209), to be significantly reshaped in relation to the Ciceronian prototype. If modesty has thus been awarded a newly privileged place, it only continues the trend begun when Ambrose commenced with silence.[65] "Silence, again, wherein all the other virtues rest, is the chief act of modesty," proclaims the bishop, reminding us once more that "Susanna was silent in danger, and thought the loss of modesty was worse than the loss of life." Modesty here translates explicitly into shame (*pudor*) and the restraint that "makes a woman unwilling to look upon men, or to be seen by them" (1.18.67). Swiftly shifting terminology yet again, Ambrose urges, "Let no one suppose that this praise belongs to chastity [*castitas*] alone," adding that modesty, shame, and purity (*pudicitia*) are all necessary collaborators with chastity. It is this winning combination of markedly sexualized womanly virtues that commends the Mother of the Lord to readers of Scripture: Ambrose emphasizes that the telling moment of the Virgin's silent response to Gabriel—verging on the impolite—could only have been the result of her maidenly modesty (1.18.69). Once again the bishop audaciously exalts the Virgin in such a way as to translate her hyperfeminine attributes into the model for a new version of masculine excellence. "A great thing, then, is modesty, which, rather negligent of its rights, seizing on nothing for itself, laying claim to nothing, and somehow rather contracted within its powers, yet is rich in the sight of God, in whose sight no one is rich," Ambrose proclaims (1.18.70). In the give and take of male competition for honor, less has definitely become more.

Modesty is written on the body, or rather—as Ambrose would have it—it is spoken by the body: "the movement of the body is a sort of voice of the soul." If "the condition of the mind [*habitus mentis*] can be seen in the attitude of the body [*corporis statu*]," this does not imply that one need only attend to one's mental habits and the body will take care of itself. On the contrary, the body becomes a site of intense and disciplined self-cultivation: if a man *seems* as he *is*, it is also the case that a man *is* what he *seems*. Extreme diligence is required to maintain modesty "in our very movements and gestures and gaits" (*Off.* 1.18.71). Not everyone masters the act. Reading the signs carefully, Ambrose has refused to ordain one man, "because his gestures were too unseemly [*dedeceret*]," while commanding another, already a member of the clergy, not to walk in front of him "because he actually pained me by the seeming arrogance of his gait." The bishop's interpretations are confirmed by subsequent events: "For both have left the church. What their gait betrayed them to be, such were they proved to be by the faithlessness of their hearts." He goes further: "In their gait was discernible the semblance of fickleness, the appearance, as it were, of fidgeting dandies [*scurrarum percursantium*]" (1.18.72). Warming to his topic, Ambrose adds contemptuously, "Some there are who in walking perceptibly copy the gestures of actors" (1.18.73). One must, then, learn to walk the walk of modesty without appearing stagy, according to this Father. Pace and timing are crucial: a false and fussy solemnity, rhythmic and slow, is as distasteful to Ambrose as is the contrived melodrama produced by a habituated haste (1.18.73–74). "A suitable gait is that wherein there is an appearance of authority and weight and dignity, and which has a calm, collected bearing." There must be no hint of "effort and conceit," no whiff of the "counterfeit." Judith Butler analyzes the ploy of such acts of naturalization: "For a performance to work . . . means . . . that a reading, an interpretation, appears to be a kind of transparent seeing, where what appears and what it means coincide."[66] "Let nature train our movements," pronounces Ambrose, adding quickly that where nature falls short, it should be corrected (1.18.75).

If "nature" for Ambrose is always also something "cultivated," some cultures of man are more refined than others, and (what is for him a restatement of the same point) some natures are likewise more natural. The anatomy of the human body—common to all—reveals a naturalized norm that closes in on itself in rejection of its own shamefully bared necessities. The highest cultures of manhood will follow nature's corporeally inscribed modesty, explains Ambrose. Nature "has left plain and open to the sight those parts which are beautiful to look upon; among which, the head, set as it were above all, and the pleasant lines of the figure, and the appearance of the face are prominent, whilst their usefulness for work is ready to hand." As for "those parts in which there is a compliance with the necessities of nature," presenting a potentially disgusting appearance, nature herself rises above her own needs partly by folding her shame within the body, and partly by teaching us to cover those parts (*Off.* 1.18.77). "Is not nature herself then a teacher of modesty? Following her example, the modesty of men . . . has covered and veiled what it has found hid in the frame of our body" (1.18.78). When it comes to certain "parts," the veil would seem to make a male body more like a female body, a man more like Mary, *inverting* the contours of masculine shame and thereby converting it to honor. Here, at any rate, it is the veiling of a not-so-hidden maleness that preoccupies the bishop, who worries aloud about Noah's exposure and also about men in the baths—especially fathers and sons, for to look on a father's nakedness is to risk failing at the duty of reverence. He reminds his readers that the priests of Israel wore linen shorts to protect their modesty (1.18.79–80). "It has given me pleasure to dwell somewhat at length on the various functions of modesty," Ambrose concludes with a sigh of satisfaction (1.19.81). However, he is not really ready to renounce his pleasure yet: this discourse on modesty will grow still longer.

If a body voices its modesty partly without recourse to words, the embodied voice must also be attended to carefully, Ambrose continues. Here he makes it even more explicit that the cultivation of masculinity per se is at stake. "The voice, too, should not be languid, nor feeble, nor womanish in its tone. . . . It should preserve a certain quality, and rhythm, and a manly vigor." A priest must not only walk the walk but also talk the talk of his manhood, and how he talks is at least as important as what he says. Ambrose "cannot approve of a soft or weak tone of voice, or an effeminate gesture of the body"; nor, at the opposite end of the spectrum, can he approve "of what is boorish and rustic" (*Off.* 1.19.84). At this point Ambrose slides into a more wide-ranging discussion of manly comportment. "Profligate men," those frivolous jokers and party-goers, "enervate that manly gravity of theirs," he notes disapprovingly, counseling clerics to avoid banquets and unchaperoned visits to the homes of virgins or widows (1.20.85–87). In general, reason should firmly govern the passions, and the bishop once again urges particular diligence in guarding against anger, which remains a man's most prominent temptation (1.21.90–97). Circling back to the topic of voice, he now muses: "I certainly think it ought to be plain and clear. . . . Let it be distinct in its pronunciation and full of a manly vigor, but let it be free from a rough and rustic twang." All of this care and control should not, however, add up to a loss of the effect of a natural simplicity in delivery: "See, too that it does not assume a theatrical accent, but rather keeps true to the inner meaning of the words it utters" (1.23.104).

"I think I have said enough on the art of speaking," notes Ambrose briefly, briskly turning the corner of yet another transition: "Let us now consider what beseems an active life" (*Off.* 1.24.105). The figures of Abraham, Jacob, Joseph, Job, and David are brought forth to demonstrate the rational control of passion and the aspects of moderation, proportion, and proper timing that define the decorous life (1.24.105–14). With this concluding recitation of scriptural *exempla* of modesty, Ambrose is ready to begin a more focused and structured discussion of the four cardinal virtues of wisdom, justice, courage, and temperance in which he will deliberately mix Ciceronian and biblical resources. Borrowing his moral typology from Cicero, he uses Scripture as an authority on "the lives of the fathers," who will continue to be held up as "a mirror of virtue"—a method that differs, he suggests, from a more abstract and "artificial" philosophic analysis, which might ignore the actor while busily categorizing the acts (*Off.* 1.24.115–16).[67] The discussions of justice (1.28.130–34.174) and courage (1.35.175–42.208) take up most of the space, as Ambrose attempts, on the one hand, to expand justice, as the civic virtue par excellence, into the spaces of its own excesses—beneficence and generosity—and, on the other hand, to encompass courage, as the preeminent military virtue, within the category of a spiritualized warfare. "If the thought of warlike matters seems to be foreign to the duty of our office," Ambrose will nonetheless point out that "our fathers . . . gained great glory also in war," albeit fighting only "when driven to it" (1.35.175–77). When Christians renounce war, it is not, then, because they lack courage but because they possess an excess of bravery. Real men, he argues, do not strive after mere bodily fortitude but rather seek fortitude of the mind. "We too must prove ourselves to our captain, so that our members may be the weapons of justice; not carnal weapons in which sin may reign but weapons strong for God, whereby sin may be destroyed" (1.37.185). Proof that a privileging of spiritual warfare does not rest on physical cowardice is offered by reference to the Maccabees, who, although soldiers, refused to fight on the Sabbath (1.40.196). Their leader eventually died gloriously in battle, but the children of Judas Maccabeus, captured and unyielding under torture, "were armed, but they conquered without arms." In the end, "the mother looked with joy on the corpses of her chil-

dren as so many trophies and found delight in the voices of her dying sons"
(1.41.199–202). Agnes and Lawrence—the latter portrayed as the loyal son
of Bishop Xystus—are offered as Christian prototypes of the martyr as
"warrior of Christ" (1.41.203–6; cf. 1.36.182). The filial depiction of Lawrence becomes a thread that weaves through the initial treatment of temperance—"let us link ourselves with older men of approved goodness"
(1.43.211)—and on into the extended discussions of decorum and the control of anger, as these apply more directly to the clerical calling. "In the clerical office . . . nothing is more rare than to find a man to follow his father's
footsteps" (1.44.217), notes Ambrose, relating this more to the observed
high demands of the office than to his own conviction that "the ministerial
office . . . must not be defiled by conjugal intercourse" (1.50.248). However
prolific some bishops may be, priestly sons are not carnally begotten but
rather, like the Levites, "chosen out of the whole number of the children of
Israel" (1.50.250), and their sonship is proven by their virtue (1.50.257).

The subsequent portions of Ambrose's *On the Duties* follow Cicero's
broad framework in introducing, first, the question of "the useful" and, second, its relation to "the virtuous." Ambrose has, as he here reminds us, already demonstrated that the virtuous and the useful are, in principle, not
"mutually opposed" but rather "one" (*Off.* 3.2.8); thus, his second and third
books do not so much problematize apparent conflicts between ethics and
expediency as concretize the first book's discussion of virtue.[68] These later
books sustain the demarcation of a pure and hidden inner self that eludes
the perception and therefore also the judgment of the public eye, while they
firmly plant the virtuous Christian subject in the life of the city. "Blessed,
plainly, is that life which is not valued at the estimation of outsiders, but is
known, as judge of itself, by its own inner feelings," proclaims the bishop at
the opening of book 2. "Thus the less it strives for glory, the more it rises
above it" (2.1.2). Book 3 commences with a still more extended reflection on
the interior life. "The prophet David taught us that we should go about in
our heart as though in a large house; that we should hold converse with it as
with some trusty companion." A medley of biblical texts suggests that the
inner self is a well; its waters are deep; it is a fountain from which strangers
are barred (3.1.1). These images are again reminiscent of the Song of Songs,
with its "garden enclosed," the "fountain sealed," which elsewhere in Ambrose's texts signifies female virginity. Moses, as well as David, has prior

claim on Scipio's insight that "he was not alone when he was alone, or that he was least at leisure when he was at leisure." Silent, Moses spoke; at ease, he labored hard, fighting, and indeed "triumphing over enemies whom he had not come near" (3.1.2). The Christian man may be quiet and appear withdrawn from public life, but in fact he is always on active duty—indeed, his agency transcends limitations of place or time. The agenda behind the Ciceronian takeoff becomes more sharply articulated: the Christian clergy are a new elite, and *officium*, in defining a higher moral duty in distinctly ascetic terms, also marks the privilege and responsibility of a ruling class. "I think, then, that one should strive to win preferment, especially in the church, only by good actions with a right aim. . . . When in office [*in ipso vero munere*], again, it is not right to be harsh and severe, nor may one be too easy; lest on the one hand we should seem to be exercising a despotic power, and on the other to be by no means filling the duty [*officium . . . implere*] we had taken up" (2.24.119–20). Achieving a governing and well-governed manhood is a matter of locating the golden mean between the effete and the vulgar, as Ambrose emphasizes again and again, and less is indeed sometimes more when cultivating a modest masculinity. Nevertheless, it is finally important that someone not just wear but fill the pants of priestly modesty. Nor is ministerial "duty" narrowly circumscribed or cleanly separated from the concerns of a civic magistrate. A cited instance of Christian "liberality" is the redemption of captives taken in the Gothic wars, and Ambrose severely criticizes those who have opposed this practice: "there were some who would have sent back into slavery those whom the church had redeemed," he notes in tones of horror, seemingly alert to the "usefulness" of such a liberated clientele (2.15.70). Elsewhere he delivers a lengthy condemnation of the urban prefect—identifiable as Symmachus himself[69] —who expelled strangers from Rome in a time of famine. This act, he argues, was not only cruel but also inexpedient: "How unprofitable for their city that so large a number should perish, who were wont to be helpful either in paying contributions or in carrying on business" (3.7.46).

Whatever its actual pedagogical uses for clergy may have been, Ambrose's treatise is, as McLynn puts it, an "exercise designed at once to make the church intelligible to the *saeculum* and to annex the latter's traditional territory."[70] Priestly pedagogy remains, however, a crucial framing device for Ambrose's annexing of the territory of a tradition of manly excellence.

Each of the last two books closes, even more pointedly than the first, with an explicit address to his "sons." "As the children of one father you have become united under the bond of brotherly affection" (*Off.* 2.30.155). "Preserve, then, my sons, that friendship you have begun with your brethren, for nothing in the world is more beautiful than that" (3.22.131). He has left his children with precepts so that they may guard them in their minds. The cited words and *exempla*, he would have them note, are drawn from "the elders": thus the moral teaching of Scripture has, in this text, neatly displaced the *mos majorum* that defined classical Roman values (3.22.138).

It seems that Ambrose does not after all omit the factor of sex—though a deliberate omission of women is undoubtedly part of the sexual politics of his mature episcopacy. It seems that he is indeed rather faithful to his Ciceronian source, and even to the more stoicizing aspects of its ethics: *naturam sequi*, to follow nature, remains a virtue in this Father's view. If he seeks to curb the excesses of anger and desire, that is only because nature has veered off its course. Once Ambrose has redirected the steps of virtue onto a higher, straighter path and restitched virile habits into *verecundia*'s virginal sheath of inviolability, a man would do well to let nature take its course. Nor are the pleasures of a pursuit of self-care marked by the stringent renunciation of virile aggression strictly deferred: by the late 380s, a modest measure of heaven's austere bliss—and firm rule—had come to settle over Milan.

Embodying the Spirit

Supplementing his manhood with the veil of virginity, Ambrose gives body to sexual difference: tracing the movement of a trinitarian erotics, his is a sex that is simultaneously one and more than one, a desire for the other that is also narcissistic self-love. In the female virgins whom he finds so alluring, the bishop sees his own reflection, and in himself he perceives the mirror of their virginity. The circulation of images between man and maidens displaces the question of origins or essences, as Ambrose borrows what is already his own projection of womanhood and projects what is already borrowed, naturalizing his highly cultivated, "femminized" style even as he cultivates his natural virtue. Wearing his hidden depths on his sleeve, he does not so much internalize the Virgin as wrap himself in the delicate perfection of her membrane, thereby miming her immaculate act of self-containment, while in that very act placing himself also elsewhere, "within." It is under the sign of the Spirit, as well as the veil of the Virgin, that Ambrose conceives his virility as a lion that, by imitating virginity, envelops itself in a woman's skin—partly inverting the familiar Herculean figure.[71] Enclosed in the womblike embrace of an eternally unbroken copulation, *this* inspired hero never leaves home. Investing himself fully in his seamless public performance of *verecundia*, he creates for himself a private "inner man" who gives rise to his own transcendence by making himself invisible.

I have suggested that Ambrose models a transvestite masculine subjectivity, as he couples the sexes through a crossing of gendered roles that repeatedly transgress, parody, and reverse—but always also partly reinstate—a naturalized hierarchy of sexual difference. This is not, however, the only way in which he can be represented as a distinctly "copulative" figure. As we have seen, the bishop of Milan also serves as a prolific translator of pro-Nicene Greek trinitarian doctrine for a Latin-speaking world, as a skillful transposer of early Roman scripts for a late-antique audience, and as a shrewd mediator of the marriage between ecclesiastical and imperial authorities, Christian and pagan cultures, and indeed (as it sometimes seemed to local spectators) heaven and earth themselves. A capacity to access an interiorized site of spiritualizing transcendence while also remaining a highly visible performer on the world's stage makes Bishop Ambrose not only a fit representative of the imperialized orthodoxy that he promotes but also a model of civic manhood. As Neil McLynn has shown,[72] even in his most wide-ranging, promiscuous borrowings and crossings, Ambrose remains enmeshed in locale, loyal to his chosen city, engaging the universalizing institutions and cultures of empire and ecumenical Christianity precisely at those points where they join the concrete concerns of the Milanese church and the challenges of his own leadership.

All of this well-directed copulating makes Ambrose not only a man of the city but also a saint. In fact, it gives him a life. Although expert in the art of what Patricia Cox Miller calls "collective biography," producing an effect of "dissonant echoing" through the repetition of fragmented and condensed figures and scenes,[73] Ambrose himself pens no literary *Vitae*. He is not the author but rather the subject of a monologic *Life*, composed within about two decades of his death by the deacon Paulinus, who purports to write at the request of Augustine—with a glance over his shoulder at the competing *Lives* of Antony, Paul, and Martin (*Vita Ambrosii* 1). The Ambrosian biography is punctuated by explicit narrativizing devices, marking time in the bishop's career. Nevertheless, as one commentator remarks, "Paulinus does not always maintain the chronological order of events, nor does he attempt to establish a connection between them; the result is a feeling that things are jumbled together."[74] Indeed, the more the biographer calls attention to chronology, the more he seems to advertise that temporal sequence is beside the point. As in Ambrose's own collective biographizing, here the reader is "required to construct narratives of theological meaning that arise from the juxtaposition of images rather than from straightforward linear development."[75] One of the most striking of such images occurs early, in an account of Ambrose's infancy. As the baby lay sleeping, open-mouthed, in his cradle in the courtyard, "a swarm of bees came and covered his face and mouth in such a way that they would go in and out," relates Paulinus. Despite his nurse's fears, the bees—inhaled and exhaled like breath, or Spirit—did not harm the child. "But after a short time passed they flew out and were lifted so high into the air that they could not be seen by the human eye." Witnessing the event (and preventing the nurse from intervening), Ambrose's father, according to Paulinus, predicted greatness for his son, a prophecy to which Paulinus adds his own retrospective interpretation: "That swarm of bees produced for us the honeycombs of his writings, which would tell of heavenly gifts and raise the minds of human beings from earthly things to heaven" (*Vita Ambrosii* 3). The writings of Ambrose, here identified with the bees' honeycombs, themselves offer bees as signs of virginity and cite the account of a swarm of bees found in the carcass of a slain lion, from whose mouth a biblical hero tastes honey. Reading the images juxtaposed within an Ambrosian corpus that now extends beyond Ambrose's own writings, we understand that the body of Ambrose's masculinity has, like Samson's (or Thecla's) lion, been transformed in Paulinus's text into a receptacle for bees, a producer of virginity's sweet honey; thus will the Spirit ascend on wings beyond the scope of the human eye, even as it is also made a spectacle of power on an earthly stage. With the rhetoric of modesty dropped from the figure of the bishop, Paulinus's account unveils Ambrose's naked authority, piling on one wonder after the other. At the same time, however, his narrative reveils the vulnerable body of Ambrose's episcopacy. Recent readers have attempted to circumvent the seeming problem of the biographer's stylistic excesses so as to steal a glimpse of the weaknesses underneath the repetitious recountings of Ambrose's displays of miraculous strength; in this they may be *partly* following the bishop's own coy invitation. Reinscribing the life of Ambrose with a renewed modesty heightens the effect of the man's remaining accomplishments, where victory was never assured. Thus, McLynn ends his own ostensibly nonbiographical account with a flourish: "It was he who at last 'created' an episcopal role for the stage of the Christian empire."[76]

Victory is never assured before the end, because only death seals the triumph of virginity, as Ambrose ever reminds his readers. The virgin is always under siege, and her ambiguous execution—rape or bridal bed?—is the hysteric's final, complicated witness to the violation of a virgin's chastity, an outrage that also encodes a threat to a woman's power of desire. Through a comparative reading of late-antique tropings of the matron and the virgin, Kate Cooper argues for the destructive volatility of the virgin as a "figure of wronged vulnerability," whose moral authority can be invoked to destabilize any consensus and who frequently functions—then, as now—to validate "what a modern humanist might call religious extremism." Lapsing momentarily into a bit of mimetic hysteria herself, Cooper counsels, "we should beware the allure of a figure who still moves among us."[77] Indeed, observing Ambrose's melodramatic antics, listening to his shrill and strident tones, I too have often sought the counterbalance of the matron's calm and steady conservatism, lest I be caught by the bishop's parodic act in a falsely sustained state of virginal alarm of my own—lest I discover myself, as "woman," not merely exploited but also trapped by the alienating "extremism" and apocalyptically world-denying terms of his feminized discourse.

And yet, like Cixous, I find that "it is impossible to have a single, rigid point of view about it," for the figure of the virgin martyr also "has its use." I confess it: sometimes, reading Ambrose's virgin, I choose to succumb to his seduction; I submit to her allure; "I become, I inhabit, I enter." Becoming the bishop's virgin, inhabiting her place, I begin to imagine how, "if the scene change[d] and if the woman [began] to speak in other ways," her hysteria "would be a force capable of demolishing those structures" that stifle her, her virginity would challenge "the illegitimate power of rape and violence." Entering her text, I perceive that "the source of [her] strength is, in spite of everything, her desire." She "is not just someone who has her words cut off, someone for whom the body speaks. It all starts with her anguish as it relates to desire and to the immensity of her desire—therefore, from her demanding quality."[78] That is to say, it all starts when, out of her anguish, the passionate Virgin voices an immense desire. A bit demanding, after so much enforced patience, she calls for the Spirit to materialize, not as a sword-thrust's end to the voluptuous life of the flesh but as "the means for matter to emerge and endure in its proper form, in its proper forms."[79] Released from the rigidity of a single point of view, the endless embrace of the copula that is not one but is both Virgin and Spirit—two petals—may simultaneously protect and traverse a difference measured not merely vertically, between created nature and divine spirit, but also across the spiritualized natures and embodied spirits of men and women.

The fathers were not simply anti- anthropomorphic

Theological Conclusion

At least a sophisticated theology of this kind could not fall into the trap of
arguing from a supposedly personal God to a male idol. One positive
feature of the feminist critique of Christian theology is that it exposes the
limitations not only of much popular Christianity but of the theistic
traditions of most modern Western philosophy of religion, as does the
Trinitarian theology of the Fathers. For they were absolutely clear
that anthropomorphism was inappropriate.

—*Frances Young,*
The Making of the Creeds

Neither the Fathers who authored trinitarian theology nor Frances Young herself would "fall into the trap" of supposing a vulgarly "personal" God and arguing from such a God "to a male idol." The Fathers themselves were acutely aware that "anthropomorphism" is "inappropriate." So what is all the feminist fuss? Young seems to be asking. We note that this passage follows, apparently inconsequently, upon Young's closing statement of the paradox of the evolution of late-ancient trinitarian doctrine, which "appears to be a process of finer and finer definition" while functioning "to preserve the mystery of God." Summoning surprise at her own conclusion, she exclaims, "The mystery of the Trinity was the outcome, yet put a step wrong in enunciating that doctrine and you become a heretic!"[1] Perhaps her point is that readers of the Fathers should stop worrying about "wrong steps" like "misogyny," lest *someone* be declared a heretic—but *who*? She goes on to note darkly, "The Fathers are less blameworthy for their misogyny than those who have exploited some of their statements in a very different context and with differing intent."[2] Ending her own digression—and thereby attempting also to put historical theology back on the right track—Young reiterates her conviction about the particular mystery that was and should remain at the center of theological contemplation: "in this period the primary issue concerned the nature of God conceived as transcendent yet in relationship with the world."[3]

Young is surely right that a narrow version of theological "anthropo-morphism" was of no interest to the Fathers of trinitarian doctrine. Their concern, as we have seen, was not to ascribe human form to God but rather to lay claim to a transcendently divine form for man, to help man "orient his finiteness by reference to infinity," so that he might "go on *be-coming,* infinitely."[4] If the horizon of human becoming is named in the terms of Father, Son, and Spirit, this does not in itself make of God a male idol—but it does, as a matter of fact, construct both an idealized mas-culinity and a masculinized transcendence. For the Fathers, femaleness is allied with the stubborn particularity of created matter, against which the unlimited realm of supposedly ungendered divinity may be defined by the-ologians who have risen above their gender as well. Have we not found that there is, after all, much to be said about this indeed rather sophisticated theological move on maleness?

But perhaps Young, while touting the Fathers' sophistication, really wants us to read them naively, supposing them sexless and veiling our eyes against the shameful evidence of their musings about masculinity—a pre-occupation that manifests itself, as I have attempted to show, in discussions of "the nature of God conceived as transcendent and yet in relation with the world." Young seems notably impatient with her public, remarking that Christian theology "cannot be worked out *de novo* time and time again," finding it "depressing how often the old heresies re-emerge and the old issues have to be redebated because of the sheer ignorance of many Christians about their own history."[5] Among her concerns is a *methodolog-ical* ignorance, of the kind practiced by interpreters who do not know the difference between creation and pure invention, when it comes to writing history.[6] But is it more depressing to confront so much supposedly igno-rant inventiveness, or to believe that there is nothing left to be worked out, that the writing of the Fathers has reached its limit by having become long ago fully known? If (as I have preferred to view it) writing "always remains to be read, studied, sought, invented," and if (still following Cixous's hints) reading is the act of "making love" that causes the page to grow and mul-tiply infinitely,[7] then there cannot possibly be any end to knowing the Fa-thers, or even to debating old issues.

Playing lightly with the structures of trinitarian doctrine itself, I have wanted to present each of the three men of this study in his irreducible particularity, while also gesturing toward a common cultural "essence" that might provisionally contain the mystery of a shared late-antique masculinity. I have cast Athanasius of Alexandria as "father" not only because he was largely responsible for the development of a concept of doctrinal paternity associated with the ecumenical Council of Nicaea and its creed, but also because some of his most distinctive and clearly articulated theological positions quickly became foundational, taking on the status of presupposition for other fourth-century thinkers. It was Athanasius who sharply inscribed onto the Christian cosmological map what Brown has named the "closing of the heavens," emphasizing the ontological gulf separating the incorruptible creator God from a material cosmos wrenched out of nothingness and inherently inclined to corruption. By depicting the incarnate Word as the site of the joining of the unchanging God with the shifty materiality of creation, he signifies the possibilities for humanity's upward mobility—or, to put it otherwise, for the *cultivation* of a human self dramatically underdetermined by its faltering *nature*. An agent of perfection and healing, the Athanasian Christ models godliness for men who might hope to be saved from the bodily ravages of change and death without shedding their status as created (and therefore corporeal) beings. According to Athanasius, the coming of Christ enables the transformation of man, who becomes, following a pattern of paradox, *virtually* divine, *virtually* incorporeal, wondrously stabilized—despite his innate tendency to succumb to the flux of a creation that ends in dissolution. The Athanasian subject thus draws himself up to his full height (and then some!), straining toward self-transcendence. Thus human salvation is already under way, as the habits of the body give rise to an ascetic self who comes very near to attaining a divinity that finally belongs to God alone, even as it remains the signifier of manhood's desired perfection.

For Athanasius, the theological distinction between native and adoptive sonship cannot be blurred, for therein lies the fertile tension from which man emerges not as a divine but yet as a divinized subject, for whom transcendence (having begun as a gift) must become second nature, founded on the suppression of another nature that came first. Human patrilineage, reflecting the ability of men to reproduce themselves as versions of the same, becomes a stage for the enactment of a provisionally stabilized corporeality that bends the creature's capacity for change to the purposes of continuity, exemplified in the succession of bishops who faithfully preserve

and transmit the seed of apostolic doctrine encoded in credal form. Athanasius erases maternity from both divine and human economies—motherhood being uneasily associated with corruptible materiality, as well as with
the introduction of multiplicity and difference into a generative process
that might thus produce not sameness of essence but mere similarity. The
only "women" in his texts are the misbegotten sons of heresy, who are
forcibly expelled from the community. *The female is entirely excluded from
rational discourse.* Athanasius's conception of masculinity is thus austerely
ascetic, with a parthenogenic capacity for self-duplication, miming the fixity of the written word. The community that he governs with the self-
righteous assertiveness of one most often ruling symbolically, from exile, is
likewise defined by the tension of a paradox—a sublime city of men located at the interpretive intersection of the desert, where carnal Alexandria
meets the imagined perfection of the heavenly *politeia.*

As "son," Gregory of Nyssa takes on the mantle of his brother Basil's ecclesiastical authority, and thereby becomes a model for a patrilineage that is
neither strictly literal nor entirely divorced from the carnal claims of familial heritage. As "son" in this book, he may *also* be seen to extend and indeed
put flesh on the theological legacy of Athanasius. Whereas Athanasius emphasized the incarnation of Christ, understanding it as the privileged site
for the exploration of human self-transcendence, Gregory focuses rather on
the paradox of a virginal maternity, borrowing Mary's female figure to articulate (and thereby further alienate) the fecund chastity of a maleness that
strives for ascetic perfection through continual transformative sublimations.
And whereas Athanasius suppressed a feminized materiality, Gregory takes
up the fluid, changeable, and often tumultuous body disowned by his predecessor—but, through a subtle process of spiraling inversions, owns it as
male, while idealizing as female the alluringly static and arid figure who occupies the gap between what a man already is and the godlike status he may
yet achieve. Drawn on by the example of this "other," Gregory continually
makes himself female so as ultimately to become more male. To do so he
not only brings to the surface the suppressed feminine in the service of
what remains for him, as it had for Athanasius, a single-sex economy of discourse, but also exploits the rich homoerotic potential of such a system.
Making himself female, this "son" receives the deposit of truth from a transcendently paternalized lover who thereby impregnates him with his own

supreme manhood. Yet here, too, Gregory plays with inversions, for the feminized lover of God is represented not only as the receptive partner but also as the pursuer, straining after God in a chase that—as he makes explicit—is necessarily unending, with man's abyssal desire for God meeting its match in the elusive transcendence of divinity.

In most respects, Gregory shares Athanasius's highly dualistic view of the tension between cosmos and creator, likewise situating a masculinized humanity at the site of that defining tension. Yet by *extending* the bifurcated verticality across which man is stretched—taking both transcendence and degradation over the edges of excess—Gregory allows the realms of the most sublime divinity and the grossest materiality to curve back toward one another. A "horizontal" version of sexual difference is of no more interest to Gregory than to Athanasius; however, in Gregory's thought, even vertical distinctions do not quite hold, as gender becomes a way to mark merely relative positionings of man and God, and finally even that relative difference is eroded by the fluid play of exchange and reversal, through which a Son may be thought "equal" to his Father. Whereas Athanasius suppresses the female along with the mutable body, Gregory retrieves these products of exclusion and puts them to use. While for Athanasius all corporeal change is for the worse and leads toward disorder and death, for Gregory all movement may be harnessed for the pursuit of perfection, through which creation's providential order is completed. In Gregory's writing, the fluid excesses of femininity and desire and the embodied sociality of familial and civic communities can all be taken up and transformed within the highly unitive economy of the divine sex that is one.

Ambrose, celebrated for his pneumatological doctrine, and here cast in the role of "spirit," may also be read as the trinitarian "third" who disrupts the misleading impression of completeness insinuated by the dyadic play of comparison and contrast between a hypermasculine and an androgynous —or feminized—maleness. While Ambrose, like Gregory, proceeds from an Athanasian scheme (indeed at points quite directly), he nevertheless encounters virginity at angles rather different from Gregory's. Like Gregory, he retrieves the femininity excluded from (and thus indirectly produced by) Athanasius's masculine subjectivity, so as to reappropriate it for men. However, in so doing, he does not set out to depict a fluid manhood overlapped and interwoven with the feminine, but rather flaunts the play of sexual difference so as to locate a male self that is constituted by, but not simply identical with, masculine and feminine roles. Protesting his beleaguered condition while still vigorously governing his ecclesiastical community, Bishop Ambrose echoes Athanasius's rhetorical self-styling, claiming a martyr's status that seems to relinquish masculine invulnerability while introducing the excuse for a scantily veiled aggression. But Ambrose is not only more immediately successful in his play for power than the repeatedly exiled Athanasius; he also cannot resist pulling out a few more rhetorical stops. Indeed, he begins to sound more like one of Gregory's disruptive virgins—yet here, too, his act seems, by comparison, hyperbolic. It is finally the radically sublimated copulative energy circulating between an aggressive masculinity and a hysterical femininity that produces Ambrose as a late-antique man, fit for the rule of a Christianized city.

Athanasius, Gregory, and Ambrose stood at a potent moment in the history of Western thought—to state my claim as broadly and baldly as possible. As the intellectual terrain shifted along newly emerged fault lines, the restructuring of knowledge that was under way suddenly became visible when truth was seen to be founded on a credal text—a development revealing the extent to which "belief itself" had become, as Luce Irigaray puts it, "the preliminary to the question of sexual difference."[8] From this point on, *pace* Young, it was not possible to speak of "the nature of God conceived as transcendent yet in relationship with the world" without at least implicitly engaging the issue of the discursive creation of maleness and femaleness. The fourth-century doctrine of a transcendent God who is Father, Son, and Holy Spirit was inextricably intertwined with the particular late-antique claims for masculinity.

The erasure of the female from representations of divine generativity framed exclusively in terms of fatherhood and sonship is crucial to a construction of transcendence that emphasizes the mystery of a God accessible only through belief. In particular, by absenting the maternal womb from theological discourse, it becomes possible not only to transform that "first veil" (which both separates and joins child and mother) into the shroud of woman's invisibility—so that there remains only one sex—but also to erect a second veil between man and a God who cannot be seen or known and is indeed distinguished by his radical difference and distance from the world.[9] That is to say, an absolutizing divine transcendence, as a

Robert Christ

product of the asserted belief in a presence fundamentally defined by its bodily absence, is conceptually analogous to, indeed dependent on, the mother's enforced absence—which likewise demands a leap of faith. This absence is itself effected by the forceful displacement of the maternal body —and then of any bodily "presence"—through the heavy investment of Christian discourse in representational practice itself, above all in the written word, wherein meaning is always veiled, lying elsewhere, beyond letter or image.

By denying sexual difference, the Fathers affirm the difference of divinity; by making maternity invisible, they privilege fatherhood on the very basis of its invisibility; by eliminating the difference between mother and child, they assert the sameness of father and son; by suppressing materiality, they push the spirit to new heights. If this is the logic of paradox, it is also the logic of belief, which is founded upon the exchange of bodily presence for absence and absence for real presence, indeed upon the atoning principle of substitution itself. In the play of such enacted substitutions, man becomes the measure of a humanity that aspires to transcend its own nature, to be what it is not; corporeality itself is refashioned as a diaphanous veil, both hiding and revealing what lies beyond, above, or within.

It is no accident that ancient Christian art consistently depicts the divine man, Christ, as copiously robed. Indeed, the preference for the generously clothed over the partially nude man is one of the very few features that consistently distinguishes Christian images from their pagan forerunners and competitors. The well-known sixth-century mosaic from the Arian baptistery in Ravenna is an exception that proves the rule: shown at the moment of his baptism, the naked Christ is submerged up to his hips in a shimmeringly translucent veil of water that yet affords a partial glimpse of his dainty penis.[10] It is also no accident that visual representations of Christ in late antiquity are sometimes sexually ambiguous, manifesting a manhood that has already incorporated the feminine. Such is the case with the Ravenna mosaic. Such is also the case with the early-fifth-century mosaic in the church of Blessed David in Thessalonica, a particularly evocative icon of late-ancient manhood. The gracefully curving posture of the luxuriantly draped Thessalonican Christ creates "the effect of movement, as if he has only just arrived," notes Thomas Mathews. At the same time, however precarious his balance, his self-assured poise also communicates a

FIGURE 1. Christ. Apse mosaic in the church of Blessed David, Thessalonica, c. 425–50. Hirmer Fotoarchiv, Hirmer Verlag München.

FIGURE 2. The Baptism of Christ. Mosaic in the Arian baptistery, Ravenna, early sixth century. Photo: John Dean.

static calm—as if he might never *depart*. Caught up in the circling embrace of a luminous cloud, Christ "perches on a most insubstantial rainbow": the artist has here translated Ezekiel's fearsome vision of whirlwind and fire (Ezek. 1:4–28) into the serene image of a softly glowing womb enclosed by a diaphanous membrane, through which one can dimly perceive the shadowy figures of the four-faced "living creatures" who seem to carry the heavenly sphere of light on their wings. The Christ figure contained within the sphere has a "soft and beardless face, encircled with light hair that falls copiously on his shoulders." As Mathews goes on to note, "his body too lacks any masculine vigor; the shoulders are narrow and sloping, and the hips are broad." (In fact, the first people to see the mosaic upon its rediscovery in 1926 took it for an image of the Virgin.) One hand reaches upward, while the other is symmetrically directed downward, holding an unfurling scroll: the divine man and his written word span the distance between heaven and earth with seeming ease. His face is impassive; his eyes are fixed on a truth that lies beyond mere appearances.[11]

Does all of this "analysis" not, finally, add up to an unveiling of the Fathers and of the trinitarian God, an unmasking intended to expose the heresy of male idolatry hidden in the mysterious heart of orthodox faith, and to shame the ancient voices into silence and replace them with something altogether new and unquestionably superior? If my answer can only be no, the reason is fairly simple: I do not "believe in" creation out of nothing. However, I have found that what is disavowed, suppressed, or dismissed as excessive in Christian discourse—seemingly so much "nothing"—provides excellent material with which to create. Furthermore, much can often be made out of very little. (This too I have learned from reading the Fathers attentively, as well as from observing the mothers at work.) The audacious act of situating desire and generativity in the realm of absolute divinity results in no mean inheritance; for a humanity said to be created in the image of God, ancient theology is a gift that keeps on giving. Whether that "gift" is a cultural "construction" or a fact of "nature," a truth "made" or "begotten," is ultimately beside the point. The font of *all* fabrications is a virginally conceiving Father, whose fertility can only be described in terms of an organic, bodily process as mysterious as it is complex. Ever begetting, this God is also ever begotten, the beloved Son who is already the Father's equal, his most sublime lover, and the womb of his creation. Breathing capaciousness through the tight coil of divine desire, the copulative Deity is simultaneously a sanctifying Spirit, setting the limit on the unholy of all "mere" materialities, guaranteeing the transcendence engendered in a recumbent love that respects particularity and a fecundity that refuses circumscription. So I read, so I am written, so I write, reluctant to make an end of it.

Still working, inevitably, from the preexistent matter of a promisingly abysmal tradition—which seems to me neither altogether formless nor absolutely fixed—I also do not "believe in" heresy. If the veil is the mark of the interval, the guardian of difference, the sign of the possibility of communion between bodies, then to *expose* a heresy is to eliminate the space required for knowing, to destroy the distinction between self and other— even (paradoxically) in the very act of hardening boundaries. I have not desired to unveil the Fathers, but rather, by catching the threads of their texts up into my own—the shining sites of translucence, the evocatively shadowy folds, the smooth expanses, the wrinkles and snags—to weave yet another fabric of difference and joining.

REFERENCE MATTER

Notes

1. McLynn, "From Palladius to Maximinus," 477–93.

2. Gwatkin, *Studies of Arianism*, 1.

3. Previous chapters of this history have been drafted by Michel Foucault, whose influential study of the desiring subject in antiquity also results in an account of the masculine subject, owing to its mimetic reperformance of the exclusion of the female and the pathic from the domain of subjectivity. See Foucault's *Use of Pleasure* and *Care of the Self.*

4. As Wiles points out, Gwatkin, despite his explicit attempt to secularize ecclesiastical history by aligning it with political, social, or economic history, continues to stress the purported illogic and unspiritual character of Arian *belief* in an effort to support a Nicene and Chalcedonian orthodoxy that he deems uniquely well positioned to meet the challenges of "modern scientific difficulties" (Wiles, *Archetypal Heresy*, 173–75). More recent studies of the Arian controversy seem to repeat, and indeed intensify, Gwatkin's pattern of combining a secularized historical method with a blatantly apologetic orthodox doctrinalism to render history virtually irrelevant to the analysis of doctrine (see Wiles, *Archetypal Heresy*, 176–81).

5. Ibid., 183.

6. Gwatkin, *Studies of Arianism*, 4.

7. Brown, *Making of Late Antiquity*, 2.

8. Cooper calls attention to the extent to which this radically transcendent conception of manhood, along with the accompanying idealization of female virginity, represented the perspective of a minority "faction" even within Christianity. She allows, however, that asceticizing reinterpretations of gender roles attained a kind of cultural hegemony in the late fourth century, evoking

a variety of responses from "traditionalist" Christians. See Cooper, *The Virgin and the Bride.*

9. Loraux, *Experiences of Tiresias,* 8.

10. Ibid., 3.

11. See also the account of Plato's antidemocratic appropriation of the female reproductive body in duBois, *Sowing the Body,* 169–83.

12. Barton, "All Things Beseem the Victor," 92.

13. On the "femminization" (*sic*) of the (masculine) subject produced within Talmudic texts, see Boyarin, *Unheroic Conduct,* 81–150. More focused reflections on gender and martyrdom can be found in Boyarin, "Martyrdom and the Making of Christianity and Judaism." See also Moore and Anderson, "Taking It Like a Man," and Burrus, "Torture and Travail." Although its readings run deliberately against the grain of historical chrono-logic, Moore's study *God's Gym* is also directly relevant to the discussion of torturously produced and ambiguously feminized early-Christian masculinities.

14. On the prevalence of positive representations of suffering in the Roman period, see Perkins, *Suffering Self.*

15. My argument here is partly anticipated by Gillian Clark, "The Old Adam."

16. Brown, *Making of Late Antiquity,* 6, 16.

17. Ibid., 12.

18. Brown, *Authority and the Sacred,* 4.

19. Brown, *Making of Late Antiquity,* 17.

20. Ibid., 100, 17.

21. Ibid., 79–80.

22. See also Brown's 1971 essay, "The Rise and Function of the Holy Man in Late Antiquity" (republished in Brown, *Society and the Holy in Late Antiquity,* 103–52), as well as his more extensive study of the rise of asceticism in Brown, *Body and Society.* In *Power and Persuasion,* Brown argues that the philosopher was displaced as political agent by "bishops and monks." In *Authority and the Sacred,* Brown reconsiders whether the cultural prominence of the "holy man," as well as the asceticizing apocalyptic narrative that partly creates this figure, has not been overplayed in his earlier works; bringing the (Eastern) "ascetic" habit of historiographic representation explicitly into play with a contrasting (Western) "Augustinian" narrative, here Brown does not so much demote as reinterpret the now-integrative figure of the "holy man" as the icon of late antiquity.

23. Brown, *Authority and the Sacred,* 4. See also the significant work of Cameron, *Christianity and the Rhetoric of Empire.*

24. Brown, *Making of Late Antiquity*, 65.

25. Ibid., 16.

26. Ibid., 98: "Some Christian theological controversies of the late fourth and early fifth centuries show how the tide had turned." Brown has in mind here the anthropologically focused Origenist and Pelagian debates, whose broader cultural implications are explored not only in Brown, *Body and Society*, but also in Clark, *Origenist Controversy*. See also the brief but highly suggestive account of the fifth-century christological controversies in Brown, *Power and Persuasion*, 152–58.

27. Brown, *Body and Society*, is the most significant exception to this general rule; yet even this work subtly resists thematizing masculine gender per se.

28. Brown, "Rise and Function of the Holy Man in Late Antiquity, 1971–1997," 356, 371.

29. Goldhill, *Foucault's Virginity*, 44. See also Vessey, "Demise of the Christian Writer." Beginning with the observation that Brown's early treatment of Augustine elides the role of the (ancient) biographer, Vessey goes on to highlight and contextualize what he takes to be "one of the most significant aspects of Peter Brown's representation of Late Antiquity: its tacit and tactical effacement, in the interests of a certain kind of vividness or (in Momigliano's phrase) social-historical 'full-bloodedness,' of the products and procedures of ancient literacy" (382–83).

30. See McLynn's suggestion that readers of Brown "instinctively, but mistakenly, classify holy men in contradistinction to bishops" and his proposal that Brown's portrait of the holy man might serve more helpfully to illumine "a continuum of 'self-created' holiness" that would include many of late antiquity's more famous urban bishops as well as the ascetics of its hinterlands. McLynn, "A Self-Made Holy Man," 464.

31. Irigaray, *Speculum*, 248.

32. Ibid., 143–44.

33. Irigaray, *This Sex Which Is Not One*, 76–77.

34. See especially Ruether's early essays—"Mysogynism and Virginal Feminism" and "Mothers of the Church"—and Clark's *Ascetic Piety and Women's Faith*. While these works have been considerably extended by more recent studies, they have not, in my view, been superseded.

35. Irigaray, *I Love to You*, 41.

36. Philosophy being defined as "the discourse on discourse," in Irigaray, *This Sex Which Is Not One*, 74.

37. Cixous, "Coming to Writing," 24.

38. Irigaray, *This Sex Which Is Not One*, 150.

39. Ibid., 171, 193.

40. See, e.g., Irigaray, *Elemental Passions.*

41. Cixous, "Coming to Writing," 45.

INTRODUCTION

1. Gleason, *Making Men,* xxvii.   2. Ibid., xxviii.

3. Ibid., xxvii.   4. Ibid., xxii, xxv.

5. Foucault, *Care of the Self,* 85.

6. Gleason, *Making Men,* xxv–xxvi.

7. Ibid., 159.   8. Ibid., 28.

9. Ibid., 166.   10. Ibid., 167–68.

11. Ibid., 166, 162.

12. She writes that Favorinus appealed "in ways we cannot quite assess," that "it is difficult to say" how the dissonance of the performance of effeminacy was resolved, and that "we may well wonder why so many dared to adopt it," but she does not herself "dare to speculate." Gleason, *Making Men,* xxviii, 129, 161–62.

13. See Barton's works *Sorrows of the Ancient Romans,* 11–81; "Savage Miracles"; and "All Things Beseem the Victor." In this context, the feminizing self-representation of the men of a marginalized Jewish culture begins to hint at continuities as well as contrasts between Judaism and the pagan "mainstream"; see Boyarin, *Unheroic Conduct,* 81–126. See also Perkins's wide-ranging study of the allure of figures of "suffering" in this period, *Suffering Self.*

14. Note the comment of Solomon-Godeau in *Male Trouble,* 40: "There is, in fact, every reason to think that like capitalism, masculinity is always in crisis, but like the phoenix—an appropriately phallic simile—it continually rises again, retooled and reconstructed for its next historical turn."

15. Gleason, *Making Men,* 166, recalling Bourdieu, *Logic of Practice,* 52–65.

16. Cameron, *Christianity and the Rhetoric of Empire,* 14.

17. Brown, *Body and Society,* 192.

18. Lim, *Public Disputation,* 22–24.

19. I have followed the Greek text and Lake's English translation in Eusebius, *Ecclesiastical History.*

20. In discussing how the letter emphasizes Paul's behavior despite its claim that his primary offense was one of belief, Norris comments: "One striking impression arises from the extant texts. This synod did not separate completely doctrine and morals, Lordship and discipleship" ("Paul of Samosata," 70).

21. In my earlier reading of this letter, I stress how Paul is represented as

plying the arts of the rhetorician as outlined in the handbooks and also slandered according to invective topoi developed in the context of traditional class rivalries between rhetoricians. See Burrus, "Rhetorical Stereotypes."

22. Polemo, *De physiognomia,* cited by Gleason, *Making Men,* 7.

23. See Sample, "Christology of the Council of Antioch (268 C.E.) Reconsidered," 24–26, on the possible significance of this controversy for the triumph of "logos Christology" over other existing christological options, e.g., Paul's purported "adoptionism," which is itself closely associated with Arian Christology by a later tradition. Burke, "Eusebius on Paul of Samosata," 19–20, hints at a possible resonance between Paul's image as a "self-made man" and his "relegation of Jesus to the human level," i.e., to the status of an inspired prophet. See also the critical assessment of the traditional association of Paul of Samosata's "low" Christology with Arius's particular subordinationism in Lorenz, *Arius judaizans?* 128–35.

24. On Eusebius's "philosophic" representation of Origen, see Cox [Miller], *Biography in Late Antiquity,* 69–101.

25. Origen's self-castration is also discussed ibid., 88–90. Cox Miller locates the problems helpfully within the tension between, on the one hand, Eusebius's desire to present Origen as a distinctly "Christian" ascetic, molding his life closely on the dictates of Scripture, and, on the other hand, his attempt to imbue Origen with the image of the self-controlled sage or "holy man" of pagan tradition.

26. Cf. Gleason, *Making Men,* 161.

27. Note the intriguing resonance, as well as the contrast, with Eusebius's insistence that while humanity "can participate in the super-human," it "otherwise cannot lawfully transcend its bounds, nor with its wingless body emulate the bird." Eusebius, *Against Hierocles* 6, cited by Cox [Miller], *Biography in Late Antiquity,* 75–76.

28. Lactantius here closely follows a passage in the stoicizing book 2 of Cicero's *De natura deorum,* but he places greater emphasis than Cicero's Stoic interlocutor on the heavenward orientation of the human body and on the mind's oversight of the body and indeed of all material creation. See Roots, "The DE OPIFICIO DEI," 476.

29. Roots points out that Lactantius's discussion of eyes relies not only on Cicero's *De natura deorum* 2.57.142–43 but also and more importantly on his *Tusculans* 1.46. Lactantius's Ciceronian defense of the view that the eyes are the "windows" of the mind is further interpreted by Roots as a refutation of Lucretius's *De rerum natura* 3.359–69: "The Lucretian and Ciceronian passages represent for Lactantius the two sides of a debate concerning the survival of

the soul and its relationship to the body—the very question behind these chapters of the *opif.*" Roots, "The DE OPIFICIO DEI," 477.

30. Nicholson points out that Lactantius quite strongly affirms "natural" passions both here and in *Institutes* 16; although *cupiditas, ira,* and *libido* may lead to vice when misdirected, to cut away such passions would also be to eradicate the human capacity for virtue. See Nicholson, "Doing What Comes Naturally."

31. Lactantius's philosophic eclecticism, in itself scarcely unusual or innovative, is expressed via a nuanced appropriation of Cicero's *De natura deorum,* through which Lactantius incorporates both the Stoicizing perspective of Cicero's Book 2 and the Academic critique of Book 3. Lactantius's strategic rhetorical use of the arguments of the Academic skeptic enables him to develop his own dogmatic position on the independence and superiority of mind or soul in relation to body. See Roots, "The DE OPIFICIO DEI," esp. 478–83.

32. Irigaray, *Speculum of the Other Woman,* 134.

33. Lactantius is discussed by Lorenz, *Arius judaizans?* 157–61. On Eusebius's position in relation to the trinitarian controversies, see Lyman, *Christology and Cosmology,* 82–123.

34. The existing literature on the Arian controversy is extensive; Hanson's *Search for the Christian Doctrine of God* is invaluable for its sheer comprehensiveness and is likely to remain a standard text for some time among English readers.

CHAPTER I

1. Brown, *Making of Late Antiquity,* 12. See also Brown, *World of Late Antiquity,* 54: "But if the demons were the 'stars' of the religious drama of Late Antiquity, they needed an impresario. They found this in the Christian Church."

2. Brown, *Making of Late Antiquity,* 85, 93–95, 98, 100.

3. Brown, in his *Making of Late Antiquity,* avoids even the bare mention of Athanasius as author of *Life of Antony* (such as is found earlier in Brown, *World of Late Antiquity,* 88, 96), while drawing on the *Apophthegmata patrum* on almost every page of chapter 4 ("From the Heavens to the Desert: Anthony and Pachomius").

4. Brown, *Making of Late Antiquity,* 89.

5. These questions have recently been approached by Brown himself, albeit somewhat obliquely, in his *Authority and the Sacred.*

6. Brown, *Making of Late Antiquity,* 17. Cf. Brown's *World of Late Antiquity,* where he glancingly associates Athanasius's *De incarnatione* with a cos-

mological interest, alluding briefly to Athanasius's "basic preoccupation" with the "'interweaving' of human and divine by visible symbols" (78).

7. Brown, *Making of Late Antiquity*, 91, 98.

8. Bell, *Jews and Christians in Egypt.*

9. Hanson, *Search for the Christian Doctrine of God*, 422, 254, 458.

10. Young, *From Nicaea to Chalcedon*, 68.

11. Cixous, "Coming to Writing," 22.

12. Note that although the broad structure of Hanson's work inclines him to regard Athanasius's thought in general and this text in particular as "immature" in relation to a fully developed "Christian doctrine of God," Hanson's *Search for the Christian Doctrine of God* (246, 417–18) follows those recent scholars who date Athanasius's early writings—*Against the Gentiles* and *On the Incarnation of the Word*—relatively late, i.e., to the years of his first exile, 335 or 336. See the discussion of dating in T. D. Barnes, *Athanasius and Constantius*, 12–13.

13. English translations of Athanasius's works generally follow the translation by Schaff and Wace in Athanasius, *Select Works and Letters.* Critical editions of the Greek texts are found in Athanasius, *Werke, 3 volumes.*

14. Hanson, *Search for the Christian Doctrine of God*, 451.

15. This phrasing is borrowed from Haraway, *Simians, Cyborgs, and Women*, 249 n. 7, as cited and critically engaged by Betcher, "Putting My Foot (Prosthesis, Crutches, Phantom) Down."

16. This is the emphasis of Roldanus, *Le Christ et l'homme.*

17. Brown, *Making of Late Antiquity*, 65, 91. But see also Roldanus, *Le Christ et l'homme*, 60: "in the thought of Athanasius, the frontiers between creator and creature can never be effaced or exceeded." Perhaps the fullest account of Athanasius's Christology as a response to the hardening of cosmological boundaries is given by Lyman in *Christology and Cosmology*, where she notes: "Athanasius' theological concerns were thus embedded in an ongoing religious and philosophical shift toward transcendence and reduced access to the divine during the fourth century" (131); "the fourth-century heavens remained open, but the process was now weighted through a corporate, ecclesiastical conduit, rather than a multiplicity of individual journeys" (159).

18. See the discussion of Roldanus, *Le Christ et l'homme*, 98–123. Lyman notes that Athanasius's tendency to attribute the fall more to the "natural instability of created being" than to a mental or volitional failure led him to emphasize the inadequacy of revelation alone: "only incarnation, not instruction, can destroy the passions of the body, thereby allowing one to become impassable and free" (*Christology and Cosmology*, 143).

19. Hanson, *Search for the Christian Doctrine of God*, 451.

20. Lyman, *Christology and Cosmology*, 153.

21. Roldanus, *Le Christ et l'homme*, 6.

22. The teaching that the cosmos was created by God out of nothing plays a role in the writings of earlier apologists and antignostic theologians; see May, *Creatio Ex Nihilo*, and the recent gloss of O'Brien, "Cumaean Sibyl." Thus, Pettersen, in *Athanasius and the Human Body*, may overstate Athanasius's originality when he asserts, "Prior to the debates of Athanasius with Arius, the theory of *creatio ex nihilo* was propounded, if at all, with uncertainty" (5). Nevertheless, Athanasius does seem to be the first to make the concept central to a cosmological model, positioning it at a stress point in the mediation of the oppositional categories of created and uncreated being.

23. Lyman, *Christology and Cosmology*, 137.

24. Roldanus, *Le Christ et l'homme*, 34–35, argues that Athanasius should not be misread as suggesting that the creation of humanity takes place in two distinct stages or moments: his distinction between "nature" and "grace" in humanity's creation is not temporal but theoretical. However, it seems clear enough that Athanasius here casts the divine gift of rationality as a proleptic response to the weakness of created nature. See Lyman, *Christology and Cosmology*, 137.

25. Athanasius does admit that humans have sunk a bit lower than even their created "nature" owing to the explicit transgression of the law (*Inc.* 5.2). However, it would seem that for Athanasius, as Lyman notes, "the essential instability of the created body . . . outweighed the disobedience of the will" (*Christology and Cosmology*, 142–43).

26. See Roldanus, *Le Christ et l'homme*, 33–36, for a discussion of Athanasius's use of the term φύσις to designate the corruptibility of all created nature (including human nature), in contrast to divinity. Counterbalancing corruptibility, as Roldanus observes, is the divine gift of rationality or creation "in the image" which distinguishes human beings from other creatures without dissolving the difference between humanity and the divine Logos or Image itself.

27. Widdicombe, *Fatherhood of God*, 1, 5.

28. Ibid., 258.   29. Ibid., 177–78.

30. Ibid., 258.   31. Young, *Biblical Exegesis*, 32.

32. In her article "Literal or Metaphorical?" Osborne observes that Athanasius's interpretation of the scriptural language of divine fatherhood is not strictly metaphorical: "the use of language familiar in a human context to refer to God is not metaphor, but rather the primary sense in a set of related and derivative meanings" (169). I would expand on this point by noting that it is the

not-quite-metaphorical reading of God as Father that gives particular force to Athanasius's redefinition of (human) "fatherhood" itself in terms of what is "primary" (shared with God) and "derivative" (not shared with God—i.e., bodily sex and sexuality).

33. Widdicombe, *Fatherhood of God*, 260.

34. Jay, *Throughout Your Generations Forever*, 116, 127.

35. T. D. Barnes, *Athanasius and Constantius*, 53, 254–55 n. 26.

36. On the Athanasian feminization of the Arian heresy, see also Burrus, "Heretical Woman as Symbol," 233–39.

37. Irigaray, *Sexes and Genealogies*, 14.

38. Lim, *Public Disputation*, 24.

39. See the incisive discussion of Athanasius's particular understanding of scriptural "canonicity" in terms of foundational authority in Brakke, "Canon Formation and Social Conflict."

40. Irigaray, *Speculum of the Other Woman*, 133.

41. Lim, *Public Disputation*, 220.

42. Ibid., 185.

43. Ibid., 186.

44. Although it appears unlikely from the manuscript tradition that Athanasius himself published these works at any point as a "collection," I tend to see some historical relation between his own production of edited collections of texts in defense of Nicaea and the early-fifth-century compilation of an edition of Athanasius's apologetic works. This collected edition was arranged and revised to provide a coherent historical account of the period from Nicaea to about 360 while avoiding a redundancy of cited documentary sources. Such a collection was probably assembled in Constantinople, where it seems to have been available to the historian Socrates. See Opitz, *Untersuchungen zur Überlieferung*, 144–58. The place of Athanasius in the early-fifth-century production of a canon of "select fathers"—with special reference to Cyril of Alexandria's appeal to Athanasius as *the* father of orthodoxy" by virtue of his defense of Nicene orthodoxy—has been discussed by Gray in his "Select Fathers," and further elaborated in his "Athanasius as Martyr." Gray, "A Star Is Born," points to the close interrelation between the work of Athanasius himself in "inventing the conciliarization of Nicaea" and the work of the later tradition in carrying out "the patrification of Athanasius." I am grateful to Patrick Gray for sharing his unpublished works with me. In the Theodosian West, a text ascribed to Athanasius already played a role in the archival strategies of the Roman episcopal court of Damasus. This was the earliest stage in the emergence of what Vessey refers to as "a new order of [Christian] books," that is, a

Christian literary practice marked by an appeal both to creeds and to a body of "what we should now call 'patristic' texts." See Vessey, "The Forging of Orthodoxy," 499–500.

45. T. D. Barnes, *Athanasius and Constantius*, 180.

46. Kannengiesser, "Athanasius of Alexandria vs. Arius."

47. Arnold, *Early Episcopal Career of Athanasius of Alexandria*, and Barnard, *Studies in Athanasius' "Apologia Secunda,"* both offer helpful analyses of the disputed issues surrounding Athanasius's election and deposition at Tyre yet are provocatively *different* from each other in their orientations and conclusions. Also indispensable is T. D. Barnes, *Athanasius and Constantius*.

48. M. R. Barnes notes in "Fourth Century as Trinitarian Canon": "While Marcellus may have consistently understood Nicaea and *homoousios* to have a broad normative intention, a careful reading of Athanasius's works reveals that it took him almost twenty years to come to this understanding of the significance of Nicaea, while he took almost another ten years to fasten upon *homoousios* as the *sine qua non* of Nicene theology" (53). Barnes emphasizes the modalist associations of Nicaea as well as the significance of the Alexandria-Rome alliance for the making of the council's reputation.

49. Note that Barnard argues, against earlier interpretations, that this letter was written while Athanasius was still in exile in Trier. See Barnard, *Studies in Athanasius' "Apologia Secunda,"* 27–29.

50. Ibid., 33.

51. Sieben, *Die Konzilsidee der alten Kirche*, 26–29.

52. As Patrick Gray notes, "That this galaxy of ideas so central to notions of traditional orthodoxy to this very day [i.e., a particular Alexandrian theology as orthodox, Nicaea as ecumenical, and its creed as uniquely authoritative] is a construction created by Athanasius (and others), and not a historical given, is demonstrated most strikingly by the fact that it was not a given for him: he himself did not begin to speak of Nicaea (council or creed) in these terms until the 350s" ("A Star Is Born").

53. Gibbon, *Decline and Fall*, 2: 333–34.

54. Sieben, *Die Konzilsidee der alten Kirche*, 35.

55. Ibid., 39.

56. T. D. Barnes, *Athanasius and Constantius*, 112.

57. The technique was just emerging with Athanasius. In the period immediately following his death, a more elaborate citational practice and deliberately demarcated literary corpus of "Fathers" developed in the East and West respectively; for accounts of these developments, see Gray, "Select Fathers," and Vessey, "The Forging of Orthodoxy."

58. Kristeva, "Revolution in Poetic Language," 113–17, provides a nuanced analysis of the relation between fetish and (poetic) text. Kristeva argues that, although it "converges with fetishism," the poetic function remains distinct insofar as it "maintains a *signification*"; that is, "the text is completely different from a fetish because . . . it is not a *substitute* but a *sign*." By claiming that the Nicene Creed *almost* becomes a fetish for Athanasius, I am suggesting that the creed converges so closely with fetishism (in the Kristevan sense) as *almost* to transgress textuality and its constitutive signifying practice. Athanasian textuality more generally derives power from its willingness to press poetic signification to the limits of fetishization.

59. Sieben, *Die Konzilsidee der alten Kirche*, 47.

60. Note that both the letter's dating and its link with Athanasius have been seriously questioned by Kannengiesser, "(Ps.-)Athanasius, Ad Afros Examined." For my own argument, the matter of authorship is neither insignificant nor absolutely decisive. I obviously disagree, however, with Kannengiesser's confident assertion that "Athanasius would never have reached the kind of juridical abstraction at work in Ad Afros" (271).

61. Commenting on the *Letter to the African Bishops*, Sieben highlights the unprecedented boldness of Athanasius's ultimate identification of Nicaea with the very Word of God as well as the basic consistency of that identification with his earlier positions: "Athanasius does not abandon his fundamental concept of the council even in this last writing dedicated to the defense of Nicaea and its faith, despite all its superlatives" (*Die Konzilsidee der alten Kirche*, 57).

62. Brakke, *Athanasius*, 168.

63. Ibid., e.g., 159–60.

64. Ibid., 81–82.

65. Gregg and Groh, *Early Arianism*, 131–59.

66. Elm, *"Virgins of God,"* 371.

67. I am here gently resisting the tug of accounts like that of Brown, *Body and Society*, 217: "The desert was a 'counter-world,' a place where an alternative 'city' could grow." Despite his emphasis on the significance of the "political" in Athanasius's thought, Brakke, *Athanasius*, is also inclined to conceptualize Athanasius's "desert city" in the dominantly contrastive terms of an "alternative." Goehring, "Encroaching Desert," makes a subtle and persuasive case for the desert as a (largely Athanasian) literary production that inscribes a symbolic opposition of city and wilderness onto what was actually a highly gradated social and topographic continuum of communal formations. Goehring remarks upon Athanasius's positive use of the trope of "city"—noting that the bishop of Alexandria "would have vested interests in avoiding the negative

view of the city" (284 n. 9)—while highlighting how the contrast of "earthly" and "spiritual" cities in the *Life of Antony* serves to critique and revise the image of the city.

68. Brakke, *Athanasius*, 90–99.

69. Brown, *Body and Society*, 214. See also the more extended discussion of Kelsey, "Body as Desert."

70. Gregg, introduction to *Athanasius*, 9.

71. Brown, *Body and Society*, 226.

72. Brakke, *Athanasius*, 132.

73. Jim Goehring called my attention to the parallel with the *Life of Pachomius*, in which the two female convents mentioned in relation to existing male communities are simply not included in the count when the number of Pachomian establishments is given.

74. The English translation follows Brakke, *Athanasius*, 292–302.

75. Elm, *"Virgins of God,"* 333.

76. Brakke, *Athanasius*, 182–83. See also Brakke, "Jewish Flesh and Christian Spirit," on Athanasius's use of Jerusalem in his festal letters as a negative emblem of Jewish particularity that "serves as a foil for Athanasius' vision of a universal Christian orthodoxy." This paper is part of Brakke's broader study of Athanasius's resistance to the localization of the holy, as further explored in his "Outside the Places, Within the Truth," which includes a treatment of the role of the *Life of Antony* in furthering Athanasius's theological and political agenda to detach holiness from the specificities of body and place. I am grateful to David Brakke for sharing his unpublished work with me.

77. Markus, *End of Ancient Christianity*, 181.

78. Brown, *Body and Society*, 32.

79. Cixous, "Coming to Writing," 3.

80. Ibid., 23.

CHAPTER 2

1. Meredith, *The Cappadocians*, 52.

2. Brown, *Body and Society*, 290, 304.

3. Pelikan, *Christianity and Classical Culture*, 8.

4. Rousseau, *Basil of Caesarea*, 17.

5. Cf. Brown, *Body and Society*, 293.

6. Meredith, *The Cappadocians*, 52.

7. Cixous, "Author in Truth," 147–48.

8. Loraux, *Experiences of Tiresias*, 13–14.

9. Ibid., 14–15.

10. English translations of *On Virginity* follow the translation by Moore and Wilson in Gregory of Nyssa, *Select Writings and Letters*, 343–71. J. P. Cavarnos's critical edition of the Greek is in Gregory of Nyssa, *Opera ascetica*, 215–343.

11. Aubineau, *Traité de la virginité*, 91.

12. Establishing a chronology of Gregory's life and works is likely to remain a vexed task. *On Virginity* is, however, the only one of his texts that can be dated with some certainty to the period before Basil's death, and was thus probably written between 370 (when Basil was consecrated as bishop) and 378 (when Basil died); see May, "Die Chronologie," 55. Aubineau is among those who have read Gregory's probable address of Basil as "our bishop and father" as implying that Gregory himself was not yet a bishop, and thereby as dating the work before 372, by which time Gregory had been appointed to the episcopacy of Nyssa (*Traité de la virginité*, 31). But as has been suggested by Gribomont, Gregory could have referred to Basil in these terms when already a bishop himself ("Le panégyrique de la virginité," 250).

13. Hart, "Gregory of Nyssa's Ironic Praise," 6–12. See also Hart's somewhat more fully contextualized treatment in "Reconciliation of Body and Soul."

14. This language was originally used in relation to "femininity" in Freud, "Femininity," 362.

15. M. R. Barnes, "Burden of Marriage."

16. Note that this is not far from Hart's position, especially as argued in his "Reconciliation of Body and Soul."

17. Hart, "Reconciliation of Body and Soul," 468–76, gives a fine account of Gregory's "ideal of marriage as public service," especially in relation to his use of the term λειτουργία in this passage.

18. This is the position taken quite forcefully by Hart, "Gregory of Nyssa's Ironic Praise," 4.

19. Gregory's Platonism, however "overt" in its reference to themes derived ultimately from texts like the *Republic*, the *Symposium*, the *Phaedo*, and the *Phaedrus*, avoids literal or explicit citation, so that it gives the impression of reflecting a rather indistinct, highly mediated, and widespread cultural *koine*. Thus Aubineau comments that perusing the Platonic texts is useful for the contemporary reader not because Gregory cites them verbatim but because "they restore a mentality, diffuse in time and space, in which Gregory shared, following so many others, and which impregnated every student who haunted the universities in the fourth century of our era" (*Traité de la virginité*, 99). In *On Virginity* 11, however, the references to the *Symposium* are unmistakable, as Aubineau himself documents (395). Cherniss argues in his much-cited study, *Platonism of Gregory of Nyssa*, that Gregory is deeply familiar with the Platonic

corpus itself, as well as with the biblical Platonism of Philo and Origen and the pagan Neoplatonic school of thought developed by Plotinus and his followers.

20. In *On the Making of Man*, Gregory is more explicit on the point that sexual difference is a secondary accretion upon humanity's original creation "in the image" of God, in whom there is no male and female. A sexed bodily nature was added to a prior sexless rational nature as an advance compromise with the need of a fallen humanity to reproduce itself in the face of mortality (*Opif.* 16). Resurrection will return humanity to its roots, eliminating marriage as the site of both sexual difference and procreation (*Opif.* 17). See Harrison's discussion in "Male and Female in Cappadocian Theology," 465–71.

21. Underlying the ambiguities of Gregory's conception of virginal desire are the ambiguities of "platonic love" as represented in some of the very dialogues of Plato of which Gregory makes heaviest use. At issue is the structure of sublimation in both linking and opposing carnal and spiritual desires, as well as an implicit question of how the homoerotic functions in ancient philosophic discourse from Plato to Gregory. In reference to the *Symposium*, A. W. Price notes that Plato "clearly believes that there is a natural connection between pederasty and pregnancy in soul," where the goal of love is defined as a mental or sublimated procreation "in beauty," structuring an erotic "succession" mimetically between like but unequal minds. "If pederastic desire is particularly susceptible to sublimation," Price continues, "then it is natural that those particularly capable of sublimation should be inclined towards pederasty." Price, *Love and Friendship in Plato and Aristotle*, 226.

22. The difficulty of interpreting *On Virginity* may also be related to what Stead refers to (with considerable philosophic dismay) as "a really extraordinary flexibility and imprecision of terminology" resulting from a tendency to slide all too easily (from Stead's perspective) between the concrete and the abstract ("Ontology and Terminology in Gregory of Nyssa," 113). Harrison takes a far more sanguine view of the matter, at the same time offering a broad but concise discussion of the relation between philosophic "concepts" and poetic "images" in Gregory's works (*Grace and Human Freedom*, 97–99).

23. See Harrison, "Gender, Generation, and Virginity," for a thoughtful account of Gregory's Mariology in the broader context of the significance of motherhood as a privileged image for spiritual generation in his thought. Plato, Philo, and Origen are discussed as the bearers of a tradition that constructs a feminized masculinity through the development of an image of spiritual childbearing in Harrison, "Allegorization of Gender."

24. Irigaray, *This Sex Which Is Not One*, 110.

25. Aubineau, *Traité de la virginité*, 66.

26. Irigaray, *This Sex Which Is Not One*, 74.

27. If Basil died in January 379, the first book of Gregory's *Against Eunomius* must have been published in 380; see May, "Die Chronologie," 57, and Vaggione, *Eunomius*, 82–89.

28. English translations of *Against Eunomius* I follow Moore and Wilson's translation in Gregory of Nyssa, *Select Writings and Letters*, 35–100. See also the more recent translation by Hall, "Contra Eunomium I." The unbracketed section numbers in my citations (as well as in Hall's edition) correspond to Jaeger's critical edition, Gregory of Nyssa, *Contra Eunomium libri, Part 1*. The bracketed numbers in my citations correspond to the divisions of the Moore and Wilson translation.

29. Bakhtin's work is suggestive insofar as his celebration of the grotesque (as it is presented in Rabelais's novels) serves to highlight the link between generativity and the degraded body in Gregory's text. Note that Vaggione, "Of Monks and Lounge Lizards," contrasts Gregory's "mordant wit" with the "Rabelesian gusto of Theodore" (184). Vaggione's aim, however, is scarcely to deny the legitimacy of a "Rabelesian" (or Bakhtinian) reading of Gregory's *Against Eunomius* but rather to place Theodore's and Gregory's texts at slightly different points on a spectrum of polemical deployments of grotesque imagery scattered throughout anti-Arian literature. These scattered passages, on Vaggione's reading, collectively indicate the Nicene party's alignment with an ascetic agenda that functioned to detach "the classical city" from its "moorings" (213). Note, however, the cautionary remarks of Richlin, *Garden of Priapus*, regarding a Bakhtinian interpretation of ancient literature: "The badness and disgustingness of what Roman satire perceives as bad and disgusting are strongly felt qualities, and the satirist is not celebrating or validating their part in life" (71–72). I am more willing than Richlin to risk seeming to attribute a false sense of "celebration" to my sources by highlighting the crucially productive role of rhetorical techniques of degradation and negation. Other recent and illuminating studies of uses of the grotesque in antiquity include Barton, *Sorrows of the Ancient Romans*, 85–189, and Boyarin, *Carnal Israel*, 197–225.

30. Bakhtin, *Rabelais and His World*, 29.

31. The English translation of letters 29 and 30 follows Gregory of Nyssa, *Select Writings and Letters*, 33–34, where they are numbered 1 and 2 respectively. The Latin is found in Pasquali's critical edition, Gregory of Nyssa, *Epistulae*, 87–91.

32. On the broader use of the soul as a container or receptacle in Gregory's thought, see Harrison, "Receptacle Imagery in St. Gregory of Nyssa's Anthropology," and Harrison, *Grace and Human Freedom*, 183–90. The sexual con-

notations of the image were easily grasped by readers educated in a philosoph-ical tradition for which Plato's *Timaeus* had long been a central text.

33. Price, *Love and Friendship*, 16.

34. Metaphors of sexual generation had also, of course, been appropriated by philosophically minded theologians. See, e.g., the recent work of Denise Kimber Buell on Clement of Alexandria's use of metaphors of procreation and filiation to describe the relationship of Christian teachers and students; Buell, *Making Christians*, 50–68.

35. If the initial hybrid "man-mother" is already comprehended as a unity ("philosopher") in the moment of Gregory's text, it is no longer perceived as grotesque. In contrast, the hybrid "man-(maternal) beast" emerges in the in-terval of the grotesque. See Harpham, *On the Grotesque*, 15–16: "The grotesque occupies a gap or interval; it is the middle of a narrative of emergent compre-hension. . . . Resisting closure, the grotesque object impales us on the present moment, emptying the past and forestalling the future."

36. Compare the discussion of the grotesque mimic in Barton, *Sorrows of the Ancient Romans*, 141: "The image in the mirror was often a grotesque or monstrous one." On Barton's reading, mimetic circulation thus casts the self as a reflection of a grotesque mime. Harpham, *On the Grotesque*, observes that "most grotesques are marked by . . . an affinity/antagonism, by the co-pres-ence of the normative, fully formed, 'high' or ideal, and the abnormal, un-formed, degenerate, 'low' or material" (9); "the sense of the grotesque arises with the perception that something is illegitimately *in* something else" (11).

37. This echoes Athanasius's depiction of Arius, e.g., *Ar.* 1.2.

38. Compare the portrayal of Paul of Samosata as a foot-stamping rhetori-cian, as discussed above in the introduction and in Burrus, "Rhetorical Stereo-types." Meredith, "Traditional Apologetic," 316, 317, also notes the parallels be-tween the polemical representation of Paul and Gregory's depiction of Eunomius. Illanes Maestre, "Sophistica y verdad en el exordio del 'Contra Eu-nomio,'" traces in Gregory's text a Christianizing deployment of the Socratic-Platonic construction of sophistry as the enemy of philosophy. Antisophistic rhetoric exaggerates decorum to the point that it becomes paradoxically both grotesque and effeminate. Thus Barton, *Sorrows of the Ancient Romans*, 120: "Inordinate refinements create monsters. The decorum of the warrior, taken to its extreme, unmans one: the heightened demands of etiquette produce the hyperurbane person, the perurbanus—the fop—who ceases by his ex-treme fastidiousness to be a fit Roman warrior and becomes instead . . . a *portentum*."

39. Eunomius seems to have claimed that his first *Apology* was delivered

publicly at the Council of Constantinople of 359 or 360 in response to accusations by Basil; see Vaggione, *Eunomius*, 5–9, and Röder, *Contra Eunomium I 1–146*, 40–56. Basil and Gregory, however, charge that Eunomius's authoring of an "apology" is a literary conceit intended to win the heretic unmerited sympathy.

40. It is this that makes possible a reconstruction of the Eunomian work, as undertaken by Vaggione, *Eunomius*, 99–127. Vaggione notes that Gregory "several times refers his readers to the original [of Eunomius's text] or assumes that they have access to it and are in a position to check him" and is generally sensitive to the distinction between direct citation and paraphrase (90).

41. Cf. the question posed by Vessey in "Holy Man Learns to Write": "When, and under what conditions, did it become possible to merge the figures of the late classical, Christian 'man of letters' and the scribe?"

42. Note, however, the relative unimportance of the term *homoousios* for Gregory and for the Cappadocians more generally. Even here (and this is one of only 25 references in Gregory's literary corpus), he suggests that the (negative) interest in *homoousios* was generated by the anti-Nicene emperor. See M. R. Barnes, "Fourth Century as Trinitarian Canon," 59–60.

43. Cf. Gregory's *Letter to Ablabius*, in which he responds directly to the charge of tritheism that had been leveled at his analogy of "Peter, James, and John." The grammatical "habit" of pluralizing "humanity," Gregory argues, is as mistaken as the practice of pluralizing "deity"—albeit less dangerously so, insofar as the former locution applies to a created nature, which lacks the inherent simplicity of divinity. Here Gregory also argues strongly for the unity of divine action, positing the perfection of divine cooperation as a crucial contrast with humanity's fragmentation. He closes by stressing the internal relationality signified by the terms "Father," "Son," and "Spirit" (as opposed to the relation of God with creation).

44. Wiles, "Eunomius," 163.

45. See also Mosshammer, "Disclosing but Not Disclosed."

46. Lim, *Public Disputation*, 149–81.

47. See, e.g., the discussion of Gregory's theory of "names" in Young, "The God of the Greeks," 67–71.

48. This is perhaps not so very far from some Orthodox interpretations of dogma as iconic in the direction of an apophatic kataphasis, as discussed by Harrison, "Relationship Between Apophatic and Kataphatic Theology."

49. Irigaray, *Speculum of the Other Woman*, 23.

50. Momigliano, "Life of St. Macrina," 335.

51. Halperin, "Why Is Diotima a Woman?" 293.

52. An entire monograph has recently been devoted to a comparative reading of the two texts: Apostolopoulos, *Phaedo Christianus.*

53. Roth, introduction to Gregory of Nyssa, *The Soul and the Resurrection,* 11. A more extended treatment of the comparison of the two dialogues is provided by Roth, "Platonic and Pauline Elements." Rowan Williams offers the following brief comments in "Macrina's Deathbed Revisited": "As in the *Symposium,* the sage is being instructed by a holy woman, whose sexual indeterminacy qua spiritual guide is here signalled by her repeated designation as *he didaskalos*—female article with male noun" (244).

54. For example, although the literary and philosophic precedents and context for Macrina's role as dialogue partner and female mystagogue are clearly of interest to Meissner, she makes virtually no mention of the *Symposium* and none at all of Diotima in her monographic study of Gregory's dialogue, *Rhetorik und Theologie.*

55. English translations of the *On the Soul and the Resurrection* follow Gregory of Nyssa, *Select Writings and Letters,* 430–68. See also the more recent renditions in Gregory of Nyssa, *Ascetical Works*; and Gregory of Nyssa, *The Soul and the Resurrection.* Numbered references in my text are to the columns in the Greek edition in Gregory of Nyssa, *Opera, Volume 3,* 11–160.

56. Compare R. Williams, "Macrina's Deathbed Revisited," 245–46: "Macrina's sense of the risks of [the *Phaedrus*'s] mythology is real enough; but she is no less haunted, on this her literary deathbed in DAR [*De anima et resurrectione*], by the same challenge, the challenge to reconceive mind itself as the ultimate—and never sated or exhausted—case of *eros.*"

57. Ibid., 231–32.

58. Smith, "Macrina, Tamer of Horses."

59. M. R. Barnes helpfully locates this discussion in the context of debates within Hellenistic philosophy about the unity of the soul, noting further that the dialogue's assertion of a sharp distinction between the rational and passionate faculties of the soul is strongly linked with the affirmation of God's impassability, where God is the paradigm for human rationality. Barnes attributes the dialogue's failure to refer to the trinitarian implications of divine impassability to the influence of the historical Macrina and her more traditional ascetic psychological views. See Barnes, "Polemical Context," 9–11.

60. Clark remarks that, although Macrina's role is modeled on "Socrates' muse Diotima of the *Symposium,*" her "words in the dialogue on the soul and the afterlife owe much to Plato's *Phaedo*" ("The Lady Vanishes," 24; see also Clark, "Holy Women, Holy Words," 424). The "words" of the *Symposium* dialogue also press themselves into Gregory's text, which—its title notwith-

standing—can be read as a discourse on desire and immortality through spiritual procreancy as much as on "the soul and the afterlife." Roth comments on "the parallels between Gregory's dialogue and the *Symposium*" in this description of the soul's ascent, also noting the allusion to the same Platonic passage in *On Virginity* ("Platonic and Pauline Elements," 23).

61. Halperin, "Why Is Diotima a Woman?"

62. Clark, "The Lady Vanishes," 25; see also Clark, "Holy Women, Holy Words," 424.

63. Irigaray, *This Sex Which Is Not One*, 76.

64. Irigaray, *Ethics of Sexual Difference*, 26.

65. English translations of the *Life of Macrina* follow Gregory of Nyssa, *Ascetical Works*, 163–91. Callahan's critical edition of the Greek is published in Gregory of Nyssa, *Opera ascetica*, 347–414.

66. See Halperin, "Why Is Diotima a Woman?" 288.

67. Gregory's attempt to suppress the tradition of ritual lament, condemning it "as pagan and effeminate," is discussed in Alexiou, *Ritual Lament*, 27–31.

68. An intriguing comparison can be made with the seemingly parodic Platonic *Menexenus*, in which Socrates borrows his speech from a memory of Aspasia's funeral oration (itself supposedly composed for Pericles' use!). If, as Loraux has argued in *Invention of Athens*, the eulogistic funeral oration is, for classical Athens, male civic speech par excellence, built on the suppression of the female discourse of lament, then Plato's dialogue is satirical not least in its inversions of gender: the woman Aspasia teaches a man how to talk like a man (*Menexenus* 236b–c). Gregg, *Consolation Philosophy*, examines the striking continuities with earlier, non-Christian Greek traditions in the consolatory letters and orations of the Cappadocians more generally.

69. Kristeva, "Stabat Mater," 174, 180.

70. I am aware that Macrina is most commonly seen as the "Christian" voice in this dialogue and Gregory as the voice of secular learning. I think the matter may be more complicated, particularly in relation to the metaphor of the charioteer.

71. Dünzl, *Braut und Bräutigam*, 369–79, provides a recent and helpful discussion of the well-known "*eros* versus *agape*" debate as it relates to Gregory's works.

72. Irigaray, *Ethics of Sexual Difference*, 21.

73. Momigliano, "Life of St. Macrina," 343.

74. English translations of the *Life of Moses* follow the translation by Malherbe and Ferguson in Gregory of Nyssa, *Life of Moses*. There are two current

critical editions of the Greek: Gregory of Nyssa, *De vita Moysis*, ed. Musurillo; and Gregory of Nyssa, *La vie de Moïse*, ed. Daniélou.

75. The dating of the treatise and the question of its "mysticism" turn out to be closely related; see, e.g., Heine, *Perfection in the Virtuous Life*, 1–26.

76. Ferguson, "Progress in Perfection," 314.

77. Heine, *Perfection in the Virtuous Life*, 102.

78. Harrison, in "Allegory and Asceticism in Gregory of Nyssa," comments: "Exegetical method thus comes to mirror ascetic behavior itself and conversely embodies a redirection of thought which can serve as a model for the corresponding redirection of human drives and activities" (114).

79. Daniélou, *Platonisme et théologie mystique*.

80. Heine's *Perfection in the Virtuous Life* follows Mühlenberg, *Die Unendlichkeit Gottes bei Gregor von Nyssa*, in challenging a narrowly "mystical" reading of Gregory's *Life of Moses* as well as his *Commentary on the Song of Songs*. Like Mühlenberg, Heine sees a close connection between the more "philosophically" framed theological and epistemological issues debated in *Against Eunomius* and the "spiritual" concept of eternal progress thematized in these less overtly polemical works. He argues, furthermore, that Gregory is at least as concerned to engage and counter Origenism's concept of spiritual "satiety" as Eunomius's concept of divine knowability. Closer attention is paid to the philosophical context of the *Life of Moses* by Böhm in his recent work *Theoria, Unendlichkeit, Aufstieg*.

81. See, for example, Böhm's careful discussion in *Theoria, Unendlichkeit, Aufstieg*, 235–64. Regarding the broader question of Gregory's "mysticism"— with which the interpretation of the *Life*'s "theophanic" passages is deeply entangled—Harrison observes with characteristic good sense that it is possible to reject a simplistic three-stage model of mysticism, accept the importance of polemical contexts, and still find in a work like the *Life of Moses* a central concern with describing "a path to participation in divine life" figured in terms of the soul's pursuit of an unmediated union with God (see Harrison, *Grace and Human Freedom*, 61–63).

82. Harpham, "Asceticism and the Compensations of Art," 366.

83. May, "Die Chronologie," 64.

84. Gregory of Nyssa, *Homily 6 on Song of Songs* 888C–93C. This English translation follows Musurillo's in Gregory of Nyssa, *From Glory to Glory*, 193–203. Note that Dünzl, *Braut und Bräutigam*, 380–88, emphasizes the intertextual complexity and fluidity of Gregory's erotic imagery in his *Commentary on the Song of Songs*, which by no means confines itself to the metaphors explicitly set out by the biblical text.

85. Irigaray, *This Sex Which Is Not One*, 210.

86. Cf. Milbank, "Gregory of Nyssa," 95: "For Gregory it is possible, at every ontological level to be in the same instance both receptive *and* donating." Although Milbank's reading of Gregory's erotic theory is close to my own, I am perplexed and indeed disturbed by his insistence that desire is for Gregory "entirely active, in no sense passive or lacking" (106). Milbank deems this crucial for the subversion of a "cult of weakness" associated with "a certain sickly version of Christian Hegelianism, exalting pathos and dialectical negativity" (109).

87. Cixous, "Tancredi Continues," 79.

88. Ibid., 84.

CHAPTER 3

1. Brown, *Power and Persuasion*, 9.

2. McLynn, *Ambrose of Milan*, xxii.

3. See Augustine, *Confessions* 6.3. As McLynn puts it, Ambrose "weathered the hostility of Jerome as impassively as he did the admiration of Augustine" (*Ambrose of Milan*, xiv).

4. McLynn insists that "the biographical approach" is "doomed to failure with Ambrose" and that his own account "is not . . . a biography" (ibid., xxii). Biography, McLynn implies, develops an interiorized subjectivity ("inner man"), and while this may be continuous with the (also deliberately staged?) effects of the literary corpora of others among Ambrose's peers—e.g., Augustine or Jerome—it is not, according to McLynn, an aspect of Ambrose's authorial self-fashioning. Ambrose is better compared with a man like the pagan letter-writer Symmachus, whom recent appreciative reassessments have credited "for his astute tactical sense and his skill in exploiting the formulae with which he worked" (xix).

5. McLynn further describes Milan as "an unusually governable capital," "a pliable stage," whose "record of docility" betrays a "civic passivity" (ibid., 223–24).

6. This phrase is from the subtitle of McLynn, *Ambrose of Milan*.

7. Brown, *Body and Society*, 346.

8. McLynn, *Ambrose of Milan*, xx, commenting on the historiographic tradition.

9. Ibid., 47.

10. Brown, *Body and Society*, 346.

11. Ambrose and the other bishops gathered at Aquileia could also describe themselves as defending "the whole body of the church," contrasting the unity

of the Western church with the disunity of the easterners. See McLynn, *Ambrose of Milan*, 138–39, citing *Epistula extra collectionem* 6 [12]. In a recent essay, "Fourth Century as Trinitarian Canon," M. R. Barnes concisely summarizes the complex coproduction of the victory of Nicaea by "westerners" and "easterners": "When an Eastern reinterpretation of Nicaea in the 370s was added to a Western reinterpretation of Nicaea in the 360s and to the vigorous pro-Nicene polemic of Alexandria and the churches in Rome and Gaul, these together produced a dominant consensus in favour of a reinterpreted Nicene Creed. In 380/381 the Western component of the consensus obtained support for a faith descriptively attached to the creed of Nicaea, particularly in its use of *homoousios*. The Eastern component of the consensus obtained support for a faith that in content went beyond Nicaea, particularly in the doctrinal significance of *hypostasis*" (61).

12. D. H. Williams, *Ambrose of Milan*.

13. Brown, *Body and Society*, 361. Cf. his interpretation of "the late Roman revolution," in Brown, *World of Late Antiquity*.

14. Brown, *Body and Society*, 364.   15. Brown, *Augustine of Hippo*, 83.

16. Brown, *Body and Society*, 343.   17. McLynn, *Ambrose of Milan*, xx.

18. Butler, *Gender Trouble*, 134.   19. Garber, *Vested Interests*, 39.

20. I borrow this suggestive phrase from the title essay in Zeitlin, *Playing the Other*, 341–74. The essay is a study in "theater, theatricality, and the feminine in Greek drama."

21. The bulges themselves are also of course borrowed in Greek comedy, where actors sport padded leather phalluses; see the discussion of transvestitism in Aristophanes in Zeitlin, *Playing the Other*, 382–86.

22. Modleski, *Feminism Without Women*, 90.

23. Note, however, that Brown emphasizes the continuity in the political role of the philosopher: "The courage of the philosopher, not the peremptory authority of a Catholic bishop, was what he wielded most effectively at that time. . . . Ambrose posed as a Christian example of the ancient *karteria*, of the inspired obstinacy with which the philosopher faced the powerful" (*Power and Persuasion*, 111). At the same time, Brown also argues for the ultimate displacement of the philosophers by Christian bishops and monks, whose strategies of self-fashioning proved better suited to the conditions of highly autocratic rule in the late Roman Empire.

24. Boyarin coins the term "femminized" to highlight gender's cultural performativity (as evoked by the terms "femme" and "butch") and disrupt the reification of the "feminine." See Boyarin, *Unheroic Conduct*, 4–5 n. 10.

25. Modleski, *Feminism Without Women*, 103.

26. Ramsey, *Ambrose*, x.

27. Butler, *Gender Trouble*, 127.

28. Duval, "L'originalité du *De uirginibus*."

29. For the texts of Ambrose, I have followed the translations by Romestin in Ambrose, *Select Works and Letters*. A more recent translation of *On Virgins* may be found in Ramsey, *Ambrose*, 71–116. For the original Latin text, see Cazzaniga's edition in Ambrose, *De virginibus*.

30. On Ambrose's use of the figure of Agnes, see also Burrus, "Reading Agnes," 30–33, and Burrus, "Equipped for Victory," 471–75.

31. Duval, "L'originalité du *De uirginibus*," 17.

32. Duval (ibid., 17) calls attention to the break in *Virg.* 1.5.21, where Ambrose shifts from the topic of virginity's provenance and parentage to that of her merits. I am suggesting that the discussion of "merits" continues and complicates the account of virginity's lineage, which itself echoes and begins to address the claim in 1.1.4 that Ambrose will "announce the family of the Lord."

33. Duval, "L'originalité du *De uirginibus*," 20.

34. Neumann, *Virgin Mary in the Works of Saint Ambrose*, 36.

35. Duval, "L'originalité du *De uirginibus*," 13 n. 31 bis.

36. As Caner argues in "Practice and Prohibition of Self-Castration," the prohibition of self-castration became commonplace in the fourth century, when the eunuch was no longer seen as an appropriate counterpart to the female virgin as a performer of an absolutized sexual continence—both because self-castration was considered too literal an interpretation of the ascetic call and because it was not literal enough (since eunuchs could often still enjoy sexual relations). Ambrose, however, is concerned neither with the possible sexual transgressions of eunuchs nor with the problem of literalism when it applies to the bodies of virginal *women*.

37. Markschies, *Ambrosius von Mailand*, 1.

38. Homes Dudden, *Life and Times of St. Ambrose*, 2.572, citing Rufinus, *Apologia* 2.23–5. Cf. Jerome's prologue to his translation of Didymus, *On the Holy Spirit*, in which he goes on to criticize Ambrose's treatise as soft and effeminate, painted and perfumed, lacking in virile argument.

39. Kristeva, "Stabat Mater," 163.

40. Markschies, *Ambrosius von Mailand*, 5, 216.

41. There seems to be no current consensus concerning the precise dating of the first two books of Ambrose's *On the Faith*. The question was reopened in the early 1970s when Gottlieb argued for a date of late spring or summer of 380 (*Ambrosius von Mailand*, 50). In response, Nautin attempted to reinstate a "traditional" date of late 378 or early 379 ("Les premières relations d'Am-

broise," 231–35). Among recent publications, McLynn, *Ambrose of Milan*, 102 n. 90, places the text before Gratian's visit to Milan in March 380. D. H. Williams, *Ambrose of Milan*, 109 n. 24, follows Nautin in dating the text earlier (378 or 379), while Markschies, *Ambrosius von Mailand*, 175, considers the date of 380, as proposed by Gottlieb, to be "more probable" but not certain. The Latin text used here is Faller's edition, Ambrose, *De fide*.

42. D. H. Williams, *Ambrose of Milan*, 153.

43. McLynn, *Ambrose of Milan*, 98.

44. Ibid., 103.

45. On Ambrose's competitive positioning of his own masculinity in *De fide*, see also Burrus, "Equipped for Victory," 463–71.

46. In addition, Ambrose's jumbling serves to jeopardize the legal standing of the "homoians" by identifying them with the "Eunomians" banned by Gratian, as McLynn points out in *Ambrose of Milan*, 103. See also the more extended discussion of Ambrose's possible motives for conflating Arians, Eunomians, and homoians—including political strategy, relative ignorance of Eunomianism, and the objective imposition of theological criteria—in Markschies, *Ambrosius von Mailand*, 180–97.

47. Irigaray, *Sexes and Genealogies*, 30–32.

48. D. H. Williams, *Ambrose of Milan*, 142–44, makes a case for a primarily local opposition at this point, which would strengthen the sense that a rhetorical "displacement" is being enacted in the text. See also Maier, "Private Space." Note, however, that Nautin, "Les premières relations d'Ambroise," had previously emphasized the significance of the opposition of the Illyrican bishops, and McLynn, *Ambrose of Milan*, 91–100, has followed Nautin's lead, suggesting more specifically (as well as speculatively) that it was Ambrose's aggressive intervention in the ecclesiastical politics of Illyricum that motivated Gratian's request.

49. As Brown notes in *Body and Society*, the word *lubricum* "carried an exceptionally heavy charge of negative meaning for [Ambrose]: it signified moments of utter helplessness, of frustration, of fatal loss of inner balance and of surrender to the instincts brought about by the tragic frailty of the physical body" (349). This remark comes close on the heels of Brown's observation that the *saeculum* was for Ambrose "a voracious sea, whipped by demonic gusts, across which there now drifted, in times of peace, the Siren songs of sensuality, of concern for worldly advantage, and of readiness to compromise with the great—beguiling, female figures who threatened always to 'effeminate' the male resolve of the mind" (348).

50. McLynn, *Ambrose of Milan*, 113–19. Cf. the more positive reading of

Gratian's reception of *On the Faith* 1–2 by D. H. Williams, *Ambrose of Milan*, 154–57.

51. The Latin text is edited by Faller in Ambrose, *De spiritu sancto libri tres*.

52. See, e.g., Basil, *On the Holy Spirit* 10.24–26.

53. Irigaray, *Sexes and Genealogies*, 31.

54. Markschies, *Ambrosius von Mailand*, 216.

55. See Irigaray, *This Sex Which Is Not One*, 170–91. The play with the term "femminized" is from Boyarin, *Unheroic Conduct*, 4–5 n. 10.

56. The critical edition is that of Testard, Ambrose, *De officiis*. Testard places the text between 386 and 389; see ibid., 1: 44–49.

57. Foucault, *Care of the Self*, 239–40.

58. Clark, "Foucault, the Fathers, and Sex," 626.

59. Foucault, *Use of Pleasure*, 82, 92.

60. Clark, "Foucault, the Fathers, and Sex," 632.

61. Cf. Song of Songs 4.12, frequently cited by Ambrose elsewhere and discussed in Power, "Ambrose's *Hortus Conclusus*."

62. Testard, "Étude sur la composition dans le *De officiis ministrorum*," 193.

63. Ibid., 167.

64. This fact had received virtually no scholarly attention before the careful study by Steidle, "Beobachtungen zu des Ambrosius Schrift *De officiis*," 20.

65. I am here in strong agreement with Steidle, "Beobachtungen zu des Ambrosius Schrift *De officiis*," concerning the significance of the prologue for interpreting the overall coherence of the first book.

66. Butler, *Bodies That Matter*, 129.

67. See Steidle, "Beobachtungen zu des Ambrosius Schrift *De officiis*," 20, on Ambrose's reworking of the function and significance of the *exemplum*.

68. For a more detailed discussion of Ambrose's strong reworking of the Ciceronian agenda in Book 2 of *On the Duties*, see Steidle, "Beobachtungen zum Gedankengang im 2. Buch von Ambrosius, *De officiis*."

69. McLynn, *Ambrose of Milan*, 272–74.

70. Ibid., 255.

71. Ambrose's virginalizing self-presentation does not, however, simply invert the Herculean image of a man wrapped in a lion's skin. As Loraux reminds us in *Experiences of Tiresias*, "as far as [Herakles'] clothing is concerned, the woman's *peplos* often competes with the lion's skin that is his official garment" (123).

72. McLynn, *Ambrose of Milan*.

73. Cox Miller, "Differential Networks," 114.

74. Ramsey, *Ambrose*, 195.

75. Cox Miller, "Differential Networks," 119.
76. McLynn, *Ambrose of Milan*, 377.
77. Cooper, *The Virgin and the Bride*, 147.
78. Cixous, in Cixous and Clément, *Newly Born Woman*, 147–48, 154–55.
79. Irigaray, *I Love to You*, 25.

CONCLUSION

1. Young, *Making of the Creeds*, 101.
2. Ibid., 102.
3. Ibid., 103.
4. Irigaray, *Sexes and Genealogies*, 61.
5. Young, *Making of the Creeds*, 103.
6. Cf. Ibid., x.
7. Cixous, "Coming to Writing," 24.
8. Irigaray, *Sexes and Genealogies*, 27.
9. Ibid., 32–34.
10. Mathews, *Clash of Gods*, 134–35.
11. Ibid., 118. Mathews suggests that "the aureole of light encircling the body of Christ was first introduced during the anti-Arian debate of the late fourth century." I am likewise gesturing toward the resonance between theological assertions of the radical transcendence of the divine Christ and visual images that locate Christ within a separate zone of heavenly light. Note, however, that my reading of the androgynous Christ differs somewhat from that of Mathews: he speculates that such an image might have appealed to either heterodox or female sensibilities, whereas I am aligning it with an orthodox masculinity.

Bibliography

Alexiou, Margaret. *The Ritual Lament in Greek Tradition.* Cambridge, Eng.: Cambridge University Press, 1974.

Ambrose. *De fide.* Ed. Otto Faller. Sancti Ambrosii Opera, Pars Octava. Corpus Scriptorum Ecclesiasticorum Latinorum, vol. 78. Vienna: Hoelder-Pichler-Tempsky, 1962.

————. *De officiis: Les devoirs.* Ed. M. Testard. Collection des universités de France. Paris: La Société d'Éditions les Belles Lettres, 1984–92.

————. *"De spiritu sancto libri tres," "De incarnationis Dominicae sacramento."* Ed. Otto Faller. Sancti Ambrosii Opera, Pars Nona. Corpus Scriptorum Ecclesiasticorum Latinorum, vol. 79. Vienna: Hoelder-Pichler-Tempsky, 1964.

————. *De virginibus.* Ed. Ignazio Cazzaniga. Turin: In Aedibus Io. Bapt. Paraviae et Sociarum, 1948.

————. *Select Works and Letters.* Trans. H. De Romestin. Nicene and Post-Nicene Fathers, Second Series, vol. 10. 1896. Reprint, Peabody, Mass.: Hendrickson, 1994.

Apostolopoulos, Charalambos. *Phaedo Christianus: Studien zur Verbindung und Abwägung des Verhältnisses zwischen dem platonischen "Phaidon" und dem Dialog Gregors von Nyssa "Über die Seele und die Auferstehung."* European University Studies, Series 20: Philosophy. Frankfurt am Main: Peter Lang, 1986.

Arnold, Duane Wade-Hampton. *The Early Episcopal Career of Athanasius of Alexandria.* Christianity and Judaism in Antiquity, vol. 6. Notre Dame, Ind.: University of Notre Dame Press, 1991.

Athanasius. *Select Works and Letters.* Trans. Philip Schaff and Henry Wace. Nicene and Post-Nicene Fathers, Second Series, vol. 4. 1891. Reprint, Peabody, Mass.: Hendrickson, 1994.

————. *Werke, 3 volumes.* Ed. Hans-Georg Opitz. Berlin: W. de Gruyter, 1935–41.

Aubineau, Michel, trans. and comm. *Grégoire de Nysse: Traité de la virginité.* Sources Chrétiennes, vol. 119. Paris: Les Éditions du Cerf, 1966.

Bakhtin, Mikhail. *Rabelais and His World.* Trans. H. Iswolsky. Bloomington: Indiana University Press, 1984.

Barnard, Leslie W. *Studies in Athanasius' "Apologia Secunda."* European University Studies, Series 23, Theology, vol. 467. Bern: Peter Lang, 1992.

Barnes, Michel R. "'The Burden of Marriage' and Other Notes on Gregory of Nyssa's *On Virginity.*" Paper presented at the North American Patristics Society annual meeting, Chicago, Ill., May 1996.

———. "The Fourth Century as Trinitarian Canon." In *Christian Origins: Theology, Rhetoric, and Community,* ed. Lewis Ayres and Gareth Jones, 47–67. London: Routledge, 1998.

———. "The Polemical Context and Content of Gregory of Nyssa's Psychology." *Medieval Philosophy and Theology* 4 (1994): 1–24.

Barnes, Timothy D. *Athanasius and Constantius: Theology and Politics in the Constantinian Empire.* Cambridge, Mass.: Harvard University Press, 1993.

Barton, Carlin. "All Things Beseem the Victor: Paradoxes of Masculinity in Early Imperial Rome." In *Gender Rhetorics: Postures of Dominance and Submission in History,* ed. Richard C. Trexler, 83–92. Binghamton, N.Y.: Center for Medieval and Early Renaissance Studies, 1994.

———. "Savage Miracles: The Redemption of Lost Honor in Roman Society and the Sacrament of the Gladiator and the Martyr." *Representations* 45 (1994): 41–71.

———. *The Sorrows of the Ancient Romans: The Gladiator and the Monster.* Princeton, N.J.: Princeton University Press, 1993.

Bell, H. I. *Jews and Christians in Egypt.* London: British Museum, 1924.

Betcher, Sharon. "Putting My Foot (Prosthesis, Crutches, Phantom) Down: Considering Technology as/and Transcendence in the Writings of Donna Haraway." Paper presented at the American Academy of Religion annual meeting, Orlando, Fla., 1998.

Böhm, Thomas. *Theoria, Unendlichkeit, Aufstieg: Philosophische Implikationen zu De Vita Moysis von Gregor von Nyssa.* Supplements to *Vigiliae Christianae,* vol. 35. Leiden: E. J. Brill, 1996.

Bourdieu, Pierre. *The Logic of Practice.* Trans. Richard Nice. Stanford, Calif.: Stanford University Press, 1990.

Boyarin, Daniel. *Carnal Israel: Reading Sex in Talmudic Culture.* Berkeley: University of California Press, 1993.

———. "Martyrdom and the Making of Christianity and Judaism." *Journal of Early Christian Studies* 6, no. 4 (1998): 577–627.

———. *Unheroic Conduct: The Rise of Heterosexuality and the Invention of the Jewish Man.* Contraversions: Critical Studies in Jewish Literature, Culture, and Society. Berkeley: University of California Press, 1997.

Brakke, David. *Athanasius and the Politics of Asceticism.* Oxford Early Christian Studies. Oxford: Clarendon, 1995.

———. "Canon Formation and Social Conflict in Fourth-Century Egypt: Athanasius of Alexandria's Thirty-Ninth *Festal Letter." Harvard Theological Review* 87, no. 4 (1994): 395–419.

———. "Jewish Flesh and Christian Spirit in Athanasius of Alexandria: The Construction of Universal Orthodoxy." Paper presented at the conference "The Origins of the Judeo-Christian Tradition Reconsidered," Trinity College, Hartford, Conn., June 1999.

———. "'Outside the Places, Within the Truth': Athanasius of Alexandria and the Localization of the Holy." In *Pilgrimage and Holy Space in Late Antique Egypt,* ed. David Frankfurter, 445–81. Religions in the Graeco-Roman World. Leiden: Brill, 1998.

Brown, Peter. *Augustine of Hippo: A Biography.* Berkeley: University of California Press, 1967.

———. *Authority and the Sacred: Aspects of the Christianization of the Roman World.* Cambridge, Eng.: Cambridge University Press, 1995.

———. *The Body and Society: Men, Women, and Sexual Renunciation in Early Christianity.* Lectures on the History of Religions. New York: Columbia University Press, 1988.

———. *The Making of Late Antiquity.* Carl Newell Jackson Lectures. Cambridge, Mass.: Harvard University Press, 1978.

———. *Power and Persuasion in Late Antiquity: Towards a Christian Empire.* Madison: University of Wisconsin Press, 1992.

———. "The Rise and Function of the Holy Man in Late Antiquity, 1971–1997." *Journal of Early Christian Studies* 6, no. 3 (1998): 353–76.

———. *Society and the Holy in Late Antiquity.* London: Faber and Faber, 1982.

———. *The World of Late Antiquity, A.D. 150–750.* New York: W. W. Norton, 1971.

Buell, Denise Kimber. *Making Christians: Clement of Alexandria and the Rhetoric of Legitimacy.* Princeton, N.J.: Princeton University Press, 1999.

Burke, John. "Eusebius on Paul of Samosata: A New Image." *Kleronomia* 7 (1975): 8–21.

Burrus, Virginia. "'Equipped for Victory': Ambrose and the Gendering of Orthodoxy." *Journal of Early Christian Studies* 4, no. 4 (1996): 403–7.

———. "The Heretical Woman as Symbol in Alexander, Athanasius,

Epiphanius, and Jerome." *Harvard Theological Review* 84, no. 3 (1991): 229–48.

———. "Reading Agnes: The Rhetoric of Gender in Ambrose and Prudentius." *Journal of Early Christian Studies* 3, no. 1 (1995): 25–46.

———. "Rhetorical Stereotypes in the Portrait of Paul of Samosata." *Vigiliae Christianae* 43 (1989): 215–25.

———. "Torture and Travail: Producing the Christian Martyr." In *The Feminist Companion to the New Testament*, ed. Amy-Jill Levine. Sheffield, Eng.: Sheffield Academic Press, forthcoming.

Butler, Judith. *Bodies That Matter: On the Discursive Limits of "Sex."* New York and London: Routledge, 1993.

———. *Gender Trouble: Feminism and the Subversion of Identity.* Thinking Gender. New York: Routledge, 1990.

Cameron, Averil. *Christianity and the Rhetoric of Empire: The Development of Christian Discourse.* Sather Classical Lectures. Berkeley: University of California Press, 1991.

Caner, Daniel F. "The Practice and Prohibition of Self-Castration in Early Christiantiy." *Vigiliae Christianae* 51, no. 4 (1997): 396–415.

Cherniss, Harold Fredrik. *The Platonism of Gregory of Nyssa.* 1930. Reprint, New York: Burt Franklin, 1971.

Cixous, Hélène. "The Author in Truth." In *"Coming to Writing" and Other Essays*, ed. Deborah Jenson, 136–81. Cambridge, Mass.: Harvard University Press, 1991.

———. "Coming to Writing." In *"Coming to Writing" and Other Essays*, ed. Deborah Jenson, 1–58. Cambridge, Mass.: Harvard University Press, 1991.

———. "Tancredi Continues." In *"Coming to Writing" and Other Essays*, ed. Deborah Jenson, 78–103. Cambridge, Mass.: Harvard University Press, 1991.

Cixous, Hélène, and Catherine Clément. *The Newly Born Woman.* Trans. Betsy Wing. Theory and History of Literature. Minneapolis: University of Minnesota Press, 1986.

Clark, Elizabeth A. *Ascetic Piety and Women's Faith: Essays on Late Ancient Christianity.* Studies in Women and Religion. Lewiston, N.Y.: Edwin Mellen, 1986.

———. "Foucault, the Fathers, and Sex." *Journal of the American Academy of Religion* 56, no. 4 (1988): 619–41.

———. "Holy Women, Holy Words: Early Christian Women, Social History, and the 'Linguistic Turn.'" *Journal of Early Christian Studies* 6, no. 3 (1998): 413–30.

————. "The Lady Vanishes: Dilemmas of a Feminist Historian After the 'Linguistic Turn.'" *Church History* 67, no. 1 (1998): 1–31.

————. *The Origenist Controversy: The Cultural Construction of an Early Christian Debate*. Princeton, N.J.: Princeton University Press, 1992.

Clark, Gillian. "The Old Adam: The Fathers and the Unmaking of Masculinity." In *Thinking Men: Masculinity and Its Self-Representation in the Classical Tradition*, ed. Lin Foxhall and John Salmon, 170–82. London: Routledge, 1998.

Colish, Marcia L. "Cicero, Ambrose, and Stoic Ethics: Transmission or Transformation?" In *The Classics in the Middle Ages: Papers of the Twentieth Annual Conference of the Center for Medieval and Early Renaissance Studies*, ed. Aldo S. Bernardo and Saul Levin, 95–112. Medieval and Renaissance Texts and Studies. Binghamton, N.Y.: Center for Medieval and Early Renaissance Studies, 1990.

Cooper, Kate. *The Virgin and the Bride: Idealized Womanhood in Late Antiquity*. Cambridge, Mass.: Harvard University Press, 1996.

Cox [Miller], Patricia. *Biography in Late Antiquity: A Quest for the Holy Man*. The Transformation of the Classical Heritage. Berkeley: University of California Press, 1983.

————. "'Differential Networks': Relics and Other Fragments in Late Antiquity." *Journal of Early Christian Studies* 6, no. 1 (1998): 113–38.

Daniélou, Jean. *Platonisme et théologie mystique: Essai sur la doctrine spirituelle de Saint Grégoire de Nysse*. 2d ed. Paris: Éditions Montaigne, 1954.

duBois, Page. *Sowing the Body: Psychoanalysis and Ancient Representations of Women*. Women in Culture and Society. Chicago: University of Chicago Press, 1988.

Dünzl, Franz. *Braut und Bräutigam: Die Auslegung des Canticum durch Gregor von Nyssa*. Beiträge zur Geschichte der biblischen Exegese. Tübingen: J. C. B. Mohr, 1993.

Duval, Yves-Marie. "L'originalité du *De uirginibus* dans le mouvement ascétique occidental. Ambroise, Cyprien, Athanase." In *Ambroise de Milan. XVIe centenaire de son élection épiscopale*, ed. Yves-Marie Duval, 9–66. Paris: Études Augustiniennes, 1974.

Elm, Susanna. *"Virgins of God": The Making of Asceticism in Late Antiquity*. Oxford Classical Monographs. Oxford: Clarendon, 1994.

Eusebius. *Ecclesiastical History*. Trans. Kirsopp Lake. The Loeb Classical Library, vol. 153. Cambridge, Mass.: Harvard University Press, 1926.

Ferguson, Everett. "Progress in Perfection: Gregory of Nyssa's *Vita Moysis*." *Studia Patristica* 14, no. 3 (1976): 305–14.

Foucault, Michel. *The Care of the Self: The History of Sexuality, Volume Three.* Trans. Robert Hurley. New York: Random House, 1986.

———. *The Use of Pleasure: The History of Sexuality, Volume Two.* Trans. Robert Hurley. New York: Random House, 1985.

Freud, Sigmund. "Femininity." In *Freud on Women: A Reader,* ed. and intro. Elisabeth Young-Bruehl, 342–62. New York: W. W. Norton, 1990.

Gallop, Jane. *Thinking Through the Body.* New York: Columbia University Press, 1988.

Garber, Marjorie. *Vested Interests: Cross-Dressing and Cultural Anxiety.* 1992. New York: Harper Collins, 1993.

Gibbon, Edward. *The History of the Decline and Fall of the Roman Empire.* 6 vols. Boston: Phillips, Sampson, 1854.

Gleason, Maud W. *Making Men: Sophists and Self-Presentation in Ancient Rome.* Princeton, N.J.: Princeton University Press, 1995.

Goehring, James E. "The Encroaching Desert: Literary Production and Ascetic Space in Early Christian Egypt." *Journal of Early Christian Studies* 1, no. 3 (1993): 281–96.

Goldhill, Simon. *Foucault's Virginity: Ancient Erotic Fiction and the History of Sexuality.* The W. B. Stanford Memorial Lectures. Cambridge, Eng.: Cambridge University Press, 1995.

Gottlieb, Gunther. *Ambrosius von Mailand und Kaiser Gratian.* Göttingen: Vandenhoek and Ruprecht, 1973.

Gray, Patrick T. R. "Athanasius as Martyr and as the Teacher of Monks: Two Topoi Used in His Patrification." Unpublished paper.

———. "'The Select Fathers': Canonizing the Patristic Past." *Studia Patristica* 23 (1989): 21–36.

———. "A Star Is Born: The Patrification of Athanasius." Unpublished paper.

Gregg, Robert C. *Consolation Philosophy: Greek and Christian Paideia in Basil and the Two Gregories.* Patristic Monograph Series. Cambridge, Mass.: Philadelphia Patristic Foundation, Ltd., 1975.

———. Introduction to *Athanasius: "The Life of Antony" and the "Letter to Marcellinus,"* trans. Robert C. Gregg. The Classics of Western Spirituality. New York: Paulist, 1980.

Gregg, Robert C., and Dennis Groh. *Early Arianism—A View of Salvation.* Philadelphia: Fortress, 1981.

Gregory of Nyssa. *Ascetical Works.* Trans. Virginia Woods Callahan. Fathers of the Church, vol. 46. Washington, D.C.: Catholic University of America Press, 1967.

————. *Contra Eunomium libri, Part 1.* Ed. Werner Jaeger. Gregorii Nysseni Opera, vol. 1. Leiden: E. J. Brill, 1960.

————. *De vita Moysis.* Ed. Herbert Musurillo. Gregorii Nysseni Opera, vol. 7.1. Leiden: E. J. Brill, 1964.

————. *Epistulae.* Ed. Georgius Pasquali. Gregorii Nysseni Opera, vol. 8.2. Leiden: E. J. Brill, 1959.

————. *From Glory to Glory: Texts from Gregory of Nyssa's Mystical Writings.* Trans. and ed. Herbert Musurillo. Sel. and intro. Jean Danielou. New York: Charles Scribner's Sons, 1961.

————. *The Life of Moses.* Trans., intro., and notes Abraham J. Malherbe and Everett Ferguson. The Classics of Western Spirituality. New York: Paulist, 1978.

————. *Opera ascetica.* Ed. Werner Jaeger, Johannes P. Cavarnos, and Virginia Woods Callahan. Gregorii Nysseni Opera, vol. 8.1. Leiden: E. J. Brill, 1952.

————. *Opera,* vol. 3: *Patrologia Graeca,* vol. 46. Paris: J.-P. Migne, 1863.

————. *Select Writings and Letters.* Trans. William Moore and Henry Austin Wilson. Nicene and Post-Nicene Fathers, Second Series, vol. 5. 1893. Reprint, Peabody, Mass.: Hendrickson, 1994.

————. *St. Gregory of Nyssa: The Soul and the Resurrection.* Trans. and intro. Catharine P. Roth. Crestwood, N.Y.: St. Vladimir's Seminary Press, 1993.

————. *La vie de Moïse.* Intro., trans., and crit. ed. S. J. Jean Daniélou. Sources Chrétiennes, vol. 1. Paris: Éditions du Cerf, 1955.

Gribomont, Jean. "Le panégyrique de la virginité, oeuvre de jeunesse de Grégoire de Nysse." *Revue d'ascetique et de mystique* 43 (1967): 251–66.

Gwatkin, Henry Melvill. *Studies of Arianism: Chiefly Referring to the Character and Chronology of the Reaction Which Followed the Council of Nicaea.* Cambridge, Eng.: Deighton, Bell, 1882.

Hall, Stuart G. "'Contra Eunomium I': Introducción y traducción." In *El "Contra Enomium I" en la producción literaria de Gregorio de Nisa: VI Coloquio internacional sobre Gregorio de Nisa,* ed. Lucas F. Mateo-Seco and Jan L. Bastero, 21–135. Pamplona: Ediciones Universidad de Navarra, S.A., 1988.

Halperin, David M. "Why Is Diotima a Woman? Platonic Erōs and the Figuration of Gender." In *Before Sexuality: The Construction of Erotic Experience in the Ancient Greek World,* ed. David Halperin, Jack Winkler, and Froma Zeitlin, 257–308. Princeton, N.J.: Princeton University Press, 1990.

Hanson, R. P. C. *The Search for the Christian Doctrine of God: The Arian Controversy, 318–381.* Edinburgh: T. and T. Clark, 1988.

Haraway, Donna. *Simians, Cyborgs, and Women: The Reinvention of Nature.* New York: Routledge, 1991.

Harpham, Geoffrey Galt. "Asceticism and the Compensations of Art." In *Asceticism*, ed. Vincent L. Wimbush and Richard Valantasis, 357–68. New York: Oxford University Press, 1995.

———. *On the Grotesque: Strategies of Contradiction in Art and Literature.* Princeton, N.J.: Princeton University Press, 1982.

Harrison, Verna E. F. "The Allegorization of Gender: Plato and Philo on Spiritual Childbearing." In *Asceticism*, ed. Vincent L. Wimbush and Richard Valantasis, 520–34. New York: Oxford University Press, 1995.

———. "Allegory and Asceticism in Gregory of Nyssa." In *Discursive Formations, Ascetic Piety, and the Interpretation of Early Christian Literature, Part I*, ed. Vincent Wimbush, 113–30. *Semeia* 57. Atlanta: Scholars, 1992.

———. "Gender, Generation, and Virginity in Cappadocian Theology." *Journal of Theological Studies*, n.s. 47 (1996): 38–68.

———. *Grace and Human Freedom According to St. Gregory of Nyssa.* Studies in the Bible and Early Christianity. Lewiston, N.Y.: Edwin Mellen, 1992.

———. "Male and Female in Cappadocian Theology." *Journal of Theological Studies*, n.s. 41 (1990): 441–71.

———. "Receptacle Imagery in St. Gregory of Nyssa's Anthropology." *Studia Patristica* 22 (1989): 23–27.

———. "The Relationship Between Apophatic and Kataphatic Theology." *Pro Ecclesia* 4 (1995): 318–32.

Hart, Mark D. "Gregory of Nyssa's Ironic Praise of the Celibate Life." *Heythrop Journal* 33 (1992): 1–19.

———. "Reconciliation of Body and Soul: Gregory of Nyssa's Deeper Theology of Marriage." *Theological Studies* 51 (1990): 450–78.

Heine, Ronald E. *Perfection in the Virtuous Life: A Study in the Relationship Between Edification and Polemical Theology in Gregory of Nyssa's "De Vita Moysis."* Patristic Monograph Series. Cambridge, Mass.: The Philadelphia Patristic Foundation, 1975.

Homes Dudden, F. *The Life and Times of St. Ambrose.* Oxford: Clarendon, 1935.

Illanes Maestre, José Luis. "Sophistica y verdad en el exordio del 'Contra Eunomio.'" In *El "Contra Eunomium I" en la producción literaria de Gregorio de Nisa*, ed. L. F. Mateo-Seco and J. L. Bastero, 237–45. Pamplona: Ediciones Universidad de Navarra, S.A., 1988.

Irigaray, Luce. *Elemental Passions.* Trans. Joanne Collie and Judith Still. New York: Routledge, 1992.

———. *An Ethics of Sexual Difference.* Trans. Carolyn Burke and Gillian C. Gill. Ithaca, N.Y.: Cornell University Press, 1993.

———. *I Love to You: Sketch of a Possible Felicity in History.* Trans. Alison Martin. New York: Routledge, 1996.

———. *Marine Lover of Friedrich Nietzsche.* Trans. Gillian C. Gill. New York: Columbia University Press, 1991.

———. *Sexes and Genealogies.* Trans. Gillian C. Gill. New York: Columbia University Press, 1993.

———. *Speculum of the Other Woman.* Trans. Gillian C. Gill. Ithaca, N.Y.: Cornell University Press, 1985.

———. *This Sex Which Is Not One.* Ithaca, N.Y.: Cornell University Press, 1985.

Jay, Nancy. *Throughout Your Generations Forever: Sacrifice, Religion, and Paternity.* Chicago: University of Chicago Press, 1992.

Kannengiesser, Charles. "Athanasius of Alexandria vs. Arius: The Alexandrian Crisis." In *The Roots of Egyptian Christianity,* ed. Birger A. Pearson and James E. Goehring, 204–15. Studies in Antiquity and Christianity. Philadelphia: Fortress, 1986.

———. "(Ps.-)Athanasius, Ad Afros Examined." In *Logos: Festschrift für Luise Abramowski zum 8. Juli 1993,* ed. Hanns Christof Brennecke, Ernst Ludwig Grasmück, and Christoph Markschies, 264–80. Beihefte zur Zeitschrift für die neutestamentliche Wissenschaft und die Kunde der älteren Kirche. Berlin: Walter de Gruyter, 1993.

Kelsey, Neal. "The Body as Desert in the Life of St. Anthony." In *Discursive Formations, Ascetic Piety, and the Interpretation of Early Christian Literature, Part I,* ed. Vincent Wimbush, 130–51. *Semeia* 57. Atlanta: Scholars, 1992.

Kristeva, Julia. "Revolution in Poetic Language." In *The Kristeva Reader,* ed. Toril Moi, 89–136. Oxford: Basil Blackwell, 1986.

———. "Stabat Mater." Trans. León S. Roudiez. In *The Kristeva Reader,* ed. Toril Moi, 160–86. Oxford: Basil Blackwell, 1986.

Lim, Richard. *Public Disputation, Power, and Social Order in Late Antiquity.* The Transformation of the Classical Heritage. Berkeley: University of California Press, 1995.

Loraux, Nicole. *The Experiences of Tiresias: The Feminine and the Greek Man.* Trans. Paula Wissing. Princeton, N.J.: Princeton University Press, 1995.

———. *The Invention of Athens: The Funeral Oration in the Classical City.* Trans. Alan Sheridan. Cambridge, Mass.: Harvard University Press, 1986.

Lorenz, Rudolf. *Arius judaizans? Untersuchungen zur dogmengeschichtlichen*

Einordnung des Arius. Forschungen zur Kirchen- und Dogmengeschichte. Göttingen: Vandenhoeck und Ruprecht, 1979.

Lyman, J. Rebecca. *Christology and Cosmology: Models of Divine Activity in Origen, Eusebius, and Athanasius.* Oxford Theological Monographs. Oxford: Clarendon, 1993.

Maier, Harry O. "Private Space as the Social Context of Arianism in Ambrose's Milan." *Journal for Theological Studies*, n.s. 45 (1994): 72–93.

Markschies, Christoph. *Ambrosius von Mailand und die Trinitätstheologie: Kirchen- und theologiegeschichtliche Studien zu Antiarianismus and Neunizänismus bei Ambrosius und im lateinischen Westen (364–381 n.Chr.).* Beiträge zur historischen Theologie. Tübingen: J. C. B. Mohr (Paul Siebeck), 1995.

Markus, Robert. *The End of Ancient Christianity.* Cambridge, Eng.: Cambridge University Press, 1990.

Mathews, Thomas F. *The Clash of Gods: A Reinterpretation of Early Christian Art.* Princeton, N.J.: Princeton University Press, 1993.

May, Gerhard. "Die Chronologie des Lebens und der Werke des Gregor von Nyssa." In *Écriture et culture philosophique dans la pensée de Grégoire de Nysse: Actes du colloque de Chevetogne (22–26 Septembre 1969)*, ed. Marguerite Harl, 51–67. Leiden: E. J. Brill, 1971.

———. *Creatio Ex Nihilo, the Doctrine of "Creation Out of Nothing" in Early Christian Thought.* Trans. A. S. Worrall. Edinburgh: T. and T. Clark, 1994.

McLynn, Neil B. *Ambrose of Milan: Church and Court in a Christian Capital.* The Transformation of the Classical Heritage. Berkeley: University of California Press, 1994.

———. "From Palladius to Maximinus: Passing the Arian Torch." *Journal for Early Christian Studies* 4, no. 4 (1996): 477–93.

———. "A Self-Made Holy Man: The Case of Gregory Nazianzen." *Journal of Early Christian Studies* 6, no. 3 (1998): 463–83.

Meissner, Henriette M. *Rhetorik und Theologie: Der Dialog Gregors von Nyssa De anima et resurrectione.* Patrologia: Beiträge zum Studium der Kirchenväter. Frankfurt am Main: Peter Lang, 1991.

Meredith, Anthony. *The Cappadocians.* Crestwood, N.Y.: St. Vladimir's Seminary Press, 1995.

———. "Traditional Apologetic in the *Contra Eunomium* of Gregory of Nyssa." *Studia Patristica* 14, no. 3 (1976): 315–19.

Milbank, John. "Gregory of Nyssa: The Force of Identity." In *Christian Origins: Theology, Rhetoric and Community*, ed. Lewis Ayres and Gareth Jones, 94–116. New York: Routledge, 1998.

Modleski, Tania. *Feminism Without Women: Culture and Criticism in a "Post-feminist" Age.* New York: Routledge, 1991.

Momigliano, Arnaldo. "The Life of St. Macrina by Gregory of Nyssa." In Arnaldo Momigliano, *On Pagans, Jews, and Christians,* 333–47. Middletown, Conn.: Wesleyan University Press, 1987.

Moore, Stephen D. *God's Gym: Divine Male Bodies of the Bible.* New York: Routledge, 1996.

Moore, Stephen D., and Janice Capel Anderson. "Taking It Like a Man: Masculinity in 4 Maccabees." *Journal of Biblical Literature* 117, no. 2 (1998): 249–73.

Mosshammer, Alden A. "Disclosing but Not Disclosed: Gregory of Nyssa as Deconstructionist." In *Studien zu Gregor von Nyssa und der christlichen Spätantike,* ed. Hubertus R. Drobner and Christoph Klock, 99–122. Supplements to Vigiliae Christianae. Leiden: E. J. Brill, 1990.

Mühlenberg, Ekkehard. *Die Unendlichkeit Gottes bei Gregor von Nyssa: Gregors Kritik am Gottesbegriff der klassischen Metaphysik.* Forschungen zur Kirchen- und Dogmengeschichte. Göttingen: Vandenhoeck und Ruprecht, 1966.

Nautin, Pierre. "Les premières relations d'Ambroise avec l'empereur Gratien: Le *De fide* (livres I et II)." In *Ambroise de Milan: XVIe centenaire de son élection épiscopale,* ed. Yves-Marie Duval, 229–44. Paris: Études Augustiniennes, 1974.

Neumann, Charles William. *The Virgin Mary in the Works of Saint Ambrose.* Paradosis: Contributions to the History of Early Christian Literature and Theology. Fribourg: University Press Fribourg, 1962.

Nicholson, Oliver. "Doing What Comes Naturally: Lactantius on Libido." *Studia Patristica* 31 (1997): 314–21.

Norris, Frederick W. "Paul of Samosata: *Procurator Ducenarius.*" *Journal of Theological Studies,* n.s. 35 (1984): 50–70.

O'Brien, D. P. "The Cumaean Sibyl as the Revelation-Bearer in the *Shepherd of Hermas.*" *Journal of Early Christian Studies* 5, no. 4 (Winter 1997): 473–96.

Opitz, Hans-Georg. *Untersuchungen zur Überlieferung der Schriften des Athanasius.* Arbeiten zur Kirchengeschichte, vol. 23. Berlin: Walter de Gruyter, 1935.

Osborne, Catherine. "Literal or Metaphorical? Some Issues of Language in the Arian Controversy." In *Christian Faith and Greek Philosophy in Late Antiquity: Essays in Tribute to George Christopher Stead,* ed. Lionel R. Wickham and Caroline P. Bammel, 148–70. Leiden: E. J. Brill, 1993.

Pelikan, Jaroslav. *Christianity and Classical Culture: The Metamorphosis of*

Natural Theology in the Christian Encounter with Hellenism. Gifford Lectures at Aberdeen, 1992–1993. New Haven, Conn.: Yale University Press, 1993.

Perkins, Judith. *The Suffering Self: Pain and Narrative Representation in the Early Christian Era.* London: Routledge, 1995.

Pettersen, Alvyn. *Athanasius and the Human Body.* Bristol: The Bristol Press, 1990.

Power, Kim E. "Ambrose's *Hortus Conclusus* and the Transmission of Classical Culture." Paper presented at the North American Patristics Society annual meeting, Chicago, Ill., May 1998.

Price, A. W. *Love and Friendship in Plato and Aristotle.* Oxford: Clarendon, 1989.

Ramsey, Boniface. *Ambrose.* The Early Church Fathers. London: Routledge, 1997.

Richlin, Amy. *The Garden of Priapus: Sexuality and Aggression in Roman Humor.* New Haven, Conn.: Yale University Press, 1983.

Röder, Jürgen-André, trans. and comm. *Gregory von Nyssa. Contra Eunomium I 1–146.* Patrologia: Beiträge zum Studium der Kirchenväter. Frankfurt am Main: Peter Lang, 1993.

Roldanus, J. *Le Christ et l'homme dans la théologie d'Athanase d'Alexandrie: Étude de la conjonction de sa conception de l'homme avec sa Christologie.* Studies in the History of Christian Thought, vol. 4. Leiden: E. J. Brill, 1968.

Roots, Peter A. "The DE OPIFICIO DEI: The Workmanship of God and Lactantius." *Classical Quarterly* 37 (1987): 466–86.

Roth, Catharine P. "Platonic and Pauline Elements in the Ascent of the Soul in Gregory of Nyssa's *Dialogue on the Soul and Resurrection.*" *Vigiliae Christianae* 46 (1992): 20–30.

Rousseau, Philip. *Basil of Caesarea.* The Transformation of the Classical Heritage. Berkeley: University of California Press, 1994.

Ruether, Rosemary. "Mothers of the Church: Ascetic Women in the Late Patristic Age." In *Women of Spirit,* ed. Rosemary Ruether and Eleanor McLaughlin, 71–98. New York: Simon and Schuster, 1979.

———. "Mysogynism and Virginal Feminism in the Fathers of the Church." In *Religion and Sexism,* ed. Rosemary Ruether. New York: Simon and Schuster, 1974.

Sample, Robert. "The Christology of the Council of Antioch (268 C.E.) Reconsidered." *Church History* 48 (1979): 18–26.

Sieben, Hermann Josef. *Die Konzilsidee der alten Kirche.* Paderborn: Ferdinand Schöningh, 1979.

Smith, J. Warren. "Macrina, Tamer of Horses and Healer of Souls: Grief and the Therapy of Hope in Gregory of Nyssa's *De Anima et Resurrectione*." Paper presented at the North American Patristics Society annual meeting, Chicago, Ill., May 1998.

Solomon-Godeau, Abigail. *Male Trouble: A Crisis in Representation*. London: Thames and Hudson, 1997.

Stead, Christopher. "Ontology and Terminology in Gregory of Nyssa." In *Gregor von Nyssa und die Philosophie: Zweites internationales Kolloquium über Gregor von Nyssa*, ed. Heinrich Dörrie and Margarete Altenburger, 107–27. Leiden: E. J. Brill, 1976.

Steidle, Wolf. "Beobachtungen zu des Ambrosius Schrift *De officiis*." *Vigiliae Christianae* 38 (1984): 18–66.

———. "Beobachtungen zum Gedankengang im 2. Buch von Ambrosius, *De officiis*." *Vigiliae Christianae* 39 (1985): 280–98.

Testard, Maurice. "Étude sur la composition dans le *De officiis ministrorum* de saint Ambroise." In *Ambroise de Milan: XVIe Centenaire de son élection épiscopale*, ed. Yves-Marie Duval, 155–97. Paris: Études Augustiniennes, 1974.

Vaggione, Richard Paul. *Eunomius: The Extant Works*. Oxford Early Christian Texts. Oxford: Clarendon, 1987.

———. "Of Monks and Lounge Lizards: 'Arians,' Polemics and Asceticism in the Roman East." In *Arianism After Arius: Essays in the Development of the Fourth Century Trinitarian Conflicts*, ed. Michel R. Barnes and Daniel H. Williams, 181–214. Edinburgh: T. and T. Clark, 1993.

Vessey, Mark. "The Demise of the Christian Writer and the Making of 'Late Antiquity': From H.-I. Marrou's Saint Augustine (1938) to Peter Brown's Holy Man (1983)." *Journal of Early Christian Studies* 6, no. 3 (1998): 377–411.

———. "The Forging of Orthodoxy in Latin Christian Literature: A Case Study." *Journal of Early Christian Studies* 4, no. 4 (1996): 495–513.

———. "The Holy Man Learns to Write: Author-Portraits in Late Antiquity." Paper presented at the College Art Association 86th annual conference, Toronto, 1998.

Widdicombe, Peter. *The Fatherhood of God from Origen to Athanasius*. Oxford Theological Monographs. Oxford: Clarendon, 1994.

Wiles, Maurice. *Archetypal Heresy: Arianism Through the Centuries*. Oxford: Clarendon, 1996.

———. "Eunomius: Hair-Splitting Dialectician or Defender of the Accessibility of Salvation?" In *The Making of Orthodoxy: Essays in Honor of Henry Chadwick*, ed. Rowan Williams, 157–72. Cambridge, Eng.: Cambridge University Press, 1989.

Williams, Daniel H. *Ambrose of Milan and the End of the Nicene-Arian Conflicts.* Oxford Early Christian Studies. Oxford: Clarendon, 1995.

Williams, Rowan. "Macrina's Deathbed Revisited: Gregory of Nyssa on Mind and Passion." In *Christian Faith and Greek Philosophy in Late Antiquity: Essays in Tribute to George Christopher Stead*, ed. Lionel R. Wickham and Caroline P. Bammel, 227–46. Leiden: E. J. Brill, 1993.

Young, Frances M. *Biblical Exegesis and the Formation of Christian Culture.* Cambridge, Eng.: Cambridge University Press, 1997.

———. *From Nicaea to Chalcedon: A Guide to the Literature and Its Background.* Philadelphia: Fortress, 1983.

———. "The God of the Greeks and the Nature of Religious Language." In *Early Christian Literature and the Classical Intellectual Tradition: Festschrift for R. M. Grant*, ed. W. R. Schoedel and Robert Wilken, 45–74. Théologie Historique. Paris: Éditions Beauchesne, 1979.

———. *The Making of the Creeds.* London: SCM Press and Trinity Press International, 1991.

Zeitlin, Froma I. *Playing the Other: Gender and Society in Classical Greek Literature.* Women in Culture and Society. Chicago: University of Chicago Press, 1996.

Index

In this index an "f" after a number indicates a separate reference on the next page, and an "ff" indicates separate references on the next two pages. A continuous discussion over two or more pages is indicated by a span of page numbers, e.g., "57–59."